Grilling Vocab

Indoor grilling — just like the outdoor variety — has its own jargon. The following terms are those you may hear tossed around by indoor grill salespeople, your local butcher, or your next-door neighbor. Don't let them throw you for a loop — they're all pretty easy to master. For more technoterms on indoor grills, check out Chapter 2.

- **Contact grill:** A type of grill in which the food is sandwiched between two grill grids. Contact grills look like a sandwich press or waffle maker.
- **Cooktop insert:** Generally refers to a cooktop or range that has a built-in grill grid (or one that can be interchanged with a griddle).
- **Domed lid:** A rounded cover that's usually seen on a charcoal kettle grill but is increasingly available on indoor grills.
- **Drip tray:** A plastic or metal, easy-to-clean, fat-draining reservoir that a sloping grill grid drains into.
- **Electric grill:** A grill that's powered by electricity (as opposed to a gas grill or charcoal grill).
- **Grill grid:** The surface on which you grill foods, which may or may not be coated with a nonstick material.
- **Grill pan:** A pan with ribs or ridges on the cooking surface that you use on your cooktop.
- **Open grill:** An indoor electric grill that doesn't have a cover.
- **Ribs:** Yummy-good eating! Oh, and also ridges that stick up on a grill grid and create grill marks on your food.
- **Variable temperature control:** A dial on a grill that allows you to control the temperature of the grill grid.

Taking Food-Handling Precautions

In addition to taking precautions against heat and fire hazards, take the following precautions when cooking meat, poultry, and seafood:

- **Thaw meat, poultry, and seafood in the refrigerator, not on a countertop.** Food can spoil rapidly when thawing. This goes for marinating foods, too.
- **Store raw seafood in your refrigerator for no more than 24 hours. Store ground meats and raw poultry for up to two days; red meat for up to five.**
- **Never use the same plate and utensils for raw foods as you do for cooked ones.** Raw meat, poultry, and seafood can contain harmful bacteria. After placing your foods on the grill, wash your plate and utensils with soapy water before using them again.
- **Keep raw meat, poultry, and seafood separate from other foods.**
- **Always wash your hands in hot, soapy water before and after handling raw meat, poultry, and seafood.**
- **When you marinate foods and then want to use the marinade to baste your food as it cooks, first boil the marinade to kill bacteria.** Better yet, whip up a separate batch of marinade to use for basting.

Indoor Grilling For Dummies®

Cheat Sheet

Staying Safe

Indoor grills don't require the lengthy list of safety precautions that outdoor grills do, but take the following precautions, nonetheless:

- ✔ **Position your indoor grill on an open countertop so that it's not under any cabinets.** The heat from the grill may overheat a cabinet that's above the grill.
- ✔ **Don't wear clothing with loose or flowing sleeves that may drag on the grill grid and burn.**
- ✔ **If you're using a larger grill, use long-handled utensils so that you don't have to reach over the grill grid to position food.** See Chapter 2 for more on grilling utensils.
- ✔ **Open contact grills away from your face and body.** Steam that collects inside a contact grill can quickly burn your skin.
- ✔ **Use an oven mitt or potholder when working with metal handles, which are commonly found on grill pans.**
- ✔ **Always keep a fire extinguisher handy and know how to use it.**

Grilling to a Safe Temperature

Grill all uncooked meats to the following safe temperatures before serving. Use a thermometer (see Chapter 2) inserted into the thickest part of the meat to measure the temperature. (Don't insert the thermometer until the outside of the food is seared, or the thermometer itself could carry bacteria into the interior of the food.)

Type of Food	Safe Temperature	Grilling Time (in Minutes)
Beef and lamb steaks and chops	145°	5–25
Finfish	145°	8–10
Shrimp and scallops	145°	2–4
Fresh pork	150°	20–30
Ground beef, ground pork, or ground lamb	160°	10–20
Ground chicken or ground turkey	165°	10–20
Poultry breasts	170°	12–25
Poultry thighs and wings	180°	10–20
Precooked sausage and hotdogs	To taste	3–5
Fruits, vegetables, and breads	To taste	3–20

Hungry Minds™

Copyright © 2001 Hungry Minds, Inc.
All rights reserved.

Cheat Sheet $2.95 value. Item 5362-3.

For more information about Hungry Minds,
call 1-800-762-2974.

For Dummies™: Bestselling Book Series for Beginners

 TM

References for the Rest of Us!®

BESTSELLING BOOK SERIES

Do you find that traditional reference books are overloaded with technical details and advice you'll never use? Do you postpone important life decisions because you just don't want to deal with them? Then our *For Dummies*® business and general reference book series is for you.

For Dummies business and general reference books are written for those frustrated and hard-working souls who know they aren't dumb, but find that the myriad of personal and business issues and the accompanying horror stories make them feel helpless. *For Dummies* books use a lighthearted approach, a down-to-earth style, and even cartoons and humorous icons to dispel fears and build confidence. Lighthearted but not lightweight, these books are perfect survival guides to solve your everyday personal and business problems.

Already, millions of satisfied readers agree. They have made For Dummies the #1 introductory level computer book series and a best-selling business book series. They have written asking for more. So, if you're looking for the best and easiest way to learn about business and other general reference topics, look to For Dummies to give you a helping hand.

Hungry Minds™

Indoor Grilling

FOR

DUMMIES®

by Lucy Wing and Tere Drenth

Hungry Minds™

HUNGRY MINDS, INC.

New York, NY ◆ Cleveland, OH ◆ Indianapolis, IN

Indoor Grilling For Dummies®

Published by:
Hungry Minds, Inc.
909 Third Avenue
New York, NY 10022
www.hungryminds.com
www.dummies.com

Library of Congress Control Number: 00-112171

ISBN: 0-7645-5362-3

Printed in the United States of America

10 9 8 7 6 5 4 3 2 1

1O/SX/QT/QR/IN

Distributed in the United States by Hungry Minds, Inc.

Distributed by CDG Books Canada Inc. for Canada; by Transworld Publishers Limited in the United Kingdom; by IDG Norge Books for Norway; by IDG Sweden Books for Sweden; by IDG Books Australia Publishing Corporation Pty. Ltd. for Australia and New Zealand; by TransQuest Publishers Pte Ltd. for Singapore, Malaysia, Thailand, Indonesia, and Hong Kong; by Gotop Information Inc. for Taiwan; by ICG Muse, Inc. for Japan; by Intersoft for South Africa; by Eyrolles for France; by International Thomson Publishing for Germany, Austria and Switzerland; by Distribuidora Cuspide for Argentina; by LR International for Brazil; by Galileo Libros for Chile; by Ediciones ZETA S.C.R. Ltda. for Peru; by WS Computer Publishing Corporation, Inc., for the Philippines; by Contemporanea de Ediciones for Venezuela; by Express Computer Distributors for the Caribbean and West Indies; by Micronesia Media Distributor, Inc. for Micronesia; by Chips Computadoras S.A. de C.V. for Mexico; by Editorial Norma de Panama S.A. for Panama; by American Bookshops for Finland.

For general information on Hungry Minds' products and services please contact our Customer Care department; within the U.S. at 800-762-2974, outside the U.S. at 317-572-3993 or fax 317-572-4002.

For sales inquiries and resellers information, including discounts, premium and bulk quantity sales and foreign language translations please contact our Customer Care department at 800-434-3422, fax 317-572-4002 or write to Hungry Minds, Inc., Attn: Customer Care department, 10475 Crosspoint Boulevard, Indianapolis, IN 46256.

For information on licensing foreign or domestic rights, please contact our Sub-Rights Customer Care department at 650-653-7098.

For information on using Hungry Minds' products and services in the classroom or for ordering examination copies, please contact our Educational Sales department at 800-434-2086 or fax 317-572-4005.

Please contact our Public Relations department at 212-884-5163 for press review copies or 212-884-5000 for author interviews and other publicity information or fax 212-884-5400.

For authorization to photocopy items for corporate, personal, or educational use, please contact Copyright Clearance Center, 222 Rosewood Drive, Danvers, MA 01923, or fax 978-750-4470.

Hungry Minds™ is a trademark of Hungry Minds, Inc.

About the Authors

Lucy Wing, former Executive Food Editor at *Country Living* magazine and Food Editor at *McCall's,* grills as part of her everyday cooking and entertaining lifestyle. She often dishes up both outdoor and indoor grilled foods in the same meal and has been known to grill even with snow piled high around the area. Whether grilling on her rooftop in New York City, farmhouse in Pennsylvania, or patio in Arizona, only high winds force her to cease grilling outdoors to retreat to fulltime indoor grilling. Passionate not only about grilling, Lucy maintains gardens where she resides and often uses the bounty of her vegetables, fruits, flowers, and herbs in her recipes and food articles. Her garden food articles have been published in *Country Living Gardener* and *Rebecca's Garden.* She has edited a number of cookbooks, including *Country Living Country Mornings, Family Circle's Delicious Desserts, The Good Housekeeping Illustrated Cookbook,* and *Campbell's Great American Cookbook.* She created recipes for Anne Willan's *Look & Cook Asian Cooking* and *Reader's Digest Quick & Delicious Cookbook,* and has contributed to Time-Life's *Great Meals in Minutes.* She was formerly a food consultant and food stylist to the Barbecue Industry Association and to many other food companies and public relations agencies.

Tere Drenth, a freelance writer and editor, has edited numerous cookbooks, including *Grilling For Dummies* and *Seafood Cooking For Dummies,* which earned the "Best Cookbook on Fish" Award at the Versailles World Cookbook Fair. She also serves as an adjunct faculty member at Franklin College (Franklin, Indiana), where she teaches freshman English. When not writing, editing, teaching, or running competitively, Tere is in her kitchen, finding new ways to prepare fast, healthy, and delicious meals.

Dedication

We dedicate this book to the grilling enthusiasts who have made indoor grilling the phenomenon that it is today.

Authors' Acknowledgments

Lucy and Tere both wish to thank Linda Ingroia, who believed in us enough to let us write this book and encouraged us throughout the project; and Elizabeth Kuball, Project Editor Extraordinaire, who edited our words, managed the book project, and made the grueling task of writing a book in four months seem painless — even fun!

We also give our heartfelt thanks to Acquisitions Coordinator Erin Connell, who made sure the bills were paid; Recipe Tester Emily Nolan and Technical Editor Majorie Cubisino, who gave extensive feedback throughout the project; Nutritional Analyst Patty Santelli, who came up with calories, fat grams, and sodium counts for over 80 recipes; illustrator Liz Kurtzman, whose artwork is absolutely adorable; and Production Coordinator Maridee Ennis, who managed the project through layout and proofreading.

Special thanks to Christine Marks at Le Creuset and Anja Thomas at Hamilton Beach for generously providing samples for our use throughout this project. Their willingness to ship products at a moment's notice was heartwarming.

Lucy also wants to thank Donna Myers, spokesperson for the Barbecue Industry Association, for her words of wisdom, recommendations, and encouragement.

Tere also wishes to thank her husband, Doug, and best friends, Elizabeth and Jan, for being such excellent distractions while writing this book.

Publisher's Acknowledgments

We're proud of this book; please register your comments through our Online Registration Form located at www.dummies.com.

Some of the people who helped bring this book to market include the following:

Acquisitions, Editorial, and Media Development

Project Editor: Elizabeth Netedu Kuball

Senior Acquisitions Editor: Linda Ingroia

Acquisitions Coordinator: Erin Connell

Recipe Tester: Emily Nolan

Technical Editor: Marjorie Cubisino

Nutritional Analyst: Patty Santelli

Editorial Manager: Pamela Mourouzis

Editorial Administrator: Michelle Hacker

Editorial Assistant: Carol Strickland

Cover Photographer: David Bishop

Cover Food Stylist: Brett Kurzweil

Production

Project Coordinator: Maridee Ennis

Layout and Graphics: Amy Adrian, Jacque Schneider, Brian Torwelle

Special Art: Elizabeth Kurtzman

Proofreaders: Valery Bourke, David Faust, Andy Hollandbeck, Christine Pingleton, York Production Services, Inc.

Indexer: York Production Services, Inc.

General and Administrative

Hungry Minds, Inc.: John Kilcullen, CEO; Bill Barry, President and COO; John Ball, Executive VP, Operations & Administration; John Harris, CFO

Hungry Minds Consumer Reference Group

    Business: Kathleen A. Welton, Vice President and Publisher; Kevin Thornton, Acquisitions Manager

    Cooking/Gardening: Jennifer Feldman, Associate Vice President and Publisher

    Education/Reference: Diane Graves Steele, Vice President and Publisher; Greg Tubach, Publishing Director

    Lifestyles: Kathleen Nebenhaus, Vice President and Publisher; Tracy Boggier, Managing Editor

    Pets: Dominique De Vito, Associate Vice President and Publisher; Tracy Boggier, Managing Editor

    Travel: Michael Spring, Vice President and Publisher; Suzanne Jannetta, Editorial Director; Brice Gosnell, Managing Editor

Hungry Minds Consumer Editorial Services: Kathleen Nebenhaus, Vice President and Publisher; Kristin A. Cocks, Editorial Director; Cindy Kitchel, Editorial Director

Hungry Minds Consumer Production: Debbie Stailey, Production Director

◆

The publisher would like to give special thanks to Patrick J. McGovern, without whom this book would not have been possible.

◆

Contents at a Glance

Cartoons at a Glance

By Rich Tennant

The 5th Wave By Rich Tennant

"Come on in. We're grilling indoors.
Doug says the radiator's almost ready."

page 7

The 5th Wave By Rich Tennant

"I'm not sure what flavor you're tasting. I
didn't use any spice rubs on the meat, however
I dropped it several times on the way to
the grill."

page 35

The 5th Wave By Rich Tennant

"I'm pretty sure it's grilled game. That
would explain the meat tasting like
a Monopoly game board."

page 163

The 5th Wave By Rich Tennant

FOR ADDED REALISM, THE BENSONS
USE ANT FARMS FOR CENTERPIECES
AT THEIR INDOOR GRILL PICNIC

What is this—some
sort of sick joke?

page 207

The 5th Wave By Rich Tennant

Eschewing the indoor covered and more
traditional stovetop varieties, Stan opts
for a 1946 Chevrolet Fleetline grill.

page 53

Cartoon Information:
Fax: 978-546-7747
E-Mail: richtennant@the5thwave.com
World Wide Web: www.the5thwave.com

Table of Contents

Introduction

*W*elcome to *Indoor Grilling For Dummies,* a book that gives you all sorts of ways to do one thing: grill great-tasting food indoors during blizzards, rainstorms, or heat waves; on porches, decks, apartment patios, or countertops; using grills that can be inexpensive to purchase, take little time to clean up, and are small enough to store out of sight.

About This Book

Heard about the phenomenon called indoor grilling? Ads and catalogs from department stores, discount stores, specialty shops — heck, even grocery stores — display all kinds of indoor grilling options: open or covered electric grills, contact grills, grill pans, and cooktop inserts. And why shouldn't indoor grills be all the rage? Indoor grills are inexpensive compared to gas and charcoal grills, are a cinch to clean up, and can fit into the tiniest spaces.

But grilling on an indoor grill doesn't always result in the best-tasting food, and that's why this book exists. Ever tasted dried out, curled up pork chops cooked on an indoor grill? Or worse, ever tried to grill steak and ended up with a steamy mess? Indoor grilling isn't rocket science, but it isn't a cakewalk, either. *Indoor Grilling For Dummies* takes the fuss out of grilling indoors, giving you more than 80 recipes for everything from basic burgers to Asian duck. And if you're a vegetarian, you're in luck: This book even includes recipes for grilling tender fruits and veggies on your indoor grill. You also find out how to select the right grill for you, how (or whether) to accessorize, and how to stay safe in a world that's afraid of chicken juices. Best of all, this book takes you from beginner to master griller with humor and good fun.

Conventions Used in This Book

Most of the recipes in this book are pretty straightforward, but we had to use a few conventions, as follows:

- ✔ Vegetarian recipes are marked with a tomato in the "Recipes in This Chapter" section on the first page of every recipe chapter.

- ✔ Each recipe contains a nutritional analysis of the calories, fat, protein, and so on in each dish. We've tried to include healthy recipes in this book but haven't gone so far that the food tastes like straw. However, if you're interested in reducing fat and calories (and who isn't these days?), you can use lighter versions of cheese, ground meats, sour cream, and other ingredients that the recipes call for. In addition, keep in mind that the nutritional analyses don't include garnishes or optional ingredients.

✔ If you're using a small indoor grill (such as a two-burger Lean Mean), you may have to work in batches to make many of the recipes in this book. If you're purchasing a new indoor grill, look for one that can cook at least four hamburgers at one time — a six-hamburger size is even better! The larger the size of the grill, the more food you'll be able to make on it at one time, and this alone may justify the cost of a larger grill.

✔ We've asked you to preheat your electric grill, grill pan, or cooktop insert for five minutes before beginning to grill, but your particular equipment may need more time. Read the information that comes with your grilling equipment, and if you aren't satisfied with the quality of your grilled dishes, increase the amount of time that you heat up your grill.

✔ Most recipes call for temperatures like "medium," "medium-low," or "high," because most grills don't have temperature gauges. When temperatures are mentioned, however, they're in degrees Fahrenheit.

✔ When a recipe calls for salt and pepper "to taste," we means about ¼ teaspoon of salt and ⅛ teaspoon of pepper. A "pinch" isn't to help you grow an inch — it's about ¹⁄₁₆ teaspoon of salt or pepper.

✔ If a recipe calls for butter (which isn't often), we mean unsalted butter, not salted butter.

Note: The recipe instructions may seem long, but don't worry . . . they're not complicated at all. We offer cooking instructions for many types of indoor grilling equipment, so just look for what applies to the equipment you're using, and you'll see that the instructions are a cinch!

Foolish Assumptions

We assume the following about you: You're interested in grilling indoors and you have either an electrical outlet (if you're planning to purchase an indoor electric grill) or a stovetop (if you're planning to use a grill pan or cooktop insert). See Chapter 2 for details on indoor grilling equipment.

Although the recipes in this book are simple, basic recipes — many of which include step-by-step instructions — if you've never set foot in a kitchen, you may want to pick up a copy of *Cooking For Dummies,* 2nd Edition, by Bryan Miller and Marie Rama (Hungry Minds, Inc.). We figure you know how to measure and make basic cuts with knives, but other than that, we take you through what you need to know about indoor grilling.

How This Book Is Organized

We've organized this book into five distinct parts (discussed in the following sections), plus an appendix that gives you additional resources for everything from where to find information on grills to how to get your hands on additional recipes.

Part 1: Mastering Indoor Grilling

This part gives you the lowdown on grilling basics and answers questions like the following: Why grill indoors in the first place? Where can you find a grill and grilling accessories? How can you stay safe as you attempt to tame indoor heat? How do you clean and maintain your grill?

Part 11: Accounting for Taste

Marinating and rubbing your foods before you grill them adds a boost of flavor to every dish, and this part shows you how to whip up tasty seasonings or use bottled favorites. In addition, your grilled meal can rival that of a restaurant meal by adding simple sauces — you'll find recipes galore for doing just that in this part.

Part 111: Getting Grilled

This part, the bulk of the book, shares dozens of recipes for everything from sausage to fajitas, barbecued pork tenderloin to brandied turkey, and grilled mushrooms to chicken Caesar salad. Simply flip to the chapter that interests you most and get ready for a fast, delicious, hassle-free meal.

Part 1V: Dressing Up for Dinner

This part helps you give your parties and meals a boost, showing you how to create mouth-watering grilled appetizers, delicious grilled desserts, and memorable meals from foods you get a chance to cook only once in a great while: lamb, whole fish, venison, and veal.

Part V: The Part of Tens

This part of handy tips and tricks takes you just a minute to read and at the end, you discover ten great reasons to start grilling indoors, ten ways to make your meals lean and healthy, and ten ways to keep people talking about your delicious meals.

Appendix

Near the back of this book, we've included an appendix filled with indoor-grilling resources. We list a number of grilling manufacturers and retailers, places on the Web to find recipes, and a listing of specialty mail-order food sources.

Icons Used in This Book

Icons are little pictures in the margins that you can think of as roadside signs: Like construction signs that suggest alternate routes, two of the icons in this book give you tips and tricks that make your travels into the world of indoor grilling seem like a walk in the park; like a stop sign, one icon tells when to stop, turn around, and go like crazy the other way; like those repetitive signs on the highway that tell you the exit really is coming up or construction really is starting, one icon gives you gentle reminders; and like historic register signs, a final icon shares some interesting tidbits that you can skip if you're in a hurry.

Pay attention to this icon for tips, tricks, and techniques that make indoor grilling a cinch for you to master.

Although most of the recipes in this book are lean and healthy, use this icon to help you cut additional calories and fat from your grilled meals.

Steer clear of potential pitfalls by heeding these signs that warn you of everything from ways to eliminate bacteria in meat to surefire tips to keep from burning tender veggies.

This icons suggests that you remember certain tidbits of information — think of this icon as the stuff to write down and post on your fridge with a magnet.

These bits of techie information are interesting to note but okay to skip if you want to. Of course, paying attention to these icons will make you seem like the smartest indoor griller on your block. . . .

Where to Go from Here

This book isn't meant to be read from cover to cover, so you can start on page 1, 62, or 189. To find out general information about indoor grilling, start in Part I. To find out about marinades and sauces that add flavor to all types of food, hop over to Chapters 4 and 5. For basics like hamburgers, hot dogs, and grilled cheese, flip to Chapter 6.

For general recipe ideas, look at the Recipes at a Glance section near the beginning of this book. If you're looking for a recipe that includes a particular type of food — say, chicken breasts or salmon or bananas with chocolate sauce, take a peek at the index or flip to the chapter that covers the type of food you're interested in.

Chapter 18 fills you in on ideas for keeping your meals light, as do most of the recipe chapters. To find out how to dress up your grilled meals, turn to Chapters 14 and 19.

Part I
Mastering Indoor Grilling

The 5th Wave   By Rich Tennant

"Come on in. We're grilling indoors.
Doug says the radiator's almost ready."

In this part . . .

*I*ndoor grilling is fun, easy, inexpensive, and healthy.
And this part shows you how to choose from an
immense variety of grills and grill pans, find accessories
that'll make your indoor grilling even easier, properly
warm up your grill, stay safe while grilling, and clean up in
a snap! You can even find a section on mastering grilling
jargon.

Chapter 1

Why Grill Indoors?

Grill indoors? Doesn't that defeat the purpose of grilling: firing up the grill and braving the elements, rain or shine? Well, maybe. Outdoor grilling is a joy when you're expecting a large group for a barbecue or picnic on a beautiful summer day. But there's plenty of work involved, too. If you have a charcoal grill, you have to purchase charcoal briquettes, natural lump charcoal, or wood chunks; prepare the fire; and control the heat. Although grilling on a gas grill is a little simpler, you still have to mess with a propane tank (which eventually runs out of fuel and needs to be refilled). And when you grill outdoors, you have to bring the food from the kitchen to the outdoor grill and back, fight off the mosquitoes, and contend with smoke blowing in your eyes.

Grilling indoors is a kinder, gentler approach to cooking. You don't have to invest a lot of money in your grilling equipment, go outside to brave the elements and mosquitoes, take the time to fire up a grill, or spend much time cleaning up. Yet you still get the same char marks as with outdoor grilling, and when you use the right recipes (hint: see Parts III and IV), you'll be eating tender food with a delightful taste. Indoor grilling, like outdoor grilling, takes you back to an age when people hunted for their own food, cooked it over an open fire, and ate it, but the entire process is much more civilized: Buy your food in a grocery store, cook it on an indoor grill, and still feel like a lusty caveman!

The idea behind indoor grilling is that you can do it every day for family meals, regardless of the conditions outside. You simply plug your grill into an outlet or place a grill pan on your stovetop, preheat it for five minutes (some grills may take a little longer — read the instruction manual for your grill), put your food on the grill, and let it cook.

If you're not sold on the concept already, in this chapter we provide some great reasons to consider bringing your grilling indoors. From weather to cost, cleanup to storage space, if there's a reason to grill indoors, you'll find it here.

No Rainouts

The major benefit of indoor grilling is that you never have to worry about the weather. Go ahead and plan a barbecue on the most beautiful day of the year, but plan to cook it indoors, so that if it rains, your plans will go off without a hitch. If you live in Minnesota, you can still grill in January. If you're in the middle of the monsoon season, you can still eat delicious grilled meals. Even when the postman is trudging through snow, rain, or gloom of night to get the mail to your door, you can be warm and cozy in your kitchen, getting that great, grilled taste from your food.

Lower Costs

Indoor grills range in price from $25 to $120, far short of the money — sometimes thousands of dollars — that you can spend on a charcoal or gas outdoor grill. And after your initial investment, you don't have to spend another dime on charcoal or propane gas. As long as you pay your electric bill on time, you'll have all the power you need.

Less Space

An indoor grill requires almost no storage space — you can store most models in a kitchen cabinet. You don't have to allot a special place on your patio or allow for storage space in your garage or basement while your grill isn't in use. **Remember:** Your grill can *always* be in use!

Indoor grills get bigger every year, and although this challenges your storage space, it's actually a good thing: The larger the *grill grid* (the area on which you cook your food), the more food you can cook at one time. Indoor grills have traditionally had about a quarter of the grill grid area that charcoal or gas grills have, but today you can find indoor grills on which you can cook enough for a large party (see Chapter 2).

Safe Balcony or Patio Grilling

Many condominiums associations, co-op boards, and apartment complexes don't allow outdoor grills on balconies or patios because the heat and flames can start a fast-spreading fire. Indoor electric grills are a safe alternative: You get the feel of an outdoor grill with the safety and convenience of an electric grill.

When your association president or apartment manager stops by, planning to slap you with a fine because of the enticing smell of your grilled food, show off your electric grill and ask him to stay for dinner.

Fast and Easy Cooking and Cleaning

Another benefit of indoor grilling is that it's fast — really fast! You can prepare and cook many dishes in less than 30 minutes (see Parts III and IV for recipes). Because you don't have all the fuss and fanfare of outdoor grilling, you can prepare tasty grilled dishes in less time than it takes to order pizza.

In addition, many models are nearly 100 percent dishwasher-safe (except for the plug and electric coil), so cleaning up is a snap. Even if your grill can't go into the dishwasher, most indoor grills comes with a nonstick surface that you can wipe off with a soapy paper towel after the grill has cooled.

Light and Healthy Eating

Many indoor grills include a system that allows fat to drain away from the food while it's cooking, so the food tastes more like food and less like fat. Unlike pan frying or deep frying, the food cooked on an indoor grill doesn't sit in grease throughout its cooking cycle, yet the food tends to stay moist, tender, and delicious.

Indoor grilling alone, however, doesn't make high-fat foods leaner. The staff at *Consumer Reports* cooked identically sized burgers on a variety of indoor grills and grill pans, as well as in a plain frying pan; then they checked the fat content. The result? They found no significant difference in the fat content of any of the burgers.

The trick, then, is to choose lean foods, including vegetables, seafood, and white-meat poultry, and take care to trim all visible fat from fattier cuts of meat (as shown in Figure 1-1). When you combine indoor grilling with seafood, vegetables, and lean cuts of well-trimmed meat and poultry, you can create a low-fat, low-calorie meal that's high in protein and complex carbohydrates.

Figure 1-1:
Trimming away fat from fattier cuts of meat keeps your grilled foods healthier.

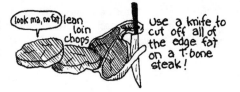

Chapter 2

Choosing Indoor Grilling Equipment and Accessories

In This Chapter

▶ Understanding the immense variety of indoor electric grills

▶ Considering a grill pan or cooktop insert

▶ Fiddling with indoor grilling accessories

*1*ndoor grills come in an amazing variety of sizes and shapes. You can find grills that plug in, and grills that are part of your stove; grills that have covers, and grills that don't; grills that you use on the stove, and grills that you use on the countertop. And although this variety allows you to adapt indoor grilling to your taste, the choices can be a bit overwhelming. This chapter gives you some tips and tricks for selecting an indoor electric grill, grill pan, or cooktop insert.

After you decide on the right grill for your cooking needs, you'll want to accessorize with tongs, thermometers, mitts, and other assorted grilling toys. Here you'll find the information you need to decide which accessories are worth purchasing.

Getting Grilled: Finding the Right Grill for You

The following sections discuss the various types of indoor grills that you plug into an outlet (as opposed to the ones that you use on a stove). See the "Out of the Fire and into the Pan" section for grilling equipment that you use on the stovetop.

Open indoor grills

Open indoor grills are grills that plug into an outlet and don't have a cover (see Figure 2-1). Using an open indoor grill is very much like using an outdoor gas grill with the cover open. You preheat the grill, set the food on the grill grid, set your timer, and check the food's temperature when the timer dings. Indoor grills come with drop trays that hold water to catch the grease and reduce smoking. And although these are called *open indoor grills,* some models do come with a cover that increases their cooking versatility.

Food cooked on an open indoor grill has those delightful char marks on the surface that has been touching the grill grid, but as with an outdoor grill, you need to flip the food halfway through the cooking cycle. In addition, while the bottom side is cooking, the top side of the food may get a little dry, just as it can on an outdoor gas grill with the cover open or when food is broiling or baking.

Figure 2-1: Open indoor grills come in a variety of sizes and shapes.

OPEN INDOOR GRILLS

When using an open indoor grill, you may want to cover the food with aluminum foil to keep it from getting too dry.

Salton has created an indoor covered grill that eliminates the problem of dry foods. The grill, the George Foreman indoor/outdoor electric grill, features a large, domed lid (refer to Figure 2-2), similar to what you see on a charcoal kettle grill. With an adjustable temperature control, adjustable steam vents in the dome, and a five-prong base that elevates the grill to waist height, it cooks surprisingly like an expensive outdoor grill, yet costs just $100 to $120. And it boasts 240 square inches of cooking space, so you can use it to host an indoor/outdoor cookout (or is that a *cook-in?*).

You can find an amazing variety of open indoor grills (see the Appendix for a list of manufacturers), but new indoor grills are always being introduced, so check your local retailer and the Internet for advances in open indoor grilling technology.

Figure 2-2:
The George
Foreman
indoor/
outdoor grill
is an open
indoor grill
with a large,
domed
cover.

Our favorite design is one that also includes a *grill/griddle surface* on one side of the grill, which allows you to cook smaller, thinner pieces of foods while grilling your main dish. This solid section of the grill grid doesn't allow food to drop through, eliminating the need for special equipment when you're grilling small-sized foods.

Open indoor grills range in price from $30 for a low-end grill to $120 for the top-of-the-line model. Look for better models at home stores, department stores, and discount chains.

Be wary of low-end models — they usually have small cooking surfaces, have lower wattage so they cook more slowly, use lots of parts that can get lost, and may not be dishwasher-safe.

Although many open indoor grills have just one heat setting (similar to a medium or medium-hot setting on a charcoal or gas grill), look for an adjustable temperature control when selecting an open indoor grill. Variable heat allows you to sear foods initially at a higher heat, and then grill them more slowly at lower temperatures, resulting in more tender dishes. Most open indoor grills at the mid to high end of the price range have adjustable temperature controls.

Contact grills

Contact grills plug into an outlet but have two sets of grill grids: one that you set the food on and another that cooks the food from the top when you close the cover (see Figure 2-3). The food is sandwiched between the two grids, speeding up the cooking process. Some models also open flat (like a book) so you have the option of cooking food on both sides of the surface, turning the product into a large open grill that then becomes an open grill.

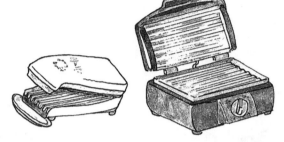

Figure 2-3:
Contact grills cook foods from both sides.

Contact grills have all the advantages of open indoor grills (see the preceding section), but the food on the grill grid doesn't require turning and cooks in usually half the time. However, in order to get those characteristic char marks on your food, you may have to turn (flip) and rotate the food at least one time while it's grilling. By opening your contact grill to turn and rotate the food, you also let out some of the steam that can get trapped in a contact grill. Like open indoor grills, new models of contact grills are introduced frequently, so check with your local retailer and the Internet before making a selection. See the Appendix for a list of grill manufacturers.

When shopping for a contact grill, look for a dishwasher-safe *drip tray,* into which fat from your foods can drain away. Also look for a nonstick grill grid and a variable temperature control. Prices range from $20 for a personal-sized model to $120 for a top-of-the-line, fully featured contact grill.

In some contact grills, the intense heat within such a small, enclosed area builds up steam, which has a hard time escaping. This can create an environment in which your food is steamed rather than grilled. Steamed food isn't necessarily bad for you or even bad-tasting, but it does tend to be rather flavorless. To keep food from steaming, make sure your *vent* (the hole in the cover that allows steam to escape) is open, and when shopping for a new contact grill, select one that offers a steam vent.

Out of the Fire and into the Pan

Indoor grilling doesn't have to involve an appliance and an outlet. For years, indoor grilling enthusiasts have used their stovetops to grill tender, delicious

foods. The two following sections introduce you to gri'
inserts. (See the Appendix for a listing of current mar'

Grill pans

A *grill pan* looks like a frying pan with raised ribs on the cooking surface, so
fats from foods drain into the bottom of the pan, between the ribs. A grill pan
gets its heat source from your stovetop, and because most models are made
of cast iron or heavy-gauge aluminum, they retain their heat well. Although
indoor grills are relatively smoke-free, stovetop grill pans tend to be smoky
during use. When using these pans, make sure you have some sort of ventilation in the kitchen. Turn the ventilation fan on or open a nearby window. And
watch out for the smoke detector — it may go off!

Most professional chefs swear by their grill pans and won't consider using
anything else. Food grilled in a grill pan tends to be tender and moist,
although grilling times may be a bit longer in a grill pan than with an open
grill or contact grill. To reduce grilling time in a grill pan, cover the food with
aluminum foil after grilling for a few minutes on each side. Also keep an eye
out for grill pans with a cover — they're becoming increasingly popular.
Many grill pans are heavy-duty, so if you maintain a high-end grill pan, it will
last a lifetime. Grill pans range from $35 to $90; opt for the best you can
afford.

Le Creuset, Calphalon, All-Clad, KitchenAid, and Lodge all make grill pans
(shown in Figure 2-4) with metal handles, so you can use the pans in the oven
as well as on the stovetop. (Professional chefs do this to finish cooking foods
and to keep foods warm.) But keep in mind that you must use a mitt or
handle glove when grasping the handle (either when it's in the oven or on the
stovetop), because it can get burning hot!

Figure 2-4:
Grill pans
allow you
to grill right
on your
stovetop.

STOVETOP GRILL PANS

Cooktop inserts

A *cooktop insert,* shown in Figure 2-5, is a component of a cooktop or range, so you have a grill grid available 24/7. Some brands are Jenn-Air, GE, and Amana. All models include a *downdraft feature* that pulls smoke away from the food (and away from your smoke detector). The grill grid can usually be removed, stored away, and replaced with a griddle or another type of cooking module.

Figure 2-5:
Consider getting a cooktop insert the next time you remodel, purchase a home, or have to buy a new range.

COOKTOP GRILL

To get a cooktop insert, you have to buy a new cooktop or a separate range with this feature. These can cost well over $1,000. We've heard people say that, after using a cooktop insert, they can't live without it, so if you're remodeling your kitchen, buying a new home, or ready to replace your old cooktop or range, consider a cooktop insert that includes a grill grid.

Accessorizing

Indoor grilling doesn't require you to use all the accessories that outdoor grilling requires, but you still need a few specific tools to make your indoor grilling experience safe and easy.

Outdoor grilling has created an entire market of long-handled tools — spatulas, forks, tongs, mitts, and brushes — because leaning in too close to an outdoor grill can toast your eyebrows. Your indoor grill may or may not require that you use these longer varieties of kitchen staples. If you're using a small indoor grill, chances are that basic kitchen tongs and spatulas will do the trick. If you opt for a larger grill, however, be sure to stick to longer-handled tools.

Many indoor grills use a nonstick coating on the grill grid, and metal tools will eventually scratch the coating. Longer-handled grilling tools, however, tend to be metal because they're designed for outdoor grills, which don't feature that nonstick coating. Manufacturers are beginning to design longer-handled nylon grilling tools — we predict that they'll become commonplace before long.

When shopping for plastic grilling tools, be sure they're labeled as being "heat resistant," preferably up to about 500 degrees. And before purchasing a plastic tool, futz with it to see how much wear and tear it can take: Bend it back and forth, twist it at the handle, and slap it against your hand to test its strength. If the tool breaks during this test, set it down, back away slowly, and stay away from that store in the future! No, seriously, take the tool to the manager and advise her about your "test results."

Tongs

Tongs are essential equipment for an indoor griller. With tongs, you can carefully lift and turn foods without piercing the surface and without scratching the grill grid. Tongs come in two distinct varieties:

- **Spring-loaded tongs:** Shown on the left side of Figure 2-6, spring-loaded tongs stay open until you squeeze the handles together. These tongs are a cinch to maneuver and are perfect for sturdy foods such as beef, pork, and chicken pieces.

- **Ice tongs:** Ice tongs, shown on the right side of Figure 2-6, don't stay open automatically; you must open and close them manually. Although ice tongs are a bit harder to use, they're perfect for delicate seafood dishes.

Figure 2-6:
Consider keeping both kinds of tongs on hand.

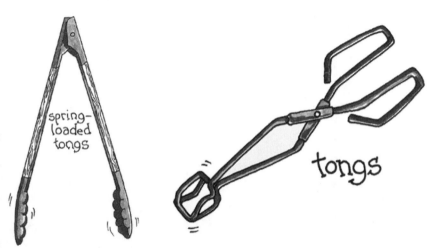

We don't recommend using a fork to move your food around on the grill or in the grill pan. A grill fork (a long fork with two tines on the end) pierces the food, letting out juices and, ultimately, flavor. Instead, use tongs or a spatula (see the following section) to maneuver your food on the grill. If, however, the grid (or ribs, on a grill pan) make using a spatula too much of a circus act, look for a sturdy, two-tined, wooden-handled fork, and take care not to scratch the grill grid's surface when spearing your food.

Spatulas

By *spatula,* we don't mean the flexible rubber-topped utensil that you use to spread frosting on a cake. Instead, we mean the kind shown in Figure 2-7, which you use to flip foods on your grill and to move food from the grill to a plate. They're especially useful for wide, heavy foods such as burgers and grilled cheese sandwiches.

The kind of spatula you buy depends on the type of grill you're using:

- **Long-handled spatula:** Use this kind for a grill with a large grill grid — one that can hold enough food for six to eight people. Otherwise, you can stick to a shorter spatula.

- **Metal spatula:** Use a metal spatula only with a grill that can't be damaged by scraping. Spatulas that are specifically meant for nonstick surfaces, usually made of heat-resistant nylon, are very popular.

Figure 2-7:
A spatula is
a critical
grilling tool.

Regardless of the type you buy, be sure the *blade* of the spatula (the wide part that's connected to the handle) is at least four inches wide at its widest point.

Mitt

A mitt protects your hand and wrist when you're moving food around on your grill grid and keeps you from singeing your hand on a hot grill pan handle.

Most indoor grills are small enough that a standard oven mitt is protection enough, but if you're using a larger indoor grill, consider purchasing a *grill mitt,* shown in Figure 2-8, which reaches to your elbow.

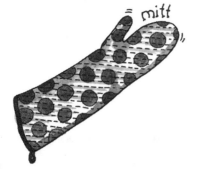

Figure 2-8:
Don't forget to put a grill mitt on your mitts!

Thermometer

Although your parents and grandparents may have cooked meat, poultry, and seafood without a thermometer and never contended with even the flu, times have changed. Meat, poultry, and seafood are likely to carry bacteria, which is destroyed only by heating foods to a certain temperature (see Chapter 3 for more information).

Look for a simple instant-read thermometer with a dial that indicates the temperature, like the one shown in Figure 2-9. Sure, you can find fancier ones, but a good-old instant read thermometer is a cheap and efficient way to ensure that your food is safely cooked.

Figure 2-9:
Use an instant-read thermometer to ensure that your meat is thoroughly cooked.

Be sure to sear the surface of your food before inserting a thermometer. Otherwise, the thermometer itself could carry bacteria into the interior of the food.

Timer

A timer and a thermometer are an inseparable pair. The timer gets you close to the proper cooking time (see Chapter 3 for an approximate listing of grilling times), letting you know when to insert the thermometer and check the temperature.

Don't go solely by time, however. Use the timer only as an approximate gauge. Continue to cook meat, poultry, and seafood until it reaches the appropriate internal temperature.

Knife

A good knife is critical to nearly every type of cooking, including indoor grilling. You don't need a zillion fancy knives, but you do need one good one. If you don't already have one, consider purchasing a chef's knife or butcher's knife. Look for one with a heavy handle that feels balanced and is proportional to your hand.

Every good knife needs a knife sharpener. Although you can get away without a knife sharpener for the first few weeks you own a new knife, soon after, the blade dulls, and cutting even thin-skinned vegetables becomes a chore. We recommend using a *sharpening steel* (a long steel rod, available where knives are sold). You simply draw the knife blade against the steel 10 or 15 times on each side of the blade. You'll be amazed at the difference!

Brushes

Brushes help you *baste* (apply marinade to food as it's cooking), adding flavor and moisture. As shown in Figure 2-10, brushes range from something that looks like a paintbrush (which helps you get into cracks and crevices in the food's surface) to a small mop (which applies a great deal of marinade to the surface of the food).

See Chapter 3 for tips on using marinades; flip to Chapter 4 for marinade recipes.

basting brushes

Figure 2-10:
Mops and brushes make easy work of basting.

Skewers

If you ever plan to make kebabs (see Part III), you need skewers. *Skewers* are metal or bamboo rods, shown in Figure 2-11, onto which you alternate layers of vegetables with meat, poultry, or seafood (you can also make all-veggie kebabs). Look for long (12- to 15-inch) metal skewers, but always use a mitt when removing them from your grill grid — metal is a great conductor of heat. If you store metal skewers where they won't get damaged and clean them after every use, they can last a lifetime.

An alternative to metal is bamboo, which doesn't last as long and tends to scorch. To make them less likely to flare up on a cooktop insert, soak bamboo skewers in water for 20 to 30 minutes before threading food onto them.

Check with the product manual for your grill before buying accessories. The manual may specify which kind of skewers work best with your grill.

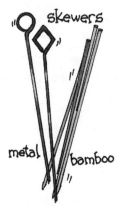

Figure 2-11:
Pick a
skewer, any
skewer, but
make sure
you use a
mitt to pick
them up
from a hot
surface!

Chapter 3

Understanding the Basic Techniques of Grilling Indoors

Successful indoor grilling requires just a few skills — ones that you can master in minutes. In this chapter, you get all the tips you need to grill indoors like a pro.

Speaking a Griller's Language

Simple as it is, even indoor grilling has a language all its own. The following alphabetical list can get you jiggy with GrillSpeak:

- **Baste:** Brush a seasoned liquid over the surface of food as it's grilling, to add flavor and moisture.

- **Contact grill:** A type of grill in which the food is sandwiched between two grill grids. Contact grills look like a sandwich press.

- **Cooktop insert:** Generally refers to a cooktop or range with a grill grid (see Chapter 2). Cooktop inserts include a downdraft feature that pulls smoke away from the cooktop insert (and away from your smoke detector).

- **Domed lid or cover:** A rounded cover that's usually seen on a charcoal kettle grill. Salton now makes an indoor/outdoor George Foreman grill with a domed lid (see Chapter 2).

- **Drip tray:** A plastic or metal, easy-to-clean, fat-draining reservoir that a sloping grill grid drains into.

- **Electric grill:** A grill that's powered by electricity.

- **George:** Reference to a George Foreman-style grill, as in, "So then I made him a phat burger on my George."

- **Grill grid:** The surface on which you grill foods. A grill grid may be coated with a nonstick material.

- **Grill griddle surface:** A solid grill grid (resembling a griddle) on one portion of an open grill that doesn't allow food to drop through the grill grid. A grill griddle surface allows you to cook thinly sliced vegetables and other small foods on a grill.

- **Grill pan:** A pan, usually made of cast iron, with ribs or ridges on the cooking surface (see Chapter 2). Grill pans get their heat from a cooktop.

- **Lean Mean:** Reference to George Foreman's Lean Mean Fat-Reducing Grilling Machine by Salton, as in, "I *so* want a Lean Mean for my birthday."

- **Marinate:** Soak food in a seasoned liquid, called a *marinade,* prior to cooking it, in order to add flavor and moisture (see Chapter 4).

- **Open grill:** An indoor electric grill that does not have a cover (see Chapter 2).

- **Ribs:** Ridges that stick up on a grill grid and create grill marks on your food. Generally used only when referencing a grill pan.

- **Rub:** A blend of herbs and spices that you rub onto the surface of foods before you cook them. (See Chapter 4.)

- **Sear:** Cooking food initially at a high temperature to seal in juices and give the food a brown, caramelized, slightly crusty look.

- **Variable temperature control:** A dial on a grill that allows you to control the temperature of the grill grid.

- **Vent:** Holes in the grill cover that allow steam to escape. Some indoor grills come with an adjustable vent, letting you control the heat of the cooking surface.

Marinating

If we had to name one secret to grilling success, it would be to marinate with a flourish. *Marinating* means soaking food prior to grilling in a seasoned liquid for anywhere from five minutes (if you're rushed) to overnight. The longer you allow the food to marinate, the more flavor the food will soak up.

You can marinate in any liquid, called a *marinade,* that enhances the flavor of your food. If you'd like to make your own marinades, Chapter 4 gives you the lowdown on which herbs to use with which foods and also gives you some terrific, simple recipes to use right away. If you're opting for an even simpler method, however, try using bottled marinades or salad dressings.

Whether you make your marinade from scratch or use a premade, bottled preparation, the marinating process is fairly simple:

1. **Place your food into a container that's not too big and not too small — just large enough to fit the food without much room to slosh around.**

   Be sure the bowl is *nonreactive* (that is, not made of a metal such as aluminum). Use glass, ceramic, or plastic containers, which won't react with the acids in the marinades (see Figure 3-1). All metal containers (except for stainless steel) react with the marinade and give an awful, metallic flavor to marinated foods.

Figure 3-1: Be sure to use only good containers for marinating.

2. **Pour the marinade over the food in the nonreactive container and place in the refrigerator.**

   If you can marinate overnight, great, but even if you're pressed for time, ten minutes of marinating is much better than none at all.

3. **Remove the foods from the container and place on a preheated grill or grill pan.**

4. **Discard the excess marinade and wash the container with soapy water.**

The easiest way to marinate food is to use a resealable bag that's just slightly larger than the food you're placing inside the bag. Simply place the food in the bag, pour in the marinade so that it covers the food, press all of the air out of the bag, and seal it shut (see Figure 3-2). Place the food on a preheated grill or grill pan. Discard the bag and the excess marinade.

Using a Plastic Bag to Marinate Food

Figure 3-2:
Marinate your foods in a resealable bag.

Place food in a plastic bag.

Pour marinade into the bag.

Press all of the air out of the bag.

Seal shut, making sure the food is surrounded by the marinade, folding over if necessary.

As your food grills, continue to marinate the food by basting it with a brush or mop (see Chapter 2). Be sure, however, not to use a marinade that has touched raw meat, poultry, or seafood. If your marinade has touched raw foods, you must first boil it to kill bacteria that may be in the meat.

A better idea is to whip up a new batch of marinade to use for basting. In fact, you can store a spray bottle (see Figure 3-3) full of marinade in your refrigerator, using it to baste foods from two or three inches away. Just be sure that the marinade is a watery mixture with no pieces of herbs, onions, or garlic and that the tip of the bottle doesn't touch any raw foods.

SPRAY BOTTLE
WITH MARINADE

Figure 3-3:
Baste your food with a spray bottle.

Warming Up

To heat an open indoor grill or contact grill, plug the unit in and preheat for the length of time the manufacturer directs, which is usually 5 minutes but can be up to 15, depending on the brand and type of grill.

To heat a stovetop grill pan, follow these instructions, based roughly on Le Creuset's guidelines and illustrated in Figure 3-4:

1. **Place grill pan over medium or medium-high (not high) heat for five minutes.**

   Don't preheat on high and then lower to medium or medium-high!

2. **Brush the grill grid lightly with vegetable oil.**

   Avoid using olive oil or butter to oil the grid — they tend to create smoke. If the surface is smoking, remove the pan from the heat and cool slightly before continuing.

   To save calories (and time and mess), use a nonstick cooking spray to oil the grill grid.

3. **When a few drops of cold water scattered over the surface spit and evaporate, the grill pan has warmed up.**

   If cold water gently hisses, heat the pan a few minutes longer.

4. **Dry food — even those that have been marinated — with a paper towel and place on the grill grid.**

5. **Leave the food on the grid, without turning it over, for one to two minutes to seal and sear the outside.**

Figure 3-4:
Warming up a grill pan involves several steps.

Staying Safe

Indoor grills don't require the lengthy list of safety precautions that outdoor grills require, but watch for the following fire and heat precautions, nonetheless:

- ✔ **Position your indoor grill on an open countertop so that it's not under any cabinets.** The heat from the grill may overheat a cabinet that's above the grill.

- ✔ **Don't wear clothing with flowing or loose sleeves that may drag on the grill grid and overheat.**

- ✔ **If you're using a larger grill, use long-handled utensils (see Chapter 2) so that you don't have to reach over the grill grid to position food.**

- ✔ **Open contact grills away from your face and body.** Steam that collects inside a contact grill can quickly burn your skin.

- ✔ **Use a mitt or potholder on metal handles, which are commonly found on grill pans.**

- ✔ **Always keep a fire extinguisher handy.**

In addition to taking precautions against heat and fire hazards, take the following precautions when cooking meat, poultry, and seafood:

- ✔ **Thaw meat, poultry, and seafood in the refrigerator, not on a countertop.** Food can spoil rapidly when thawing. This goes for marinating foods, too.

- ✔ **Store raw seafood in your refrigerator for no more than 24 hours.** Store ground meats and raw poultry for up to two days; red meat for up to five.

- ✔ **Never use the same plate and utensils for raw foods as you do for cooked ones.** Raw meat, poultry, and seafood can contain harmful bacteria. After placing your foods on the grill, wash your plate and utensils with soapy water before using them again.

- ✔ **Keep raw meat, poultry, and seafood separate from other foods.**

- ✔ **Always wash your hands in hot, soapy water before and after handling raw meat, poultry, and seafood.**

- ✔ **When you marinate foods and then want to use the marinade to baste your food as it cooks, first boil the marinade to kill bacteria.** Better yet, whip up a separate batch of marinade to use for basting.

- ✔ **Cook all meat, poultry, and seafood to a safe temperature (see Table 3-1).** Use a thermometer (see Chapter 2) inserted into the thickest part of the meat to measure the temperature.

Don't insert the thermometer until the outside of the food is seared or the thermometer itself could carry bacteria into the interior of the food.

Table 3-1	U.S.D.A. Grilling Temperature Recommendations
Type of Food	*Safe Temperature*
Beef and lamb steaks and chops	145°
Finfish	145°
Shrimp and scallops	145°
Fresh pork	150°
Ground beef, ground pork, or ground lamb	160°
Ground chicken or ground turkey	165°
Poultry breasts	170°
Poultry thighs and wings	180°
Precooked sausage and hot dogs	To taste
Fruits, vegetables, and breads	To taste

TECHNICAL STUFF

Watching your PAHs and HCAs

You may have heard reports over the last few years of cancer risk from heterocyclic amines (HCAs) that are created when meat and poultry are cooked at high temperatures and polycyclic aromatic hydrocarbons (PAHs) that form when fat drips onto a heating element, such as that in your electric indoor grill. According to the Center for Science in the Public Interest, the jury is still out on whether HCAs and PAHs are a health threat to humans, but these chemicals have caused cancer in laboratory animals. Here's the advice the Center for Science in the Public Interest gives on cutting your risk:

✔ **Marinate your food.** The marinade sets up a barrier against heat.

✔ **Don't try to save time by cooking your food at a high temperature.** After initially searing each surface, use a medium temperature to cook your foods.

✔ **Choose seafood, vegetables, and fruits.** They produce few or no HCAs and PAHs.

✔ **Choose smaller, lean cuts of meat and poultry.** Lean cuts produce fewer PAHs, and smaller cuts give HCAs less time to form (because they cook faster).

✔ **Thaw frozen meat (in the refrigerator) before you cook.** This helps prevent the surface of the meat from being overexposed to high temperatures while allowing the inside to cook slowly.

✔ **Avoid eating charred or blackened food.**

Perfecting Your Timing

To grill food to perfection, you need two tools: a timer and a thermometer (see Chapter 2). Use Table 3-2 and your timer to approximate the cooking times for your foods; use a thermometer and Table 3-1 to double-check whether your food is ready to savor.

Don't cook at a high heat. You'll end up with a charred outer surface and an uncooked interior. Instead, preheat your grill grid for at least five minutes, and then sear all surfaces of your foods on the grill grid. After you've seared every surface, locking in juices and flavor, cook foods at a moderate temperature setting.

Keep in mind that if your grill doesn't have an adjustable temperature control, the heat is automatically set to medium or medium-high heat.

Table 3-2	Grilling Times
Food	*Approximate Grilling Time (In Minutes)*
Shrimp and scallops	2–4
Precooked sausage and hot dogs	3–5
Fruits, vegetables, and breads	3–20
Beef and lamb steaks and chops	5–25
Finfish	8–10
Ground beef, ground pork, or ground lamb	10–20
Ground chicken or ground turkey	10–20
Poultry thighs and wings	10–20
Poultry breasts	12–26
Fresh pork	20–30

Maintaining Your Grill

The best way to clean your grill is to make a deal with your cooking partner that if you cook, he or she cleans up. Short of such a bargain, keep in mind that indoor grills are generally a joy to clean.

To clean an open indoor grill, contact grill, or a cooktop insert, do the following:

1. **Unplug the unit or remove it from the heat and allow it to cool.**

2. **Remove the drip tray (if your unit has one), dispose of the liquid, and wash the reservoir.**

   Many drip trays are dishwasher-safe.

3. **Remove the grill grid (and any other removable parts) and hand wash.**

   Check the instructions that come with your indoor grill to see if the grill grid is dishwasher-safe. Even if it is, however, you may decide to hand wash your grill grid because of the space it takes up in your dishwasher.

   If your unit doesn't have a removable grill grid, use a sponge to wipe food particles from the grid's surface.

   Don't use any metal or abrasive pads, because they may scratch the surface. A sponge or nylon brush is all you need to clean your indoor electric grill.

4. **Dry thoroughly and store.**

To clean a grill pan, follow these steps:

1. **Remove from heat and allow to cool.**

2. **Fill the grill pan with warm water and soak for 15 minutes.**

   Don't plunge a hot grill into cold water or fill it with cold water. However, if you wait for your grill pan to cool completely before soaking or washing it, food residue will really stick to the surface.

3. **After soaking, scrub the grill pan with a sponge or nylon brush.**

   Don't use any metal or abrasive pads, because they may scratch the surface.

   Most grill pans are dishwasher-safe; however, using a dishwasher for your grill pan reduces the amount of brownish-black film on the surface of the grill pan. Although it may sound disgusting, this film is a good thing: The more buildup you have on the surface of your grill pan, the more efficient your pan is. Your pan will also require less oil each time you use it.

4. **Dry thoroughly and store.**

Part II
Accounting for Taste

The 5th Wave   By Rich Tennant

"I'm not sure what flavor you're tasting. I didn't use any spice rubs on the meat, however I dropped it several times on the way to the grill."

In this part . . .

In this part, you find ways to add flavor to your grilled food through marinades, rubs, and sauces (both homemade and bottled). Although grilled food has a delicious flavor all its own, a little boost of flavor — whether from marinating before you grill or adding a dollop of special sauce to a finished dish — takes a meal from pretty great to out-of-this-world. This part shares plenty of recipes that will make your grilled meal something to rave about.

Chapter 4

Making Marinades and Rubs

In This Chapter

▶ Adding a bevy of flavor to your grilled foods with marinades

▶ Massaging taste into food with homemade rubs

Marinades and rubs are *the* secret to grilling: No other technique adds as much to the flavor of your grilled foods as soaking your food in seasoned marinades or massaging the surface of your foods with dry or pasty rubs. This chapter shares some tasty recipes and also gives you tips on creating your own, personalized seasonings.

Soaking Up Flavor with Marinades

A *marinade* is a seasoned liquid in which you soak your foods before grilling them. Although marinades vary wildly in taste, they share three key ingredients: herbs, an oil, and an acid (such as citrus juice, wine, vinegar, or yogurt).

You're not cheating by using prepared marinades, you're simply being efficient! Be creative as you look around for marinade ideas in salad dressings, soy sauce, wines, oils, ketchup, mustard, citrus fruits, garlic and onion, and yogurt. You'll need about a cup of marinade for every pound of food.

Marinades are simple to make. We recommend whipping up the recipes in this section as a starting point and then branching out to mix your own flavors. Figure 4-1 helps you identify some well-known herbs and Table 4-1 matches those herbs to foods.

Table 4-1	Matching Herbs to Foods
Herb	*Use with These Foods*
Basil	Tomatoes, poultry, meat
Bay leaf	Poultry, seafood, meat
Chervil	Combine with other herbs to increase potency
Chives	Vegetables
Cilantro	Vegetables
Dill	Tomatoes, seafood (especially salmon), poultry
Marjoram	Meat, seafood, tomatoes
Mint	Vegetables, meat, poultry, lamb
Oregano	Zucchini, beef, lamb
Parsley	Vegetables (especially potatoes), seafood
Rosemary	Chicken, pork, duck, lamb, potatoes
Sage	Seafood, poultry, pork, sausage
Savory	Poultry, meat
Tarragon	Seafood, chicken
Thyme	Seafood, poultry, lamb, tomatoes, broccoli

For the best flavor, use fresh herbs whenever possible. If your supermarket or specialty shop doesn't carry fresh herbs year-round, consider growing a few of your favorites in a pot on your kitchen windowsill. Cut, washed, and dried herbs will stay fresh in the crisper drawer of your refrigerator for a few days; they last even longer if you store them between strips of paper towel instead of in plastic bags. When you're ready to use the herbs in a recipe, first chop them roughly and then use a rocking motion with your knife to chop them finely, releasing their savory flavors (see Figure 4-2). Freeze chopped basil, chives, dill, or fennel by mixing with a bit of water and placing in a freezer-safe container. You can also freeze parsley, but it doesn't require additional water for freezing.

Dried herbs are another alternative, but you won't get as much of a flavor-packed punch from dried herbs as you will from fresh. That said, dried herbs are more concentrated than fresh, so use about one-third the amount of dried herbs as you would fresh.

Chopping Parsley & Other Fresh Herbs

Figure 4-2:
Chopping
herbs for
best flavor.

1.

Rinse and dry well

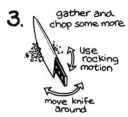

2. chop roughly

✳NOTE:
For herbs like rosemary
and thyme, remove and chop
leaves. Discard thick stem.

3. gather and chop some more

Use rocking motion

move knife around

Bird Bath

Any marinade for poultry should complement or enhance the bird rather than mask it. Citrus juices provide the acidity in this delicate, general-purpose seasoning liquid.

Tools: *Jar with tight-fitting lid*

Preparation time: *10 minutes*

Yield: *1 cup (16 tablespoons)*

½ cup orange juice

¼ cup fresh lemon juice (about 2 lemons)

¼ cup olive oil

2 tablespoons chopped fresh or 2 teaspoons
dried tarragon or thyme leaves

1 teaspoon salt

¼ teaspoon paprika

¼ teaspoon Tabasco sauce

1 In a jar with a tight-fitting lid, shake together all ingredients.

2 Use the mixture to bathe 2 pounds boneless chicken breasts; 8 quail; 4 Cornish hens; or 1 cut-up, whole chicken. Marinate at least 1 hour or up to 24 hours before grilling.

Nutrition at a glance (per 1 tablespoon): calories 35; calories from fat 31; fat 3 g; saturated fat 1 g; cholesterol 0 mg; sodium 146 mg; carbohydrates 1 g; dietary fiber 0 g; protein 0.1 g

Meat Soaker

The bold flavor of this wine-based marinade makes it ideal for lamb and any less-than-tender cuts of beef. Choose a red wine that has some body such as a cabernet sauvignon. It doesn't have to be an expensive wine, just good enough to sip.

Tools: *Jar with tight-fitting lid*

Preparation time: *5 minutes*

Yield: *2 cups (32 tablespoons)*

1⅔ cups dry red wine	*1½ teaspoons salt*
⅓ cup olive oil	*½ teaspoon ground black pepper*
¼ cup cut chives or chopped small scallion	
2 tablespoons chopped fresh or 2 teaspoons dried oregano leaves	

1 In a jar with a tight-fitting lid, mix all ingredients.

2 Pour 1 cup of the mixture over 1½ to 2 pounds of meat. For best results, marinate meat in the refrigerator for 4 hours or overnight but no longer than 24 hours. If possible, turn the meat in the marinade a few times during its soaking time. Store unused marinade in the refrigerator.

Nutrition at a glance (per 1 tablespoon): *calories 29; calories from fat 20; fat 2 g; saturated fat 0 g; cholesterol 0 mg; sodium 110 mg; carbohydrates 0 g; dietary fiber 0 g; protein 0 g*

Mixin' and matchin'

Consider mixing up batches of the following dried herb mixes to use at a moment's notice. (Don't worry if you can't pronounce these herb mixes — they're all French. Apparently, the French spend more time mixing herbs than the rest of the world does — or at least they're better at naming them first — so classic herb mixtures generally don't have names like "Bob's Spicy Herb Mix.")

✔ **Herbes de Provence:** thyme, oregano, rosemary, and savory

✔ **Bouquet garni:** parsley, thyme, and a bay leaf

✔ **Fines herbs:** parsley, chervil, chives, and tarragon

Carolina Spray Mop

This watery, tangy sauce was originally concocted in the Carolinas to moisten a whole hog while it smoked over a long period of time. Texans also mopped their barbecued beef briskets with a spicy version. Typically applied with a long-handled brush or small cotton mop (see Chapter 2), you can spray this thin basting sauce from a spray bottle (see Chapter 3) onto today's leaner pork, chicken breasts, and turkey. Just be sure to use a spray bottle that's meant for food rather than one that's meant for household chemicals!

Tools: *Small mixing bowl, whisk*

Preparation time: *5 minutes*

Yield: *1⅛ cups (18 tablespoons)*

1 cup cider vinegar	*1 teaspoon Worcestershire sauce*
3 tablespoons sugar	*¼ teaspoon hot pepper sauce, or to taste*
1 teaspoon salt	

1 In a small mixing bowl, whisk together all ingredients until sugar dissolves.

2 Pour into bottle with a sprayer. If the sprayer gets clogged, remove from bottle and rinse under warm water, spraying until it is cleared.

Vary It! *For an Asian Mop, combine 1 cup pineapple juice, ¼ cup naturally brewed soy sauce, 2 tablespoons sugar, 2 tablespoons rice vinegar, 1 teaspoon ground ginger, and ¼ teaspoon garlic powder. Yields 1½ cups (24 tablespoons).*

Nutrition at a glance (per 1 tablespoon): *calories 9; calories from fat 0; fat 0 g; saturated fat 0 g; cholesterol 0 mg; sodium 114 mg; carbohydrates 3 g; dietary fiber 0 g; protein 0 g*

Rubbing Your Food the Right Way

A *rub* is a combination of herbs and spices that you massage onto the surface of the food you're preparing to grill. Rubs come in two varieties: dry and wet.

- ✔ **Dry rubs:** Dry rubs generally call for more spices than herbs, because spices don't char the food's surface. The amount of dry rub to use is a matter of personal taste; count on 1 to 2 tablespoons for every pound of food. You can store dry rubs indefinitely in an airtight container.

- ✔ **Wet rubs:** A wet rub is usually a dry seasoning that has oil or fresh herbs added to create a paste. Rubbing with a wet herbal paste adds a vibrant flavor to all kinds of food.

Poultry Dust

This dry rub, also called a *dust*, is a perfect complement to chicken, turkey, game hens, and duck. If the poultry is lean, such as boneless skinless chicken breast or turkey cutlets, rub the food with oil before sprinkling with the dust. Foods with skin (chicken wings, game hens, or duckling) need no oiling.

Tools: *Plastic zipper bag*

Preparation time: *5 minutes*

Yield: *14 teaspoons*

2 tablespoons kosher or sea salt	2 teaspoons onion powder
1 tablespoon sugar	1 teaspoon ground white pepper
2 teaspoons rubbed or finely crumbled dried sage	1 teaspoon paprika

1 Combine all ingredients in a small plastic zipper bag.

2 Coat the food lightly with oil (if necessary) before rubbing.

3 Taking a small amount of the mixture in your hand, massage the rub into the surface of 2 to 2½ pounds of poultry before grilling.

Nutrition at a glance (per 1 teaspoon): *calories 6; calories from fat 0; fat 0 g; saturated fat 0 g; cholesterol 0 mg; sodium 481 mg; carbohydrates 1 g; dietary fiber 0 g; protein 0 g*

Backbone of Rubs

Use this herbal paste with nearly any meat or poultry. Your foods taste sooo good after this rubdown!

Tools: *Small jar*

Preparation time: *10 minutes*

Yield: *½ cup (8 tablespoons)*

⅓ cup extra virgin olive oil

¼ cup finely chopped fresh herbs (1 tablespoon each of parsley, rosemary, basil, and oregano) or ¼ cup chopped fresh parsley plus 1 teaspoon dried basil, ½ teaspoon dried rosemary, and ½ teaspoon dried oregano

2 tablespoons red wine vinegar or balsamic vinegar

1 teaspoon dry mustard

½ teaspoon salt

1 In a small jar, combine all ingredients.

2 Take a few spoonfuls and massage the rub into 2 pounds of vegetables, meat, or seafood, making sure that all sides are coated.

Nutrition at a glance (per 1 teaspoon): calories 27; calories from fat 27; fat 3 g; saturated fat 0.5 g; cholesterol 0 mg; sodium 49 mg; carbohydrates 0 g; dietary fiber 0 g; protein 0 g

Chapter 5

Serving Up Sauces

Sauces are a perfect way to add color, flavor, texture, and variety to your grill dishes. In many cases, you can whip up a sauce (or walk to your pantry and open a jar) in less time than you need to grill your main dish. This chapter shares both homemade and store-bought sauce ideas.

Shh! Don't Tell: Using Bottled Sauces

Bottled sauces that you pick up at your supermarket are a quick and easy way to sauce up your grilled dishes. To keep your secret safe, pour the sauce into a small dish or pitcher before serving.

- ✔ **Barbecue sauce:** Try heating bottled barbecue sauce in the microwave for a close-to-homemade flavor enhancer.

- ✔ **Chutneys:** Chutneys combine chunks of fruits or vegetables with vinegar, a sweetener, and some sort of spicy flavor like onions or hot peppers. Like salsa, chutneys are a wonderful companion to a variety of grilled foods, including pork, lamb, and beef.

- ✔ **Horseradish sauce:** Bottled horseradish sauce complements the flavor of sausage, burgers, and seafood. For a flavor variation, add chunks of vegetables such as tomatoes, cucumbers, and green peppers to bottled sauce.

- ✔ **Pesto:** The tangy zip of basil, pine nuts, and olive oil are a tasty companion to any seafood dish.

- ✔ **Salad dressings:** With flavors from Thousand Island to ranch to sun-dried tomato with basil, you can find a dressing made up of your favorite flavors.

✔ **Salsa:** Salsa, now America's favorite condiment, is a winner on burgers, steaks, fish, and poultry, as well as in wraps. Choose your heat when cooking for yourself, but when entertaining guests, stick with the mild variety.

✔ **Tabasco sauce:** This spicy condiment adds tangy flavor to grilled foods of all kind. Leave a bottle on the table so that everyone can apply enough to suit his own tastes.

The Secret's in the Homemade Sauce

If you can spare the time, homemade sauces are a supreme flavor enhancer. The sauces in this section require from 15 to 30 minutes of preparation time, but the results are worth it: Family, dinner guests, and your canine companion (who may get a few scraps after dinner) will all rave about the flavor and color these sauces add to your grilled dishes.

Basic Barbecue Sauce

This delectable sauce adds a smoky outdoor flavor to any cut of beef, pork, or poultry grilled in your kitchen.

Tools: *Medium saucepan*

Preparation time: *28 minutes*

Yield: *1¾ cups (28 tablespoons)*

1 tablespoon vegetable oil	¼ cup packed light brown sugar
1 small or ½ medium onion, finely chopped (¼ to ⅓ cup)	2 teaspoons liquid smoke seasoning (see the "Smoke in a bottle" sidebar)
1½ cups ketchup	½ teaspoon salt
¼ cup Worcestershire sauce	

1 In medium saucepan, heat oil over medium heat. Add onion and cook until softened, about 2 to 3 minutes. Add remaining ingredients.

2 Bring to a simmer and cook over low heat 20 minutes, stirring occasionally. Remove from heat and let stand at room temperature to cool.

3 Serve immediately or pour into a container with a lid. Cover and refrigerate up to a week. Warm a chilled sauce slowly over low heat to serve on brisket, ribs, chicken, shredded pork, or burgers.

Vary It! To kick the heat up a notch in this sauce, add 2 teaspoons chili powder, 1 teaspoon ground pure hot red chili, ½ teaspoon ground red pepper (cayenne), or ½ teaspoon Tabasco sauce to the basic sauce.

Nutrition at a glance (per 1 tablespoon): calories 28; calories from fat 5; fat 1 g; saturated fat 0 g; cholesterol 0 mg; sodium 222 mg; carbohydrates 6 g; dietary fiber 0 g; protein 0 g

Orange Soy Glaze

Many commercially prepared teriyaki sauces contain a lot of sodium due to the soy sauce. In this homemade version, orange juice, which replaces some of the high-sodium soy sauce that most recipes call for, cuts the sodium level considerably. Apply this glaze to grilled chicken, beef, pork, salmon, and vegetables such as eggplant.

Tools: *Medium saucepan*

Preparation time: *15 minutes*

Yield: *1⅔ cups (26 tablespoons)*

1 cup orange juice	1 tablespoon finely grated fresh ginger
½ cup naturally brewed soy sauce	2 tablespoons dry sherry or sake
⅓ cup sugar	2 teaspoons cornstarch

1 In a medium saucepan, combine orange juice, soy, sugar, and ginger. Heat to boiling. Meanwhile, mix sherry and cornstarch until smooth. Stir into orange mixture and heat to boiling. Boil glaze 1 minute. Remove from heat and let stand at room temperature to cool.

2 Serve immediately or pour into a jar with a lid. Cover and refrigerate up to a week. Use glaze to brush on foods the last five minutes they grill, or serve with grilled meat, fish, or poultry.

Vary It! To turn this recipe into a marinade, omit the cornstarch and combine ingredients in a glass dish or resealable plastic bag. Place food in marinade, cover, and marinate 2 hours. Great for flank or top round steak.

Nutrition at a glance (per 1 tablespoon): calories 18; calories from fat 0; fat 0 g; saturated fat 0 g; cholesterol 0 mg; sodium 283 mg; carbohydrates 4 g; dietary fiber 0 g; protein 1 g

Smoke in a bottle

Liquid smoke is made by burning wood such as hickory or mesquite and trapping the smoke, which condenses and is collected as a liquid. Often used by commercial food makers, who add it to barbecue sauces, smoked cheese, and processed meats and fish, bottled liquid smoke is available on most supermarket shelves in either the spice or barbecue sauce section. A small amount (1 teaspoon per pound of meat or cup of sauce) is all you need to give an outdoor smoky flavor to your dish.

When selecting fresh ginger, choose plump pieces of root that are over 1 inch thick and 3 to 4 inches long without too many knobs (the knobs get in the way of peeling — see Figure 5-1). Peel ginger with a vegetable peeler or knife. Grate ginger by using a sharp metal grater with ⅛-inch holes placed over a bowl. You'll get finely grated pieces, ginger juice, and some fibers on top of the grater. Squeeze the leftover fibers into the bowl to get every drop of ginger juice, and then compost the fibers. Use both grated ginger and juice when measuring ginger for the Orange Soy Glaze. Grated ginger freezes well in small plastic containers. Storing pieces or slices of peeled fresh ginger in a jar of sherry is another way to kept ginger fresh, but the ginger will have a definite sherry flavor.

Figure 5-1:
Look for fresh ginger without a lot of knobs.

Parsley Puree

This classic Argentine sauce called *chimichurri* functions not only as a table condiment but as a marinade for beef or firm fish.

Tools: *Food processor*

Preparation time: *15 minutes*

Yield: *1 cup (16 tablespoons)*

2 cups flat-leaf parsley leaves without stems	*2 tablespoons fresh lemon juice*
1 medium onion, cut into chunks	*2 tablespoons red wine vinegar*
2 cloves garlic	*1 teaspoon salt*
⅓ cup extra virgin olive oil	*¼ teaspoon ground red pepper*

In food processor, combine all ingredients and process until mixture forms a paste-like consistency, stopping occasionally to scrape the contents from the side of the container. Transfer puree to jar; store refrigerated for up to a week or freeze up to a month.

Nutrition at a glance (per 1 tablespoon): calories 45; calories from fat 41; fat 5 g; saturated fat 1 g; cholesterol 0 mg; sodium 150 mg; carbohydrates 1 g; dietary fiber 0 g; protein 0 g

Squirt-bottle cuisine

Purees first appeared in the mid 1970s to sauce foods during the time of *cuisine minceur* (low-caloried) French cooking by Chef Michel Guerard. Chefs resorted to plastic squeeze bottles (like those used to squirt ketchup or mustard) to store the sauces in and then to decorate the plates with, creating drips, dots, and lines just before a dinner plate was filled. Chefs and pastry chefs use the sauces — whether vegetables, berries, mango, or even melted chocolate — to direct precise flavoring to their masterpieces.

At home, you can create a special plate by using a squirt bottle. Just don't go crazy with it, though: Use the vibrant colors of the sauce to enhance, not obliterate your food. Use the bottle to make a bull's-eye circle of sauce, then put your grilled food on top.

Spicy Peanut Sauce

This Asian-inspired dipping sauce for skewered poultry or pork may be prepared several days in advance. Refrigerate and serve at room temperature. If sauce is too thick when serving, thin with more water. The sauce becomes thicker upon chilling.

Tools: *Small mixing bowl, whisk*

Preparation time: *5 minutes*

Yield: *1¼ cups (20 tablespoons)*

⅔ cup crunchy peanut butter

⅔ cup boiling water

2 tablespoons naturally brewed soy sauce or
1 tablespoon Asian fish sauce

2 tablespoons light or dark brown sugar

1 tablespoon fresh lemon or lime juice

¼ teaspoon crushed red pepper flakes

Combine ingredients in a small mixing bowl. The consistency should be a pourable sauce. Because brands of peanut butter vary in texture, if this sauce is too thin or watery, stir in more peanut butter. Pour sauce into small bowl to serve.

Nutrition at a glance (per 1 tablespoon): *calories 57; calories from fat 39; fat 4 g; saturated fat 1 g; cholesterol 0 mg; sodium 135 mg; carbohydrates 3 g; dietary fiber 1 g; protein 2 g*

Tropical Fruit Salsa

Tomato salsas have become as common as ketchup in today's pantry. Fruit versions are still a novel and tasty alternatives. Serve this one with grilled pork, ham, or poultry.

Tools: *Small saucepan*

Preparation time: *25 minutes*

Yield: *2 cups (32 tablespoons)*

1 teaspoon olive oil	*2 kiwifruit, peeled and diced*
¼ cup chopped red onion or sweet red pepper	*3 tablespoons chopped fresh cilantro or parsley*
1 small jalapeno pepper, seeded and chopped	*1 tablespoon fresh lime juice*
1 large ripe or 2 small mangos (about 1 pound)	*¼ teaspoon salt*

1 In a small saucepan, heat the oil over medium-low heat. Add the onion and jalapeno; cook and stir just until vegetables are softened, about 2 minutes. Do not allow the vegetables to turn brown.

2 Remove the saucepan from the heat and cool the onion mixture. Meanwhile, peel, pit, and dice the mango (see Figure 5-2). Place the mango in a mixing bowl or storage container and stir in the onion mixture and remaining ingredients. Cover and refrigerate salsa until serving time.

Vary It! *Substitute about 1½ cups of diced fresh pineapple for the mango.*

Nutrition at a glance (per 1 tablespoon): *calories 10; calories from fat 2; fat 0 g; saturated fat 0 g; cholesterol 0 mg; sodium 19 mg; carbohydrates 2 g; dietary fiber 0 g; protein 0 g*

How to Cut a Mango

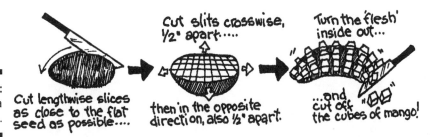

Figure 5-2: Cutting up a mango.

Cut lengthwise slices as close to the flat seed as possible....

Cut slits crosswise, ½" apart.....

then in the opposite direction, also ½" apart.

Turn the 'flesh' inside out...

...and cut off the cubes of mango!

Veggie Coulis

A classic French sauce of pureed cooked vegetables (or fresh fruit), *coulis* is easily prepared in an electric blender or food processor. This low-calorie, delicately flavored sauce is nutritious and a great companion to grilled seafood.

Tools: *Small saucepan, blender or food processor*

Preparation time: *30 minutes*

Yield: *2½ cups (40 tablespoons)*

1 tablespoon olive oil

3 shallots, peeled and chopped, or ¼ cup chopped white part of scallions

1 pound carrots, peeled and cut into ¼-inch slices

1 cup chicken broth

½ teaspoon salt

½ cup low-fat sour cream

1 In a small saucepan, heat oil over medium-low heat. Add shallots and cook 2 minutes. Add carrots, broth, and salt and bring to a boil over high heat. Reduce heat to low, cover and simmer about 15 minutes or until carrots are very tender when pierced with a fork.

2 Transfer the carrots and the broth to an electric blender or food processor. Add the sour cream and puree on low speed just until the sour cream is mixed in. (Because the mixture is hot, be careful with the blender. You may have to remove the center part of the cover to allow some steam to escape.) Then puree the mixture on high speed until smooth. If the sauce is too thick, stir in some more broth or water. Keep sauce warm over hot water. To serve, spoon or squirt sauce from a bottle onto serving plates and top with grilled food.

Vary It! *Substitute 2½ cups 1-inch cubed fresh cauliflower for the carrots but cook 10 minutes. Two cups (about 10 ounces) of thawed frozen peas may also be cooked to make coulis.*

Nutrition at a glance (per 1 tablespoon): *calories 14; calories from fat 8; fat 1 g; saturated fat 0 g; cholesterol 3 mg; sodium 63 mg; carbohydrates 2 g; dietary fiber 0 g; protein 0 g*

Part III
Getting Grilled

The 5th Wave   By Rich Tennant

Eschewing the indoor covered and more traditional stovetop varieties, Stan opts for a 1946 Chevrolet Fleetline grill.

In this part . . .

This part is the meat of the book (pun intended!), with recipes that range from basic grilled favorites like hamburgers and grilled cheese to delicious meals that feature steak, pork, poultry, and seafood. We've also included a chapter on grilling vegetables and one on making salads and wraps from grilled foods. And with many of the recipes you find in this part, we've cued you in to some great dishes that partner well with these foods, as well as some ways to vary the recipes if you're so inclined.

Chapter 6

Quick and Easy Favorites

In This Chapter

▶ Using your grill to make fast, simple dishes

▶ Creating the world's best burgers

▶ Preparing hot dogs and sausages with style

▶ Whipping up gourmet grilled cheese

▶ Grilling ham to perfection

*T*his chapter contains the simplest, most basic recipes we know: burgers, hot dogs and sausages, grilled cheese, and grilled ham steaks.

Burgers

Hamburgers are a culinary classic that range from everyday to highbrow. By changing the type and quality of ground meat, the type of bun, the ingredients added to the ground meat, and the toppings, your burger can be anything from a quick meal for kids to a gourmet delight.

Every burger, however, requires the following care (illustrated in Figure 6-1), regardless of its pedigree:

- ✔ **Make sure the burger size is uniform and not too thick (no more than ¾-inch thick).** A burger that's thicker in the middle than on the edge — or is just uniformly huge — won't grill evenly.

- ✔ **Mix the burger ingredients just enough to combine them.** Overmixing toughens the meat.

- ✔ **Don't use a spatula to flatten the burger as it cooks.** You'll end up with a tough burger. Instead, gently lift and flip the burger with a spatula or with tongs (see Chapter 2).

Figure 6-1:
Shaping a
burger into
patties.

Selecting the best ground meat

When choosing ground meat for your burgers, keep in mind that the "name" of the ground meat has little to do with its leanness or its quality. For the record, what's often labeled as *ground beef* is the fattiest of all meats (as much as 30 percent fat) and tends to taste greasy. Ground chuck contains 20 to 25 percent fat; ground round, 15 to 20 percent fat; and ground sirloin boasts 10 to 15 percent fat. Most experts agree that meat that has about 15 percent fat makes the best-tasting burgers.

No federal regulations govern the labeling of fat content for ground meat. Food labeled *lean* or *extra lean* can contain over 22 percent fat. To better inform yourself, look for "% lean" to determine the quality of the meat: Consider "10% lean" or better to be fairly low in fat; "5% lean" or better is extra-lean meat.

Take care when substituting other ground meats for ground beef, because many are as high (or higher) in fat. If you're trying to eat in a way that contributes to a healthier lifestyle, steer clear of ground lamb and use only ground turkey breast or ground chicken breast, which are both quite lean.

What does all that other labeling mean?

In addition to the cut of meat and the percent fat or percent lean, you may also find the following labeling on ground beef, which may or may not be important to you:

✔ **Hormone-free:** No synthetic growth hormones were fed or injected into the livestock.

✔ **Antibiotic-free:** No antibiotics were used in the feed or care of the livestock.

✔ **Organic:** Livestock feed was grown without the use of synthetic pesticides or fertilizers; livestock was not given synthetic hormones or treated with antibiotics.

✔ **Grass-fed:** Livestock was fed on grass in a pasture instead of feeding on corn and other grains.

✔ **Free-range:** Livestock roamed around the farm and was not restricted to a small pen.

Taking your burger's temperature

The U.S. Department of Agriculture (USDA) recently advised using only the internal temperature of a beef patty — and not the color of the interior of a cooked patty — to determine whether a burger is safe to eat. Here's their advice:

✔ **Cook burgers to an internal temperature of 160°.** Keep in mind that, at that temperature, the cooked patty may look brown, pink, or brown *and* pink. Remember that even burgers that are cooked to a temperature less than 160° can be brown throughout the patty, so color isn't the most accurate indicator of doneness.

✔ **Wash the thermometer immediately after testing an undercooked burger and also when the burgers are ready to eat.**

✔ **When you *can't* take the temperature of a burger, go by the color.** Never eat burgers that are pink or red in the middle.

Varying the routine

Add some variety to your burgers by changing the following:

✔ **Type of ground meat:** Consider using ground lamb, turkey, or chicken.

✔ **Type of bun:** Use whole-grain buns, Italian bread, pita bread, tortillas, or bagels.

✔ **Ingredients added to the ground meat:** Add dried fruit, jalapenos, dried tomatoes, chopped boiled eggs, diced vegetable pieces, fresh or dried herbs, or spices.

✔ **Toppings:** Use salsa, a variety of cheeses, bacon, mushrooms, tomatoes, or other vegetables.

Simple Burgers with Special Sauce

This American classic is so simple, you really don't need a recipe. But watch that you don't overhandle the ground meat and other ingredients. To avoid tough burgers, sprinkle the seasonings on the meat, gently toss with a fork, and then shape into patties.

Tools: *Grill, small mixing bowl*

Preparation time: *10 minutes*

Grilling time: *15 to 20 minutes*

Yield: *4 servings*

4 sesame seed sandwich buns, split

1 teaspoon dried thyme leaves, crumbled

½ teaspoon salt

½ teaspoon garlic powder (optional)

¼ teaspoon ground black pepper

1½ pounds ground chuck

Special Sauce (see the following recipe) or ketchup or ranch salad dressing

Lettuce leaves and tomato slices

1 Spray the grill grid with nonstick cooking spray or brush with oil to prevent food from sticking. Heat an indoor electric grill, grill pan, or cooktop insert over medium-high heat for 5 minutes.

2 Place 2 buns, cut sides down, on the grill and cook, uncovered, just until warmed or lightly browned. Place the grilled buns on a plate, cover with foil, and keep warm. Repeat with the other two buns. If using a large electric grill or cooktop insert, grill all the buns at the same time.

3 In a small mixing bowl, combine the thyme leaves, salt, garlic, and pepper. Sprinkle the meat with seasonings. Shape the ground beef into four patties, each ¾-inch thick in the center and at the edge. (Even thickness ensures even grilling.)

4 Place the patties on the grill. Grill 5 to 7 minutes per side in a grill pan, on an open grill, or on a cooktop insert (for medium doneness). For a contact grill, grill patties for 3 minutes, turn patties, and grill covered 2 minutes longer to brown lightly.

5 To serve, spread cut surfaces of buns with Special Sauce. Top each bottom bun half with lettuce, beef patty, tomato, and top of bun.

Nutrition at a glance (per serving without condiments): calories 454; calories from fat 215; fat 24 g; saturated fat 8 g; cholesterol 108 mg; sodium 631 mg; carbohydrates 23 g; dietary fiber 1 g; protein 34 g

You can substantially reduce the calories, fat, and saturated fat by using ground turkey breast or 90-, 92-, or 96-percent lean beef.

Special Sauce

Tools: *Small mixing bowl*

Preparation time: *2 minutes*

Yield: *½ cup (8 tablespoons)*

½ cup low-fat mayonnaise

1 tablespoon ketchup

1 tablespoon drained pickle relish.

In a small mixing bowl, combine all ingredients.

Nutrition at a glance (per 1 tablespoon): *calories 30; calories from fat 9; fat 1 g; saturated fat 0 g; cholesterol 0 mg; sodium 178 mg; carbohydrates 5 g; dietary fiber 0 g; protein 0 g*

Safety precautions for ground meat

Ground beef is more likely to harbor *E. coli* than any other food. (*E. coli* is a common bacteria found in the intestinal tract of warm blooded animals; it can cause illness — and sometimes even death — if it is consumed.) Although this may sound startling, you can take simple precautions to ensure that your burgers are safe to enjoy:

- Thaw burgers in the refrigerator, not on a countertop.

- Store fresh ground meat in your refrigerator for no more than two days.

- Never use the same plate and utensils for raw burgers as you do for cooked ones.

- After placing your foods on the grill, wash your plate, mixing bowl, and utensils with soapy water before using them again.

- Keep raw ground meat separate from other foods.

- Always wash your hands in hot, soapy water before and after handling raw ground beef.

- Cook ground beef, pork, and lamb to 160°, as measured by a thermometer. Cook ground chicken or turkey to 165°.

TIP

Great side dishes for quick meals

Any of the following dishes make a terrific (and quick) complement to burgers, hot dogs, sausages, grilled cheese, and grilled ham:

- Red potato salad
- Oven "fried" potatoes
- Baked potatoes
- Baked beans
- Ravioli or tortellini topped with tomato sauce

- Cold pasta salad
- Corn on the cob
- Soup
- Chili
- Steamed vegetables
- Lettuce salad
- Raw veggies and dip
- Fruit salad

Stuffed Burgers

Sandwiched between two thin beef patties is a pocket of cheese and dried tomato filling. This elevates the humble burger into a special meal.

Tools: *Grill*

Preparation time: *15 minutes*

Grilling time: *15 to 20 minutes*

Yield: *4 servings*

8 slices brioche or crusty peasant bread
(about 4 inches in diameter)

1¾ pounds lean ground beef

4 slices goat cheese (¼ inch thick by 1¼ inch
in diameter)

4 teaspoons chopped, drained, oil-packed
sun-dried tomatoes

4 teaspoons chopped flat-leaf parsley

½ teaspoon salt

¼ teaspoon ground black pepper

Arugula or red leaf lettuce

1 Spray the grill grid with nonstick cooking spray or brush with oil to prevent food from sticking. Heat an indoor electric grill, grill pan, or cooktop insert over medium-high heat for 5 minutes.

2 Place the bread slices, four at a time, on the grill and toast on both sides until lightly browned, about 2 to 3 minutes. Transfer the bread to a plate, covering with foil to keep warm. If using a large grill or cooktop insert, toast all the bread at the same time.

3 On waxed paper or a plate, divide and shape the ground beef into eight patties, each about 4 inches in diameter. Place 1 cheese slice, 1 teaspoon chopped tomato, and 1 teaspoon chopped parsley in the center of each of the four patties. Top with the remaining patties. Press the edges firmly together to seal the stuffed patties (see Figure 6-2). Gently pat to an even ¾-inch thickness. The patties should appear as if there is no filling. Sprinkle the patties with salt and pepper.

4 Place patties on the grill. Grill 5 to 7 minutes per side in a grill pan, on an open grill, or on a cooktop insert (for medium doneness). For a contact grill, grill patties covered 3 minutes, then turn the patties and grill covered 2 minutes longer to brown lightly.

5 To serve, top each of the four toasted bread slices with arugula, a stuffed beef patty, and a slice of bread.

Vary It! *Use mozzarella cheese instead of goat cheese, chopped prosciutto instead of dried tomatoes, and basil instead of parsley.*

Nutrition at a glance (per serving): calories 733; calories from fat 357; fat 40 g; saturated fat 18 g; cholesterol 198 mg; sodium 912 mg; carbohydrates 40 g; dietary fiber 2 g; protein 51 g

 Reduce the calories, fat, and saturated fat by using ground turkey breast or 90-, 92-, or 96-percent lean beef.

HOW TO STUFF A BURGER

Figure 6-2: Stuffing a beef patty.

1. START WITH 2 THIN BEEF PATTIES

2. PLACE FILLING ON 1 PATTY.

3. PRESS THE 2 PATTIES TOGETHER.

4. NO FILLING SHOWS.

5. PRESS AND SHAPE TO AN EVEN THICKNESS.

Sausage and Hot Dogs

Sausage and hot dogs are, quite possibly, the world's simplest foods to prepare on a grill. Because they're precooked, you don't have to worry about cooking them to the proper temperature, and they cook in minutes!

Uncooked sausage is a little more temperamental. Whether you use turkey, pork, or beef sausage, cook it for 15 to 25 minutes to an internal temperature of 160° (beef and pork) and 165° (turkey).

Grilled Dogs with Onions

By nature, hot hogs (frankfurters) are salty, and when you top them with sauerkraut, you add even more sodium to your diet. But onions are a great alternative.

Tools: *Grill, medium mixing bowl*

Preparation time: *10 minutes*

Grilling time: *15 minutes*

Yield: *4 servings*

4 hot dog buns, split open

1 large onion, halved lengthwise and sliced across (see Figure 6-3)

1 tablespoon vegetable oil

½ teaspoon paprika

4 all-beef hot dogs

Mustard, ketchup, pickle relish

1 Heat an indoor electric grill, grill pan, or cooktop insert over medium-high heat for 5 minutes. Place two buns, cut sides down, on the grill. Grill, uncovered, just until warmed, about 2 minutes. Place grilled buns on a plate, cover with foil, and keep warm. Repeat with the other two buns. If using a large grill or cooktop insert, you can grill all the buns at the same time.

2 In a medium mixing bowl, toss the onion half-slices with oil and paprika. Grill the onions on medium heat for 5 minutes in a grill pan, stirring occasionally, or 3 minutes for a contact grill. If using an open grill or cooktop insert, cook the onions in a large skillet.

3 Meanwhile, with a knife, split each hot dog lengthwise without cutting all the way through. Move the onions to one side of the grill. If your grill is too small to fit the hot dogs with the onions, cook the onions a few minutes longer or until tender and remove to a bowl. Grill the dogs 4 to 6 minutes with onions, turning once in a grill pan, on an open grill, or on a cooktop insert, or without turning if using a contact grill, until lightly browned. Serve grilled dogs on buns with onions, mustard, ketchup, or pickle relish.

Nutrition at a glance (per serving without condiments): calories 350; calories from fat 206; fat 22.9 g; saturated fat 8 g; cholesterol 35 mg; sodium 810 mg; carbohydrates 25 g; dietary fiber 2 g; protein 11 g

To reduce fat and calories, use low-fat or nonfat hotdogs.

Peppered Turkey Sausages

Opting for turkey sausages instead of pork links greatly reduces the calories in this recipe.

Tools: *Grill, medium mixing bowl*

Preparation time: *15 minutes*

Grilling time: *15 to 25 minutes*

Yield: *4 servings*

1 large red bell pepper

1 large green bell pepper

2 tablespoons Backbone of Rubs (see Chapter 4) or bottled low-fat or nonfat Italian salad dressing

1¼ pounds or 8 sweet or hot Italian-style turkey sausages

1 Spray the grill grid with nonstick cooking spray or brush with oil to prevent food from sticking. Heat an indoor electric grill, grill pan, or cooktop insert over medium-low heat for 5 minutes.

2 While the grill is heating, seed and cut the peppers into strips (see Figure 6-4). In a medium mixing bowl, toss the peppers with Backbone of Rubs or salad dressing until well coated.

3 Place the sausages on the grill and cover with aluminum foil. Grill 15 to 18 minutes, turning occasionally, in a grill pan, on an open grill, or on a cooktop insert, until no longer pink in the center (cut into the center of a sausage with a knife to test doneness). For a contact grill, grill the sausages covered 10 minutes. Remove the cooked sausages to a plate; cover to keep warm.

4 Increase heat to medium-high. Add the peppers to the grill and cook 5 minutes, stirring occasionally, in a grill pan, on an open grill, or on a cooktop insert (or 3 minutes, stirring occasionally for a contact grill), until tender-crisp. If using an open grill or cooktop insert, cook the peppers in a large skillet.

5 Serve the sausages with the grilled peppers.

Vary It! *Serve grilled sausages in toasted hero rolls with a spoonful of warmed, bottled spaghetti sauce or cut up sausages and heat with peppers in a pot of spaghetti sauce and serve over pasta or polenta. Check out* Cooking For Dummies, *2nd Edition, by Bryan Miller and Marie Rama (Hungry Minds, Inc.) for some great recipes.*

Nutrition at a glance (per serving): *calories 252; calories from fat 140; fat 16 g; saturated fat 4 g; cholesterol 61 mg; sodium 966 mg; carbohydrates 8 g; dietary fiber 2 g; protein 20 g*

To reduce fat and calories, look carefully at the turkey sausage label. Calorie count and fat grams vary widely from brand to brand.

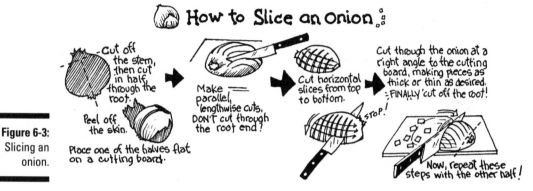

Figure 6-3: Slicing an onion.

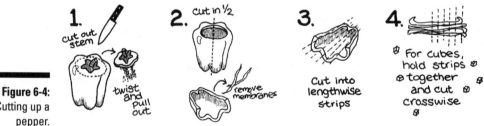

Figure 6-4: Cutting up a pepper.

Grilled Cheese and Ham

What makes a great grilled cheese sandwich is a matter of debate. The American classic is made of sliced processed cheese sandwiched between soft bread that's often smothered with butter. The French make grilled *croque monsieur,* which consists of ham and Gruyere cheese topped with a creamy white sauce.

Some grilled-cheese addicts argue that the sandwiches must be grilled in a sandwich press (although we disagree here — an indoor grill does just fine). Other devotees call for tomatoes or insist on the addition of boiled ham. We don't try to settle the argument in this section; instead, we give you two simple recipes to try at home, adapting as you see fit.

Grilled Cheese Sandwiches

Looking for a reduced-fat version of the old classic? Look no further. This recipe doesn't call for a coating of butter on the bread.

Tools: *Grill*

Preparation time: *5 minutes*

Grilling time: *8 to 15 minutes*

Yield: *4 servings*

8 slices firm white or whole wheat sandwich bread

8 thin slices cheese (American, Swiss, or cheddar)

4 thin slices smoked ham or 4 large slices ripe tomato

1 Heat an indoor electric grill, grill pan, or cooktop insert over medium-high heat for 5 minutes. Grill four bread slices 2 minutes, turning once. Remove toasted bread. Repeat to warm the other bread slices. On 4 slices, place 1 slice of cheese and ham or tomato, then top each with a slice of cheese and bread.

2 If using a grill pan, open grill, or cooktop insert, place sandwiches, on grill and cook until lightly browned, then turn and brown the other side. If using a contact grill, grill sandwiches for 3 minutes. The sandwiches will be pressed and the cheese will melt nicely.

Vary It! *Italian-style, use slices of Italian bread (5 inches in diameter) and coat on the inside with homemade or purchased Basil Pesto. Top with slices of mozzarella, tomato, and Grilled Zucchini (see Chapter 11). Grill sandwiches until cheese melts.*

Nutrition at a glance (per serving): *calories 332; calories from fat 120; fat 13 g; saturated fat 7 g; cholesterol 36 mg; sodium 981 mg; carbohydrates 36 g; dietary fiber 2 g; protein 16 g*

To reduce fat and calories, use low-fat or fat-free cheese slices and substitute turkey-ham for ham.

Honey Mustard Grilled Ham

Ready-to-eat ham steak needs only a few minutes on the grill to brown lightly. In this recipe, the ham steaks are accompanied by pineapple slices and a sweet, tangy sauce.

Tools: *Grill, small mixing bowl, whisk*

Preparation time: *15 minutes*

Grilling time: *15 to 20 minutes*

Yield: *4 servings*

¼ cup mild-flavored honey

2 tablespoons Dijon-style or spicy brown mustard

1 tablespoon pineapple juice (reserved from drained pineapple below)

1 teaspoon balsamic or cider vinegar

1 center-cut smoked cooked ham steak, about ½-inch thick (about 1⅓ pounds)

1 can (20 ounces) sliced pineapple packed in juice, drained, or 1 container peeled fresh pineapple, drained, sliced, and cored

1 In a small mixing bowl, whisk the honey, mustard, pineapple juice, and vinegar until well mixed. Cut the ham into 4 pieces, discarding its round bone and any fat.

2 Spray the grill grid with nonstick cooking spray or brush with oil to prevent food from sticking. Heat an indoor electric grill, grill pan, or cooktop insert over medium-high heat for 5 minutes.

3 Pat the pineapple slices dry on paper towels.

4 For a grill pan, an open grill, or a cooktop insert, grill the ham 3 minutes per side, turning once. To create decorative grill marks, grill 2 minutes and rotate the ham at a right angle to the first grill marks, then grill another 1 minute. If using a contact grill, grill the ham covered for 3 minutes. Lift the cover and rotate the ham, then cover and grill 2 minutes longer.

5 Transfer the ham to a plate, cover, and keep warm. Place the pineapple slices on the grill and grill 5 minutes per side or until lightly browned and heated. If slices don't fit in a single layer, grill them in two batches. Arrange the grilled pineapple on the plate with the ham and drizzle all with some of the honey mustard. Serve with the remaining honey mustard.

Nutrition at a glance (per serving): *calories 286; calories from fat 55; fat 6 g; saturated fat 2 g; cholesterol 56 mg; sodium 1775 mg; carbohydrates 34 g; dietary fiber 1 g; protein 25 g*

Chapter 7

Beefing Up Your Repertoire

In This Chapter

▶ Knowing what to look for as you shop for beef cuts

▶ Following beef safety guidelines

▶ Grilling beef cuts with delicious recipes

Recipes in This Chapter

▶ The Original London Broil

▶ Cowboy Steaks

▶ Skirt Steak Fajitas

▶ Beef and Vegetable Kebabs

▶ Thai Basil Beef

▶ Tuscan Strip House Special

▶ Peppery Beef Tenderloin

▶ Chimichurri Round Steak

Think *grilling* and chances are, you also think *beef*. Beef is delicious, hearty, and healthy. Did we really say *healthy?* Sure! Lean beef is a high-quality source of protein, B-vitamins, zinc, and iron. In fact, calorie for calorie, beef is one of the best sources of B-vitamins, including riboflavin, niacin, vitamin B6, and vitamin B12, while a 3-ounce portion of beef provides 32 percent of the U.S. Daily Recommended Allowance (RDA) of zinc.

Grilled beef can also be low in fat and calories, but you must shop carefully. Look for cuts of beef that have "loin" or "round" in the name: for example, sir*loin,* top *loin,* tender*loin,* and top *round.* Table 7-1 compares the calories and fat found in 3 ounces of various cuts of grilled "loin" and "round" beef, with all the visible fat trimmed before cooking. You can find out more about these cuts of meat in the "Selecting Beef Cuts and Grades" section, later in this chapter.

Table 7-1	Grilled Beef Nutrition Chart		
Variety of Beef	*Calories*	*Total Fat*	*Saturated Fat*
Bottom round	175	6	2
Eye of round	140	4	2
Round tip steak	160	6	2
Sirloin steak	170	6	2
Tenderloin steak	180	9	3
Top loin steak	180	8	3
Top round steak	150	4	1

In general, a 3-ounce cooked portion, which is about the size of a deck of cards, started with 4 ounces of raw beef. When you compare the figures in Table 7-1 to 3 ounces of skinless chicken breast (120 calories, 2 grams of fat, 1 gram of saturated fat) and skinless chicken thigh (150 calories, 7 grams of fat, 2 grams of saturated fat), beef begins to look pretty lean.

Staying Safe with Beef

Like all meats, beef can contain surface bacteria that are eliminated by grilling it to the proper temperature. Because of these bacteria, however, take care when selecting and storing cuts of beef. In particular, when shopping, select meat last (just before checking out) so that your meat stays as cold as possible. Look for beef that is bright red in color, avoiding cuts with gray or brown spots. Beef should be firm to the touch, not soft or mushy. A package of meat should be cold to the touch and tightly wrapped — don't buy beef that has juices leaking out of the package. (Make sure frozen beef is frozen solid.) Check the "sell by" date to make sure the meat hasn't expired.

When you get home, place the meat in the meat drawer or on the lowest shelf, near the back of the fridge. And don't cram the package in. Make sure air can circulate around the package. Never thaw frozen meat and then refreeze it.

Keep the following shopping, handling, and preparation tips in mind when grilling with beef:

- ✔ **Wash your hands with hot, soapy water before and after handling cuts of beef.** Hot, soapy water kills bacteria.

- ✔ **Wash cutting boards, knives, and countertops in hot, soapy water after contact with beef.** Choose plastic cutting boards over wood, if possible, because bacteria can get caught in the cracks that develop in wood cutting boards over time. If you have a dishwasher, run your plastic cutting board through the wash cycle before using it again.

✔ **If you're using tongs or a spatula to turn raw beef, be sure to wash the tool with hot soapy water before using the same tool to remove cooked food from the grill.** Consider using two tongs: one to handle raw foods and the other to handle cooked foods. Wash the raw-food tongs with soapy water after you're finished grilling.

✔ **Never place cooked foods, vegetables, bread, or any other ready-to-eat food on an unwashed plate that was used for raw beef.** You may spread bacteria from the uncooked meat to the ready-to-eat food.

✔ **Defrost beef in the refrigerator, not on the countertop.** At room temperature, bacteria can build up during the thawing process.

✔ **Marinate beef in the refrigerator.** Always dispose of the marinade after use — it may contain bacteria. (See Chapter 3 for more on marinade safety.)

Grill beef to an internal temperature of at least 145°. See the "Grilling Beef for Dinner and Other Meals" section, later in this chapter, for more information.

Selecting Beef Cuts and Grades

Cuts of beef are *graded* by the U.S. Department of Agriculture (USDA), using standards based on tenderness, juiciness, and flavor. The top three grades of beef include the following:

✔ **Prime:** Prime has the most *marbling* (lines of fat running through it) and is usually sold to fine restaurants and specialty meat markets.

✔ **Choice:** Choice is less tasty than prime, but is usually the tastiest cut of beef sold in supermarkets.

✔ **Select:** Select has the least amount of marbling, making it leaner than choice or prime. You may find, however, that select cuts aren't as tender, juicy, or flavorful as choice and prime cuts of beef.

In addition to USDA grades, you can find a tremendous variety of beef cuts, illustrated in Figure 7-1. All should be cut to at least ¾-inch thickness so that the meat doesn't burn on the grill. If you see only ½-inch thicknesses at your meat counter, ask your butcher if he has thicker cuts of meat available.

One of the most popular cuts of beef is called *top loin steak* (also called *strip steak* or *New York strip*), which is tender and juicy. Another good choice, albeit expensive, is *tenderloin,* which is actually a large piece of beef that's usually cut into sections and sold as smaller pieces. All parts of the tenderloin are tender and tasty, but *filet mignon,* which is cut from the small end of the tenderloin, is the most tender beef you can buy — and the most expensive. (A small portion is considered a delicacy.) *Chateaubriand* is a large tenderloin steak. *Sirloin steak* is boneless and tender — it's a good buy for your money. *Round cuts,* including *eye of round* and *round tip,* tend to be a bit less expensive than tenderloin and are generally tasty and tender.

Figure 7-1:
This well-dressed cow demonstrates where cuts of beef originate.

For kebabs, you can buy cuts labeled "beef for kebabs." This meat, which is boneless, is usually cut from sirloin or round portions of beef, making them lean and tender, but they can be cut from any portion of the beef except the shank. Marinating helps tenderize the beef. Look for packages with uniform cubes, about 1 to 1½ inches thick. You can also make your own kebabs from almost any cut of beef by purchasing beef that's at least 1 inch thick and cutting it into cubes. Check out the Beef and Vegetable Kebabs recipe later in this chapter.

These various cuts of beef can be classified as *tender* or *tough,* as shown in Figure 7-2. Tender cuts tend to be more expensive, but are often worth the higher price because the flavor is so much better. If you have tougher cuts on hand, however, use the recipes in this chapter to grill them to their tender best.

> ✔ **Tender cuts:** Tender cuts include tenderloin, filet mignon, top loin, sirloin, ribeye, T-bone and porterhouse, round tip steak, and chateaubriand. As long as these cuts are sold in at least ¾-inch thickness (and thicker is

better!), you can hardly go wrong with them, no matter which recipe you use. In this chapter, the recipe for Strip House Special calls for top loin steak; Thai Basil Beef calls for sirloin steak; Peppery Beef Tenderloin calls for filet mignon.

Note that ribeye can also be a tougher cut of meat if it's cut from the end closer to the chuck area, farther from the loin area (refer to Figure 7-1). Ask your butcher for assistance in choosing the more tender cuts.

✓ **Tougher cuts:** Tougher cuts are labeled as brisket, chuck, flank steak, skirt steak, and top round. Scoring and marinating flank steak makes for a delicious beef entrée. Use flank steak for The Original London Broil recipe (in this chapter) or substitute chuck or top round. In the Cowboy Steaks recipe, beef chuck is marinated for at least eight hours, creating a tender entrée from an inexpensive and not-so-tender cut. Well-marinated, thin strips of skirt steak are delicious in fajitas — check out the Skirt Steak Fajitas recipe in this chapter. Top round steak is marinated for at least eight hours in the Chimichurri Round Steak recipe, again creating a delicious meal with a less expensive cut of beef.

Figure 7-2:
If you can spare the change, choose tender cuts of beef.

Beef Cuts

Grilling Beef for Dinner and Other Meals

Grilling beef is a cinch: A little marinade, a thermometer, and an indoor grill come together with your favorite cut of beef to create a quick, delicious meal. The recipes in this section begin with slightly tougher, less expensive cuts of beef and move into increasingly tender, more expensive cuts. The last recipe, Peppery Beef Tenderloin, calls for filet mignon, the most expensive cut you can buy, but makes a delicious treat for a celebration or small party.

You can grill beef to any level of doneness, based on the internal temperature of the cut of beef and on the meat's interior color. All cuts, however, should be cooked to at least 145°.

Here's the lowdown on levels of doneness:

- ✔ **Rare:** Rare beef is bright red and quite juicy. Because it's cooked to only 140°, however, you may not eliminate all surface bacteria with this level of doneness. Opt for medium-rare, instead.

- ✔ **Medium-rare:** Beef cooked to medium-rare has a red center with light-brown or pink edges, and is nearly as juicy as rare beef. Because it's cooked to 145°, it's your safest choice for juicy grilling.

- ✔ **Medium:** Medium beef, cooked to 160°, is pink in the center with light-brown edges, and still tastes juicy.

  If you don't like to see any red but don't like tough or crisp beef, consider cooking your beef to what may be called *medium-well,* which would be about 165°, but isn't usually specified as a level of doneness.

- ✔ **Well-done:** Well-done beef is brown or brownish-gray throughout. It tends to be tougher than other levels of doneness and is cooked to an internal temperature of 170°.

- ✔ **Very well-done:** Otherwise known as *burnt,* very well-done beef is cooked to an internal temperature of 180° and has some blackened areas on it.

After you remove meat from the grill, the internal temperature will rise 5 to 7 degrees. Be sure to take meat off the grill when it's about 5 degrees below the desired temperature. Let the meat rest, covered loosely with foil, for 5 minutes before serving or carving.

Preheating times vary among indoor grill manufacturers. Five minutes should be enough to adequately preheat your grill, but check the use and care book that came with your grill — your particular grill may take a bit longer to heat up.

The Original London Broil

Nowadays, London broil refers to certain lean, boneless beef cuts that can be broiled or grilled and then carved across the grain into thin slices. Originally, however, it was a marinated flank steak, called "London Broil." A recipe for this classic beef entrée first appeared in 1931 in the U.S., taking its name from London, England. Other cuts often used in place of flank steak include top round, sirloin, or beef chuck shoulder steak. Because the steak is relatively thin and porous, the simple marinade penetrates the meat quickly.

Tools: Grill, nonreactive dish or large resealable plastic bag

Preparation time: 10 minutes

Marinating time: 15 minutes

Grilling time: 12 to 15 minutes

Yield: 4 servings

1¼ to 1½ pounds beef flank steak	1 teaspoon dry mustard
2 tablespoons Worcestershire sauce	¼ teaspoon salt
1 tablespoon vegetable oil	¼ teaspoon ground black pepper

1 With a knife, cut and remove any pieces of fat from the steak. To score the surface of the steak on each side, carefully make cut lines about 1¼ inches apart and about ⅛ inch deep to form a diamond pattern, as shown in Figure 7-3.

2 Place the steak in a nonreactive dish or a large, resealable, plastic bag. Drizzle with Worcestershire sauce and oil. Sprinkle with mustard, salt, and pepper. Rub the mixture into steak. Cover the dish or seal the bag and let the steak stand 15 minutes to marinate.

3 Heat the indoor electric grill, grill pan, or cooktop insert over medium-high heat for 5 minutes. If using a grill pan, open grill, or cooktop insert, grill the steak 5 to 6 minutes. If using a contact grill, grill covered for 3 minutes. Turn the steak over and grill 5 minutes longer in a pan or 3 minutes longer in a covered grill. (Meat will be rare; add a minute or two for medium rare. Flank steak should never be cooked more than medium well. Actual cooking time depends on the thickness of the steak and intensity of the heat.) Use a sharp knife to make a small incision in the center of the steak to test doneness. The meat should be browned on the outside and pink and juicy inside. When done, move the steak to a carving board and cover with foil; let rest for a few minutes and then slice thinly across the grain. If using a contact grill, pour the drippings from the drip pan over the meat before serving.

Vary It! The mild marinade allows the flavor of the beef to project. If you like, brush grilled steak with Orange Soy Glaze (Chapter 5) before slicing. You can use your favorite steak marinade, but those containing red wine may give the steak a bitter aftertaste.

Nutrition at a glance (per serving): calories 266; calories from fat 133; fat 15 g; saturated fat 5 g; cholesterol 73 mg; sodium 319 mg; carbohydrates 2 g; dietary fiber 0 g; protein 30 g

HOW TO SCORE FLANK STEAK

Figure 7-3:
Score one
for the
Gipper.

1. CUT PARALLEL LINES ABOUT 1¼" APART AND ⅛" DEEP.

2. THEN, CUT AT AN ANGLE TO THE FIRST LINES TO FORM A DIAMOND PATTERN.

Cowboy Steaks

Beef chuck is considered an inexpensive but tough cut of meat. Soaked in a wine marinade overnight, however, it becomes palatable and tasty, especially when it's served with a devilish sauce, which you can serve cold, as you would a barbecue sauce, or reheat it to serve it hot, so it doesn't chill the steak slices. In some markets, this cut is known as beef shoulder London Broil.

Tools: *Grill, nonreactive dish or large resealable plastic bag, saucepan*

Preparation time: *25 minutes*

Marinating time: *8 hours or overnight*

Grilling time: *15 to 25 minutes*

Yield: *5 servings*

1 boneless beef chuck shoulder steak, cut about 1-inch thick (about 1½ pounds)	*¼ cup lightly packed dark brown sugar*
1 cup Meat Soaker (see Chapter 4)	*¼ cup spicy brown mustard*
½ cup bottled steak sauce	*¼ cup Worcestershire sauce*
	Salt and pepper to taste

1 Working on a cutting board, trim all pieces of fat from the steak. In a nonreactive dish or a large, resealable plastic bag, place the steak and 1 cup of Meat Soaker. Turn the steak over to coat evenly with the marinade. Cover the dish or close the bag securely and refrigerate for 8 hours or overnight.

2 For the sauce, in a saucepan, heat the steak sauce, brown sugar, mustard, and Worcestershire to boiling, stirring to dissolve the sugar. Cool the sauce to room temperature and refrigerate until you're ready to serve the steak.

3 Remove the steak from the refrigerator and let stand while heating the grill. Spray the grill grid with nonstick cooking spray or brush with oil to prevent food from sticking. Heat an indoor electric grill, grill pan, or cooktop insert over medium-low heat for 5 minutes. Remove the steak from the marinade, discarding the marinade. Pat the steak dry on paper towels. Season the steak with salt and pepper to taste. Grill the steak in a grill pan, on an open grill, or on a cooktop insert for 5 minutes, turn, and grill another 5 minutes. Turn again, but rotate the steak at a right angle to the grill marks, and grill for 4 minutes. Repeat to grill the other side again for medium-rare doneness or grill 6 to 7 minutes per side for medium. Check for doneness by making a small cut into the center of the meat with a sharp knife. (For best results, less-tender steaks should be cooked from medium-rare to medium.) If using a contact grill, grill the steak 5 minutes, lift the cover, turn the steak over and rotate at a right angle to the grill marks and grill covered for 2 minutes longer or to desired doneness.

4 Transfer the steak to a cutting board, cover loosely with foil, and let the steak rest for a few minutes before thinly slicing across the grain. Serve steak with the sauce.

Vary It! Serve the steak slices and sauce in sandwich buns.

Go-With: Serve with baked beans and coleslaw.

Nutrition at a glance (per serving): calories 394; calories from fat 213; fat 24 g; saturated fat 9 g; cholesterol 93 mg; sodium 853 mg; carbohydrates 18 g; dietary fiber 1 g; protein 27 g

Skirt Steak Fajitas

For cowhands in Texas, fajitas (fah-HEE-tahs) meant a piece of beef such as skirt steak (which was often discarded because it wasn't marketable) grilled over the campfire, sliced, and served in a flour tortilla. *Fajita* actually means "belt" and describes the appearance of raw skirt steak. This beef cut from the chest of the animal (refer to Figure 7-1) has a rich beefy flavor though a chewy texture. The long thin beef strip needs to be marinated and sliced across the grain after grilling. A special chili sauce marinates these fajitas and also works as a sauce.

Tools: *Grill, food processor, nonreactive dish or large resealable plastic bag, small saucepan (optional)*

Preparation time: *45 minutes*

Marinating time: *4 hours or overnight*

Grilling time: *10 to 18 minutes*

Yield: *4 servings*

¼ cup dark seedless raisins

2 tablespoons chopped white part of scallions

2 cloves garlic

One 8-ounce can tomato sauce

½ cup beef broth

1 tablespoon unsweetened cocoa

1 tablespoon Worcestershire sauce

1 tablespoon vegetable oil

1 canned chipotle chile plus 1 tablespoon adobo sauce (see the "Hotly chipotle" sidebar in this chapter)

1⅓ to 1½ pounds skirt steak

8 large wheat flour tortillas (each about 8 inches in diameter)

Grilled Sweet Peppers (see Chapter 11)

Guacamole (optional)

1 To make a chili sauce marinade, in a food processor, place the raisins, scallions, and garlic. Process until finely chopped. Add the tomato sauce, broth, cocoa, Worcestershire sauce, oil, and chile and adobo sauce mixture. Process until the sauce is smooth. Pour ¼ cup sauce into a nonreactive dish or a large, resealable plastic bag. Trim any pieces of fat from the steak. Cut the steak strip into 4 or 5 inch pieces and add to the marinade and turn, coating the steak with the marinade. Cover the dish or seal the bag, and refrigerate for at least 4 hours or overnight. Pour the remaining sauce into a storage container or jar; cover and refrigerate.

2 Remove the steak from the refrigerator and let stand while heating the grill. Spray the grill grid with nonstick cooking spray or brush with oil to prevent food from sticking. Heat the indoor electric grill, grill pan, or cooktop insert over medium-high heat for 5 minutes. Heat the tortillas, one at a time, on the grill, turning them over several times until warm and softened, about 1 minute per tortilla. Stack the warmed tortillas on a sheet of foil, wrap them, and keep them warm.

3 Prepare and then grill the peppers according to the recipe in Chapter 11. Transfer to a dish; cover and keep warm.

4 Grill the steak in a grill pan, on an open grill, or on a cooktop insert 3 to 4 minutes per side for medium-rare doneness or 5 to 7 minutes for medium. For a contact grill, grill the steak covered 2½ to 3 minutes per side (turning them over once) for medium-rare or 7 to 8 minutes total for medium. (The cooking time will depend on the thickness of the steak and intensity of the heat.) Use a knife to make a cut in the center of the steak to test for doneness. The meat should be browned on the outside yet pink and juicy inside. Transfer the steak to a cutting board; cover with foil to keep warm.

5 Just before serving, in a small saucepan over low heat, heat the remaining sauce until hot. When ready to serve, slice the meat thinly across the grain.

6 To assemble the fajitas, place a few slices of meat and some of the grilled peppers on each tortilla. Top with a spoonful of warm sauce and guacamole, if desired, before rolling them up.

Go-With: *Serve with shredded lettuce and cubed tomatoes.*

Nutrition at a glance (per serving): *calories 659; calories from fat 222; fat 25 g; saturated fat 6 g; cholesterol 77 mg; sodium 1487 mg; carbohydrates 76 g; dietary fiber 7 g; protein 37 g*

Hotly chipotle

Chipotle is a dried, smoked jalapeno chile pepper that is available dried or canned in a sauce. The canned chile is packed in a wonderful smoky-flavored sauce. There is no real good substitute for the smoky chile except using a dried red chile that is soaked to soften, and then removing its seeds, and adding it to the sauce along with a drop of Liquid Smoke seasoning (see Basic BBQ Sauce in Chapter 5).

Beef and Vegetable Kebabs

These kebabs combine tender beef with brightly colored squash, making an attractive entrée. Grilling the meat on a separate skewer from the vegetables assures that the meat will not be overcooked.

Tools: *Grill, mixing bowl, medium saucepan*

Preparation time: *25 minutes*

Marinating time: *15 minutes*

Grilling time: *20 to 25 minutes*

Yield: *4 servings*

1⅓ to 1½ pounds boneless sirloin steak or beef top loin, cut 1¼ inches thick

3 tablespoons bottled teriyaki sauce

1 teaspoon dark (toasted) sesame oil

2 dozen (about ¾ pound) green or yellow baby pattypan squash (1¼-inch diameter) or 4 small (6 inches long) zucchini

12 small boiling or pearl onions (1¼ inch diameter)

2 tablespoons olive oil

2 cloves garlic, finely chopped

2 teaspoons chopped fresh or 1 teaspoon dried oregano leaves

½ teaspoon salt

1 Working on a cutting board, trim all pieces of fat from the steak. Cut meat into 1-inch chunks and place in bowl. Add teriyaki sauce and sesame oil. Toss the meat until it is coated with sauce; set aside 15 minutes to marinate.

2 Meanwhile, fill a medium saucepan with 2 inches of water, and heat to boiling. Trim the ends off the squash. If using zucchini, trim the ends and cut the squash crosswise into 1-inch pieces. Add the squash to the boiling water and return the water to boiling; cook the squash 2 to 3 minutes or just until softened. With a slotted spoon, transfer the squash to a bowl and set aside. Add the onions to the boiling water and heat to boiling; boil the onions for 3 to 4 minutes. Drain, rinse with cold water, and pat thoroughly dry. Peel the onions and cut off their root ends. Add the onions to the bowl with the squash. Add the oil, garlic, oregano, and salt; toss the vegetables.

3 Spray the grill grid with nonstick cooking spray or brush with oil to prevent food from sticking. Heat an indoor electric grill, grill pan, or cooktop insert over medium-high heat for 5 minutes. On four 10-inch metal skewers, alternately thread the beef with onions. On four more skewers, thread the squash so that the cut surfaces are exposed so that they will be flat against the grill. (See Figure 7-4 for ways to skewer vegetables.)

4 Grill the squash kebabs 8 to 10 minutes in a grill pan, on an open grill, or on a cooktop insert, or 4 to 5 minutes for a contact grill, turning several times, or until lightly browned. Transfer the kebabs to a plate; cover with foil to keep warm. Grill the beef and onion skewers for about 10 minutes for medium-rare doneness or 12 minutes for medium in a grill pan, on an open grill, or on a cooktop insert, turning every 3 or 4 minutes. For a contact grill, grill the beef covered 5 to 8 minutes total time (turning them over several times) for medium-rare or 8 to 10 minutes total for medium. Use a knife to make a cut in the center of the beef chunk to test for doneness. The meat should be browned on the outside yet pink and juicy inside. Transfer the kebabs to the plate with the squash kebabs and serve.

Go With: *Serve with hot cooked rice or warm couscous.*

Nutrition at a glance (per serving): *calories 323; calories from fat 140; fat 16 g; saturated fat 4 g; cholesterol 99 mg; sodium 498 mg; carbohydrates 8 g; dietary fiber 2 g; protein 37 g*

Figure 7-4:
Use these skewering techniques to keep foods from falling off.

Thai Basil Beef

In this recipe, typical southeast Asian ingredients, including fish sauce, soy sauce, and chile paste, give grilled beef slices a delightful taste combined with flavorful basil. We suggest using a grill pan, open electric grill, or cooktop insert to cook this dish; a contact grill doesn't work as well because you need a fairly high heat.

Tools: *Grill, nonreactive mixing bowl*

Preparation time: *25 minutes*

Marinating time: *15 minutes*

Grilling time: *3 to 5 minutes*

Yield: *4 servings*

1¼ pounds boneless sirloin steak, cut 1 inch thick

2 tablespoons vegetable oil

2 teaspoons naturally brewed soy sauce

2 cloves garlic, finely chopped

½ cup low-sodium beef broth

1 tablespoon sugar

2 tablespoons Asian fish sauce (nam pla or nuoc nam) or 1 tablespoon soy sauce mixed with 1 tablespoon water

½ teaspoon Asian chile-garlic paste

2 teaspoons fresh lime juice

1 cup Thai basil leaves, torn into small pieces

1 Working on a cutting board, trim all pieces of fat from the steak. With a very sharp knife, cut steak across the grain into ¼-inch-thick slices and place in a nonreactive bowl. (If you have time, freeze the meat for 30 to 40 minutes to firm it up a little and make slicing easier.) Add the oil, soy sauce, and garlic. Toss until the meat is coated with sauce; set aside 15 minutes to marinate.

2 In a measuring cup, combine the broth, sugar, fish sauce, chile-garlic paste, and lime juice; set aside.

3 Spray the grill grid with nonstick cooking spray or brush with oil to prevent food from sticking. Heat an indoor electric grill, grill pan, or cooktop insert over medium-high heat for 5 minutes. Grill half the beef strips placing them in a single layer in a grill pan, on an open grill, or on a cooktop insert. Grill the beef 1 to 1½ minutes, turn and grill the other side just until lightly browned. Transfer the strips to a bowl; repeat to grill the other half of the beef.

4 Pour the broth mixture over the grilled beef and add basil. Toss until just mixed and serve.

Note: *Asian fish sauce, made by fermenting salted fish, is considered the salt of the Southeast Asian cuisines. In Thailand, this thin, brownish liquid with a unique aroma is called nam pla, or nuoc nam in Vietnam. Fish sauce as well as chile paste are sold in Asian specialty markets or ethnic food sections of many large supermarkets.*

Go-With: *Serve with hot, cooked jasmine rice or rice noodle.*

Vary It! *Thai basil is a highly aromatic variety of basil with purple stems. In its place, you can use cilantro, mint leaves, or Italian basil.*

Nutrition at a glance (per serving): *calories 258; calories from fat 95; fat 11 g; saturated fat 4 g; cholesterol 96 mg; sodium 840 mg; carbohydrates 4 g; dietary fiber 0 g; protein 34 g*

Tuscan Strip House Special

A strip steak is actually a boneless top loin steak. It may also be called shell steak, Kansas City steak, New York steak, or boneless club steak. A popular steak in steak-houses across the U.S., this dish is topped with a classic garlicky Italian-style tomato sauce called *puttanesca*. The sauce is often served hot over pasta. This Tuscan version is made with grilled tomatoes that you serve at room temperature over steak. Be sure to use sun-ripened tomatoes for the best flavor.

Tools: *Grill, mixing bowl*

Preparation time: *25 minutes*

Marinating time: *15 minutes*

Grilling time: *10 to 18 minutes*

Yield: *4 servings*

8 large ripe plum tomatoes

¼ cup extra virgin olive oil

2 large cloves garlic, finely chopped

8 large fresh basil leaves, torn into small pieces

1 tablespoon chopped flat-leaf parsley

¼ cup sliced pitted black olives (use Gaeta or Kalamata)

1 tablespoon small capers, rinsed in water and drained

¼ teaspoon crushed red pepper flakes

½ teaspoon salt

4 well-trimmed boneless beef top loin steaks, cut ¾-inch thick (about 2 pounds)

Salt and pepper to taste

1 Spray the grill grid with nonstick cooking spray or brush with oil to prevent food from sticking. Heat an indoor electric grill, grill pan, or cooktop insert over medium-high heat for 5 minutes. Meanwhile, cut each tomato lengthwise in half. With your fingers, remove all the seeds and pulp from the tomato halves. (Freeze the pulp for soup stock, if desired.)

2 Grill tomatoes in a grill pan or on an uncovered electric grill, skin sides down, until lightly charred, about 5 minutes. Turn the tomatoes and grill until cut sides are lightly browned. Transfer the tomatoes to a chopping board and cool until they're easy to handle.

3 Meanwhile, let the grills cool and clean them to grill the steaks.

4 Remove the skins from the tomato halves. Chop the tomatoes. In a bowl, combine the tomatoes, oil, garlic, basil, parsley, olives, capers, red pepper, and salt.

5 Spray the grill grid with nonstick cooking spray or brush with oil to prevent food from sticking. Heat an indoor electric grill, grill pan, or cooktop insert over medium-high heat for 5 minutes. Sprinkle the steaks with salt and pepper to taste. Grill the steaks in a grill pan, on an open grill, or on a cooktop insert for 3 minutes per side for medium-rare doneness or 4 to 5 minutes for medium. For a contact grill, grill the steaks covered 2½ to 3 minutes, turn the steaks over, rotate at a 45-degree angle, and grill covered 2 minutes longer for medium-rare or 7 to 8 minutes total for medium. (The cooking time will depend on the thickness and temperature of the steaks and the intensity of the heat.) Use a knife to make a cut in the center of the steak to test for doneness. The meat should be browned on the outside yet pink and juicy inside.

6 Transfer the steaks to serving plates and top each with some puttanesca sauce.

Nutrition at a glance (per serving): calories 492; calories from fat 248; fat 28 g; saturated fat 7 g; cholesterol 149 mg; sodium 729 mg; carbohydrates 7 g; dietary fiber 2 g; protein 52 g

Peppery Beef Tenderloin

Tasty and easy to prepare, this beef dish topped with mushroom slices is fit for company. Be sure to have the side dishes cooking or done before grilling the steaks.

Tools: *Grill, mixing bowl*

Preparation time: *15 minutes*

Marinating time: *15 minutes*

Grilling time: *10 to 18 minutes*

Yield: *4 servings*

2 to 4 teaspoons whole black peppercorns

1 teaspoon salt

4 beef tenderloin (filet mignon) steaks (6 to 8 ounces each, cut about 1½ inches thick)

¾ pound fresh button mushrooms

2 tablespoons olive oil

Salt and pepper to taste

1 Crack the peppercorns (use 2 teaspoons if you want only a mild amount of spiciness and 4 teaspoons for pepper heads) into coarse particles (see Figure 7-5). Sprinkle salt on both sides of each steak. Spread the cracked pepper evenly onto both sides of each steak, pressing it into the surface with the palm of your hand. Allow the steaks to stand 15 minutes.

2 Rinse the mushrooms under cold running water. Drain well and pat thoroughly dry. With a knife, cut and discard a thin slice from the stem end of each mushroom. Cut each mushroom into ¼-inch slices. In a bowl, toss the mushrooms with oil.

3 Spray the grill grid with nonstick cooking spray or brush with oil to prevent food from sticking. Heat an indoor electric grill, grill pan, or cooktop insert over medium-high heat for 5 minutes. Grill the steaks in a grill pan, on an open grill, or on a cooktop insert for 4 to 5 minutes per side for medium-rare or 5 to 7 minutes for medium doneness (internal temperature should be 140° to 145° for medium rare, but temperature will rise upon standing so remove steaks from heat a few degrees below that temperature). For a contact grill pan, grill the steaks covered for 3 minutes, lift the cover, turn the steaks over and rotate at a right angle to the grill marks. Grill 2 minutes longer for medium rare. Transfer the steaks to a platter; cover them with foil to keep them warm while the mushrooms grill.

4 After the steaks are removed from the grill, add the mushrooms to the grill. If your grill has open grids through which the mushrooms may fall, use a large skillet to sauté the mushrooms over high heat. Cook and stir for 5 minutes in a grill pan or 3 minutes in a covered grill. Season mushrooms with salt and pepper to taste. Serve the mushrooms over the grilled steaks.

Go-With: *Serve with baked potatoes and a tomato mixed green salad.*

Nutrition at a glance (per serving): *calories 350; calories from fat 177; fat 20 g; saturated fat 6 g; cholesterol 106 mg; sodium 810 mg; carbohydrates 4 g; dietary fiber 1 g; protein 38 g*

How to Crush Peppercorns

Figure 7-5: Crack peppercorns into coarse particles.

gather whole peppercorns in the middle of a cutting board.

Roll up a towel and... use it to surround the peppercorns so they don't fly off the cutting board.

Use the heel of your hand to press down the edge of a small pot on to the peppercorns.

Repeat steps one and two until the peppercorns are crushed to a desired size...

Chimichurri Round Steak

Grilled beef has always been popular in Argentina, where this recipe originates, and is often served with parsley sauce. In this recipe, a parsley paste clings to the steak as it grills to season it.

Tools: *Grill, nonreactive dish or large resealable plastic bag*

Preparation time: *25 minutes*

Marinating time: *8 hours or overnight*

Grilling time: *15 to 25 minutes*

Yield: *5 servings*

Parsley Puree (see Chapter 5)

1 boneless beef top round steak, cut 1-inch thick (1½ pounds)

1 Prepare Parsley Puree.

2 Working on a cutting board, trim all the pieces of fat from the steak. In a nonreactive dish or a large, resealable plastic bag, place the steak and add ¼ cup Parsley Puree. Turn the steak over to coat evenly with the puree. Cover the dish or close the bag securely and refrigerate for 8 hours or overnight. Refrigerate the remaining Parsley Puree.

3 Remove the steak from the refrigerator and let stand while heating the grill. Spray the grill grid with nonstick cooking spray or brush with oil to prevent food from sticking. Heat an indoor electric grill, grill pan, or cooktop insert over medium-low heat for 5 minutes. Grill the steak in a grill pan, on an open grill, or on a cooktop insert 5 minutes, turn and grill 5 minutes. Turn again, but rotate the steak at a right angle to grill marks and grill 4 minutes. Repeat to grill the other side again for medium-rare doneness or grill 6 to 7 minutes per side for medium. If using a contact grill, grill the steak 5 minutes, lift the cover, turn the steak over, rotating at a right angle to the grill marks. Grill covered for 2 minutes longer or to desired doneness.

4 Transfer the steak to a plate; cover with foil and let it stand a few minutes. Carve the steak into thin slices across the grain and serve with the remaining Parsley Puree.

Go-With: *Serve with any of the vegetables in Chapter 11.*

Nutrition at a glance (per serving): *calories 326; calories from fat 177; fat 19 g; saturated fat 4 g; cholesterol 85 mg; sodium 541 mg; carbohydrates 4 g; dietary fiber 1 g; protein 33 g*

Chapter 8

Pork-Barrel Projects

In This Chapter

▶ Choosing from a variety of pork cuts

▶ Understanding how to handle pork safely

▶ Grilling up delicious pork recipes

Recipes in This Chapter

▶ Asian Butterflied Pork Loin

▶ Maple Glazed Pork Chops with Apples

▶ Barbecued Pork Tenderloin

▶ Southeast Asian Satay

▶ Miami Spice Pork-on-a-Stick

▶ Jamaican Jerk Pork

*P*ork is an easy meat to grill (and, when done right, is tender and juicy). Recently, pork prices have fallen dramatically, and although this doesn't bode well for pig farms (which are disappearing at a record rate), it does mean that pork dinners can meet your budget.

Surprisingly, certain cuts of pork are also pretty healthy: Pork tenderloin has just 140 calories per 3-ounce serving and just 4 grams of fat: That's less than nearly all lean cuts of beef! (You can find information about 3-ounce servings of other cuts of pork in Table 8-1.) After you get out of the loin area of the pig (see the "Shopping for Pork Cuts" section), pork becomes rather calorie-laden and high in fat.

Table 8-1	Grilled Pork Nutrition Chart		
Variety of Pork	*Calories*	*Total Fat*	*Saturated Fat*
Tenderloin	140	4	1
Top loin roast, boneless	170	6	2
Top loin chop, boneless	170	7	2
Loin center chop	170	7	3
Sirloin roast	180	9	3
Loin rib chop	190	8	3
Pork shoulder blade steak	190	11	4

Handling Pork Safely

Use the same care with pork as you do with poultry (see Chapter 9). However, although you take care with *poultry* because of bacteria such as E. coli, with *pork,* the culprit is a small parasite that thrives in uncooked pork and makes its way into the human body, where it can cause a disease called *trichinosis,* which is often fatal. The good news? Trichinae is destroyed at about 140°, so pork cooked to around 150° is perfectly safe — not to mention delicious — to eat.

Using a meat thermometer (see Chapter 2) is critical for grilled pork. Undercooked pork, less than 150°, can be unhealthy; overcooked pork will make you a pork-hater in no time: It turns dry, gray, and tough. Check the internal temperature of the meat and remove it from the grill a few degrees below the desired degree of doneness. Let it rest, covered loosely with foil, 5 minutes before serving.

In addition, follow some simple rules for handling pork:

✔ **Wash your hands with hot, soapy water before and after handling pork.** This includes applying rubs to the surface of pork loin and chops.

✔ **Wash plastic cutting boards, knives, and countertops in hot, soapy water after contact with pork.** Plastic cutting boards can also be run through the dishwasher. If you use sponges to clean up raw pork juices, run the sponge through the dishwasher cycle or wash in very hot, soapy water.

✔ **If you're using tongs or a spatula to turn raw pork, be sure to wash the tool with hot soapy water before using the same tool to remove cooked food from the grill.** Consider using two tongs: one to handle raw foods and the other to handle cooked foods. Wash the raw-food tongs with soapy water after you're finished grilling.

✔ **Wash any plate on which you place raw pork.** Never place cooked or ready-to-eat food on an unwashed plate that was used for raw pork, because you may spread trichinae from the uncooked meat to the ready-to-eat food.

Shopping for Pork Cuts

Pork has few available cuts, and they're easily summed up in Figure 8-1. For grilling, use loin cuts, especially tenderloin and loin chops. For kebabs, however, you can use pork shoulder or butt, which, oddly enough, comes from the shoulder of the pig!

Figure 8-1:
This little pig has plenty of pork and ham cuts for your indoor grill.

Look for pork that doesn't look mushy or soft. It should be pink, with white fat that your butcher can trim off for you. Don't purchase pork that looks gray or has yellow fat — it's past its prime. Look carefully, too, at expiration dates.

Grilling the Other White Meat

To eliminate your risk of trichinosis, always take pork's temperature before eating and check to make sure that no pink shows in the meat. For medium doneness, pork should register 160°; for a well-done cut, 170°. (See the "Handling Pork Safely" section for further details.) To ensure that you don't overcook pork, cut into the meat near the end of the estimated cooking time to see if any pink shows. If it does, cook for another minute and check again; if not, and if juices are clear, you're ready to eat.

Use rubs, which stick to pork better than marinades do, liberally on all pork (see Chapter 4). Marinades taste great, too, but you may need to marinade all day or overnight to infuse pork with the flavor of the marinade. If you're rushed for time, use a rub just before grilling and you'll be rewarded with full flavor and a crispy outer surface. Be sure to wash your hands with hot, soapy water after applying a rub.

For a really quick fix, purchase pork tenderloin or loin chops on your way home, asking the butcher to trim all fat. At the same market, pick up a box of Shake 'n' Bake, a box of quick-cooking wild-rice mixture, and some salad fixings or fresh vegetables. After you arrive home, heat your grill over medium-low to medium heat. As your grill preheats, remove the plastic shaking bag that comes in the box; place the pork in the bag with the coating, shake for a few seconds, and place the now-coated pork on your grill for 20 to 25 minutes, checking for doneness after 18 minutes. While the pork grills, fix the rice and mix up a salad or steam the vegetables for 5 to 7 minutes. With minimal expense, time, and mess, you've got yourself a delicious meal.

Preheating times vary among indoor grill manufacturers. Five minutes should be enough to adequately preheat your grill, but check the use and care book that came with your grill — your particular grill may take a bit longer to heat up.

Asian Butterflied Pork Loin

In this recipe, lean pork loin is topped with a garlicky Hoisin Barbecue Sauce that creates a delicious dish. Note that after cutting and grilling this pork loin, it resembles London broil — it's sliced across the grain into thin slices.

Tools: *Grill, nonreactive dish or large resealable plastic bag, small saucepan*

Preparation time: *25 minutes*

Marinating time: *2 hours or overnight*

Grilling time: *20 to 30 minutes*

Yield: *5 servings*

1¼ pounds center-cut boneless pork loin	1 cup ketchup
1 teaspoon five-spice powder	½ cup hoisin sauce
1 teaspoon sugar	2 tablespoons naturally brewed soy sauce
¼ teaspoon salt	5 tablespoons honey
1 teaspoon vegetable oil	2 tablespoons rice wine or dry sherry
2 cloves garlic, finely chopped	2 teaspoons dark (toasted) sesame oil

1 With a sharp knife, working on a cutting board, trim all fat from pork. To butterfly, or partially split the loin, starting from one of the long sides, cut through the center of pork horizontally to within 1 inch of the opposite side, being careful not to cut all the way through. Open the pork like a book and press the uncut long edge to flatten the meat as much as possible (see Figure 8-2).

2 Place the pork in a nonreactive dish or a large, resealable plastic bag. In a cup, combine the five-spice powder, sugar, and salt. Sprinkle the pork with the spice mixture and rub the spices in well on all sides. Cover the dish or close the bag securely and refrigerate for 2 hours or overnight.

3 Meanwhile, prepare the Hoisin Barbecue Sauce: In a small saucepan, heat the oil and add the garlic. Cook a few seconds, just until the garlic is golden. Do not allow the garlic to brown. Stir in the ketchup, hoisin sauce, soy, honey, wine, and sesame oil. Heat and stir the sauce until bubbly. Remove from the heat and cool the sauce to room temperature. Cover and refrigerate the sauce until you're ready to grill the pork.

4 Remove the pork from the refrigerator and let stand while heating the grill. Spray the grill grid with nonstick cooking spray or brush with oil to prevent food from sticking. Heat an indoor electric grill, grill pan, or cooktop insert over medium-low heat for 5 minutes. Place the pork flat, cut side down, on the grill grid. Grill the pork in a grill pan, on an open grill, or on a cooktop insert for 5 minutes. Turn and grill 5 minutes. Cover with foil. If the pork is browning too much, reduce the heat if possible. Grill 10 to 15 minutes longer. The pork is done when you see only a hint of pink in the center or until an instant-read thermometer inserted into the thickest part of the tenderloin registers 150°. If using a contact grill, grill the pork covered for 10 minutes, lift the cover and turn and rotate the pork; grill covered 5 minutes longer.

5 Transfer the pork to a cutting board, brush with some Hoisin Barbecue Sauce; cover loosely with foil and let it stand a few minutes.

6 Carve the pork into thin slices across the grain and serve with the remaining sauce.

Go-With: *Serve with hot cooked rice. If you're using a contact grill, after the pork is cooked, add ½ head green cabbage, cored and cut into ½-inch slices, to the grill and cook covered about 5 minutes or until tender, stirring once.*

Nutrition at a glance (per serving): *calories 446; calories from fat 158; fat 18 g; saturated fat 6 g; cholesterol 82 mg; sodium 1661 mg; carbohydrates 44 g; dietary fiber 1 g; protein 29 g*

How To 'Butterfly' Pork

Figure 8-2: Here's a riddle: How does a pig become a butterfly?

1. FAT SIDE UP

CUT FROM A LONG SIDE TO WITHIN ONE INCH OF THE OPPOSITE SIDE

2.

OPEN THE LOIN LIKE A BUTTERFLY...

DO **NOT** CUT FROM THE TOP OF THE LOIN DOWN!

Maple Glazed Pork Chops
with Apples

Grilled apple slices make a colorful, tasty accompaniment to these marinated chops.

Tools: *Grill, small mixing bowl, resealable plastic bag or baking dish*

Preparation time: *15 minutes*

Marinating time: *1 hour*

Grilling time: *25 minutes*

Yield: *4 servings*

¼ cup maple syrup

2 tablespoons cider vinegar

1 tablespoon chopped fresh or 1 teaspoon dried thyme leaves

½ teaspoon salt

4 large boneless loin pork chops, cut ¾-inch thick (1⅓ pounds total)

3 golden delicious or other firm cooking or baking apples

1 tablespoon sugar

¼ teaspoon ground nutmeg

1 For the Maple Glaze, in a small bowl, whisk the maple syrup, vinegar, thyme, and salt. Trim all visible fat from each chop. Place the chops in a resealable plastic bag or a shallow baking dish. Pour glaze over the chops. Seal the bag or cover the dish and refrigerate 1 hour.

2 Core the apples (see Figure 8-3) and cut each apple crosswise into ½-inch-thick round slices, discarding the ends. In a cup, mix the sugar and nutmeg. Remove the chops from the marinade, shaking off most of the excess; discard the marinade. Pat the pork dry with paper towels.

3 Spray the grill grid with nonstick cooking spray or brush with oil to prevent food from sticking. Heat an indoor electric grill, grill pan, or cooktop insert over medium heat for 5 minutes.

4 If using a grill pan, open grill, or cooktop insert, grill pork 5 to 6 minutes per side, turning once. To create decorative grill marks, grill the chop 3 minutes and rotate the chop at a right angle to the first grill marks, then grill another 3 minutes. Turn the chop over and repeat. Cut to determine doneness or use an instant-read thermometer inserted into the side of the chop. The chops are done when the meat has a light pink blush or an internal thermometer reads 150°. If using a contact grill, grill the chops covered for 5 minutes. Lift the cover and turn the chops over and rotate at a right angle to create crossed grill marks; cover and grill 3 minutes longer or until done.

5 Transfer the chops to a plate; cover and keep warm. Place the apple slices on the grill and grill 5 minutes per side or until tender. If using a contact grill, grill the apples 2 to 3 minutes. If the apples don't fit in a single layer, grill them in batches. Arrange the grilled apples on a plate and sprinkle with the sugar mixture. Serve the chops with the apples.

Nutrition at a glance (per serving): *calories 319; calories from fat 90; fat 10 g; saturated fat 4 g; cholesterol 97 mg; sodium 144 mg; carbohydrates 22 g; dietary fiber 3 g; protein 34 g*

Barbecued Pork Tenderloin

One of the leanest cuts of pork, this tenderloin is perfect for two or three persons. You can easily double the recipe to serve more because this pork cut is often packaged with two loins. It dries out easily, so a spritz of the Spray Mop keeps it moist as it is grilling.

Tools: *Grill*

Preparation time: *25 minutes*

Grilling time: *20 to 35 minutes*

Yield: *3 servings*

Carolina Spray Mop (see Chapter 4)   *1 pork tenderloin (about 1 pound)*

Basic Barbecue Sauce (see Chapter 5)

1 Prepare Carolina Spray Mop and Basic Barbecue Sauce.

2 With a sharp knife, working on a cutting board, trim all the fat and the tendon from the pork. Spray the grill grid with nonstick cooking spray or brush with oil to prevent food from sticking. Heat an indoor electric grill, grill pan, or cooktop insert over medium-low heat for 5 minutes.

3 Grill the pork in a grill pan, on an open grill, or on a cooktop insert 5 minutes, turn and squirt with Carolina Spray Mop. Cover the pan with foil and grill the pork 25 minutes longer or until done, turning and squirting with Carolina Spray Mop occasionally. (The internal temperature should be 150°.) If using a contact grill, grill the pork 5 minutes, squirt, and grill (covered) for 5 minutes. Grill the pork until done, about 3 minutes longer. Transfer the pork to a cutting board; cover with foil and let it stand a few minutes.

4 Carve the pork into thin slices across the grain and serve with Basic Barbecue Sauce.

Nutrition at a glance (per serving): *calories 226; calories from fat 54; fat 6 g; saturated fat 2 g; cholesterol 90 mg; sodium 445 mg; carbohydrates 10 g; dietary fiber 0 g; protein 32 g*

How to Core an Apple

Figure 8-3: Building *esprit de core!*

Run a paring knife clockwise around the core (leaving ¼" at the bottom)...

...and pop out the core!

POP-

Southeast Asian Satay

Satay, a popular southeast Asian skewered food that resembles kebabs, may be made with chicken or beef as well as pork. In Thai versions, coconut milk and fish sauce are typical ingredients. This Malaysian-inspired dish is based on soy sauce and curry, a spice blend. Serve it as an appetizer, snack, or part of a meal with rice.

Tools: *Grill, bamboo skewers*

Preparation time: *15 minutes*

Marinating time: *2 hours or overnight*

Grilling time: *15 to 20 minutes*

Yield: *4 servings*

1½ pounds boneless pork butt or loin

3 cloves garlic, finely chopped

3 tablespoons naturally-brewed soy sauce

1 teaspoon curry powder

Spicy Peanut Sauce (see Chapter 5)

2 cucumbers

1 small red chili pepper (Thai bird or Mexican serrano), seeded and chopped, or ½ small red onion, thinly sliced

2 tablespoons sugar

2 tablespoons rice vinegar or distilled white vinegar

½ teaspoon salt

1 With a sharp knife, trim and remove any excess pieces of fat from the pork. Cut the pork into ¼-inch-thick strips about 3 or 4 inches long. (If you have time, freeze the meat 30 to 40 minutes for easier slicing.) In a nonreactive dish or a large, resealable plastic bag, combine the pork strips, garlic, soy, and curry. Rub the mixture into the strips. Cover the dish or seal the bag and refrigerate for at least 2 hours or, if possible, overnight, to marinate. Soak 12 (8-inch) bamboo skewers in water for 30 minutes prior to grilling.

2 Meanwhile, prepare Spicy Peanut Sauce.

3 To prepare a cucumber relish, peel the cucumbers and cut each in half lengthwise. Scoop out the seeds (see Figure 8-4). Cut the cucumber halves crosswise into thin slices. In a medium mixing bowl, combine the cucumbers, pepper or onion, sugar, vinegar, and salt. Cover and refrigerate until serving time.

4 Drain and dry bamboo skewers. Thread 2 to 3 pork strips accordian style onto each bamboo skewer, dividing strips evenly among the skewers.

5 Heat an indoor electric grill, grill pan, or cooktop insert over medium-high heat for 5 minutes. If using a grill pan, an open grill, or a cooktop insert, grill the pork 5 to 6 minutes, turning skewers frequently. If using a contact grill, grill 3 minutes, lift the cover and turn the skewers over and grill covered 1 or 2 minutes longer, pressing the cover down firmly to char the top of the pork. With a covered grill, serve the drippings with skewers.

6 Drain the cucumbers just before serving and transfer to a small dish. Accompany satay with cucumber relish and Spicy Peanut Sauce.

Go-With: Serve with hot cooked jasmine rice or any other variety of rice.

Nutrition at a glance (per serving): *calories 410; calories from fat 199; fat 22 g; saturated fat 8 g; cholesterol 103 mg; sodium 663 mg; carbohydrates 13 g; dietary fiber 2 g; protein 39 g*

How to Seed a Cucumber

Figure 8-4:
Seeding a
cucumber
with ease.

Remove the peel with a knife or peeler.

Cut in half, lengthwise...

and scoop out the seeds with a small spoon.

Miami Spice Pork-on-a-Stick

If you visit Miami Beach, you may find this great nosh being grilled by a street vendor in a street-side grill cart. Skewered chunks of garlicky pork are served up in hot dog buns. Our version is an adaptation with the tomato relish topping added.

Tools: *Grill, garlic press, mixing bowl, nonreactive dish or large resealable plastic bag, skewers*

Preparation time: *15 minutes*

Marinating time: *Overnight*

Grilling time: *15 to 23 minutes*

Yield: *4 servings*

2 cloves garlic, pressed or minced

1 teaspoon ground oregano or cumin

1 teaspoon salt

¼ teaspoon ground black pepper

2 tablespoons fresh lime or lemon juice

1 tablespoon cider vinegar

1 tablespoon olive oil

1¼ pounds boneless pork butt or lean pieces of pork shoulder, cut into 1-inch cubes

4 hoagie or submarine rolls (6 inches long), split

Tomato Relish (see following recipe)

1 Prepare the garlic marinade: In a mixing bowl, combine the garlic with the oregano, salt, pepper, lime juice, vinegar, and oil.

2 Place the pork cubes in a nonreactive dish or a large, resealable plastic bag. Add the garlic marinade and mix well. Cover the dish or seal the bag and marinate the pork in the refrigerator overnight. (If you use wooden skewers, soak them for 30 minutes in cold water prior to grilling.) Thread the pork cubes on four skewers. (Don't pack the meat too tightly on the skewers but allow a little space in between each piece to let heat circulate and ensure even cooking.)

3 Heat an indoor electric grill, grill pan, or cooktop insert over medium-low heat for 5 minutes. If using a grill pan, an open grill, or a cooktop insert, grill the skewers 15 to 18 minutes or until pork is firm but still pale pink in the center, turning the skewers every 3 to 4 minutes. If using a contact grill, grill for 5 minutes. Turn the skewers over and grill 5 minutes longer in a covered grill. (Use a sharp knife to make a small incision in the center of a pork cube to test for doneness. The meat should be browned on the outside and pink and juicy inside.) If using a contact grill, pour the drippings from the drip pan over the pork before serving in rolls topped with Tomato Relish.

Nutrition at a glance (per serving without condiments): calories 644; calories from fat 210; fat 23 g; saturated fat 7 g; cholesterol 87 mg; sodium 1410 mg; carbohydrates 70 g; dietary fiber 4 g; protein 36 g

Tomato Relish

You can make this relish ahead of time and refrigerate until needed.

Tools: *Mixing bowl*

Preparation time: *20 minutes*

Yield: *1¾ cups (28 tablespoons)*

2 medium tomatoes, chopped	1 tablespoon lime juice
1 small onion, finely chopped (¼ cup)	1 tablespoon vegetable oil
1 clove garlic, minced	½ teaspoon salt
¼ cup finely chopped cilantro	1 small, ripe Hass avocado (about 5 ounces)

In a mixing bowl, combine all the ingredients except the avocado. Right before serving, cut 1 small avocado in half, remove the pit, peel, and cut the avocado into ½-inch cubes. Gently fold the diced avocado into the tomato mixture.

Nutrition at a glance (per 1 tablespoon): *calories 118; calories from fat 89; fat 10 g; saturated fat 2 g; cholesterol 0 mg; sodium 162 mg; carbohydrates 8 g; dietary fiber 5 g; protein 2 g*

Jamaican Jerk Pork

A dry rub of allspice with a touch of spiciness characterizes this Caribbean pork dish. *Allspice* is a dried bean from an evergreen tree that resembles a peppercorn, but tastes like a mixture of cinnamon, cloves, and nutmeg, hence its name.

Tools: *Grill, nonreactive dish*

Preparation time: *5 minutes*

Marinating time: *2 hours*

Grilling time: *13 to 20 minutes*

Yield: *4 servings*

2 teaspoons dried oregano leaves, crumbled	*½ teaspoon salt*
1 teaspoon ground allspice	*½ teaspoon ground red pepper*
1 teaspoon brown sugar	*4 boneless pork butt steaks or center-cut loin chops, cut ¾-inch thick*
1 teaspoon garlic powder	

1 In a cup, combine the oregano, allspice, sugar, garlic, salt, and pepper.

2 With a sharp knife, working on a cutting board, trim as much fat as possible from the pork. Place the pork in a nonreactive dish. Sprinkle the spice mixture evenly on all sides of the pork. Cover the dish and refrigerate for 2 hours.

3 Remove the pork from the refrigerator and let stand while heating the grill. Spray the grill grid with nonstick cooking spray or brush with oil to prevent food from sticking. Heat an indoor electric grill, grill pan, or cooktop insert over medium-low heat for 5 minutes. Grill the pork in a grill pan, on an open grill, or on a cooktop insert for 5 to 6 minutes per side, turning once. Because of the spice rub, the pork will appear blackened. With a knife, make a cut to determine doneness or use an instant-read thermometer. The inside should have a slight blush of pink in the center or should reach an internal temperature of 150°. If using a contact grill, grill the pork for 5 minutes, lift the cover, turn the pork over, and rotate the pork at a right angle to the grill marks. Grill covered for 3 minutes longer or until done.

Go-With: *Serve with Tropical Fruit Salsa (see Chapter 5).*

Nutrition at a glance (per serving): calories 155; calories from fat 53; fat 6 g; saturated fat 2 g; cholesterol 59 mg; sodium 335 mg; carbohydrates 3 g; dietary fiber 1 g; protein 22 g

Chapter 9

Getting a Bird's-Eye View of Poultry

*P*oultry — from chicken to turkey, game birds to duck — is tender, juicy, and easy to grill. It's also pretty inexpensive, and because it freezes well, you can buy it on sale and store it in your freezer to use as needed. White meat poultry cooks quickly on the grill, and although dark meat takes a little longer, it tastes succulent when grilled.

This chapter contains recipes for chicken and turkey, as you may expect, but also for Cornish game hens, which you can find in your grocer's freezer section; and quail and duck, which may be available at your super- market or at a gourmet store. If you can't find quail and duck where you live, they can be procured online, at the following Web sites:

▶ **D'Artagnan,** out of Newark, New Jersey, sells fresh duck and quail, as well as a variety of other game birds and other animals. Visit its site at www.dartagnan.com.

▶ **Select Gourmet Foods, Inc.,** in Kenmore, Washington, sells a variety of game. Visit selectgourmetfoods.com for information.

▶ **Culver Duck,** in Middlebury, Indiana, sells duck breasts and whole duck. Go to www.culverduck.com to browse and buy.

Poultry can also be quite healthy, ranging from a slim 120 calories for a 3-ounce portion of chicken breast to 220 for the same amount of duck, as shown in Table 9-1. The trick, however, is to always remove the skin from poultry before grilling. Skin adds from 40 to 60 calories and 5 grams of fat for every 3-ounce portion of poultry. If you want to leave the skin on during grilling to add moisture, be sure to remove it before eating.

Table 9-1	Grilled Poultry Nutrition Chart		
Variety of Poultry	*Calories*	*Total Fat*	*Saturated Fat*
Chicken breast	120	2	1
Chicken thigh	150	7	2
Cornish game hen	45	1	0.5
Duck	220	12	4.5
Ground turkey	195	12	5
Quail	64	1.5	0.5
Turkey breast	120	1	0
Turkey thigh	140	5	2

Grilling Poultry Safely

Poultry is especially vulnerable to surface bacteria, but the good news is that the bacteria is eliminated by grilling it to the proper temperature. Because of this bacteria, however, take care when selecting and storing poultry. In particular, when shopping, select your poultry last (just before checking out) so that your meat stays as cold as possible. Be sure that packaged poultry is cold to the touch and tightly wrapped — don't buy poultry that has juices leaking out of the package. Check the "sell by" date to make sure it hasn't passed.

When you get home, place the poultry in the meat drawer or on the lowest shelf, near the back of your refrigerator. Be sure to allow air to circulate around the package.

Because poultry — especially chicken and turkey — occasionally go on sale, you can purchase three months' worth of meat and freeze it. You're better off buying fresh poultry and freezing it yourself, but make sure it wasn't previously frozen. (Never thaw frozen meat and then refreeze it.) If you buy frozen poultry, make sure it's frozen solid and if you have a long trip and the weather is hot, keep it frozen on your way home by packing it in an ice-filled cooler. Before freezing, place poultry in a resealable freezer bag or wrap in heavy-duty aluminum foil. Use poultry within three months of freezing it.

Keep the following shopping, handling, and preparation tips in mind when grilling poultry:

✔ **Wash your hands with hot, soapy water (which kills bacteria) before and after handling poultry.**

✔ **Wash plastic cutting boards, knives, and countertops in hot, soapy water after contact with poultry or run plastic cutting boards through a dishwasher.**

✔ **Use paper towels to clean up countertop spills.** If you use sponges to clean up raw poultry juices, run the sponge through the dishwasher cycle.

✔ **If you're using tongs or spatula to turn raw poultry, be sure to wash the tool with hot soapy water before using the same tool to remove cooked food from the grill.** Consider using two tongs: one to handle raw foods and the other to handle cooked foods. Wash the raw-food tongs with soapy water after you're finished grilling.

✔ **Never place cooked or ready-to-eat food on an unwashed plate that was used for raw poultry.** Doing so may spread bacteria from the uncooked meat to the ready-to-eat food.

✔ **Defrost frozen poultry in the refrigerator, not on the countertop.** At room temperature, bacteria can build up during the thawing process. If you use a microwave to defrost frozen poultry, grill it as soon as it's thawed.

✔ **Marinate poultry in the refrigerator, not on the countertop.** Always dispose of the marinade after use, because it may contain bacteria. (Flip to Chapter 3 for the lowdown on marinade safety.)

✔ **Insert a meat thermometer (see Chapter 2) into the thickest part of the meat to ensure you've cooked it to the appropriate temperature.** Grill turkey or chicken white meat to an internal temperature of 170°. Grill dark-meat poultry, including duck, to 180°. (This will be well-done; if you like duck on the pink side, grill to 160°.)

Preheating times vary among indoor grill manufacturers. Five minutes should be enough to adequately preheat your grill, but check the use and care book that came with your grill — your particular grill may take a bit longer to heat up.

Counting On Chicken

In this section, you can find a velvety chicken breast recipe that uses honey and lavender; a tangy tomatillo, jalapeño, and chicken breast recipe; a delicious pairing of chicken tenderloins and pasta; a paprika-ginger recipe for chicken thighs; and a delightful chicken-thigh kebab recipe. In addition to the recipes in this section, use the rubs and marinades in Chapter 4 to jazz up otherwise plain chicken breasts and thighs.

Chicken drumsticks tend not to grill well because they're too thick to cook thoroughly without burning. Chicken wings can also be a challenge, but if you choose to try grilling chicken wings, leave the skin on, rub them with a dry or wet rub (see Chapter 4), and grill them over a medium-high heat. Turn them with tongs every couple minutes. Grill for 10 to 15 minutes. Check for doneness by cutting into the thickest part of the wing: You shouldn't see any sign of pink. The last minute, brush with a sauce before serving.

In addition to the following recipes, try the Grilled Chicken Caesar Salad recipe in Chapter 12.

Lemon Lavender Chicken

This recipe was created to serve at a floral luncheon that Lucy hosts and caters at the Boyce Thompson Arboretum in Arizona for their annual February Language of Flowers program. Although it was grilled outdoors there, it can easily be grilled indoors anytime. Just take care not to overcook or the chicken will be dry. We prefer Meyer lemon juice for this recipe, which is less acidic, but you can use any other lemon variety.

Herbes de provence is a mixture of herbs typically used to flavor foods in the south of France — see Chapter 4. You can produce your own version by combining dried thyme, basil, fennel seeds, savory, rosemary, tarragon, and lavender. Look for dried lavender at your local health food store, co-op, or wherever else you can purchase dried spices and herbs in bulk. Make sure to buy the untreated kind, so that you avoid the lavender treated with scent. If you can't find lavender, you can prepare this recipe without it, but the lavender flavor will be less pronounced.

Tools: *Grill, resealable plastic bag or nonreactive container*

Preparation time: *20 minutes*

Marinating time: *1 hour*

Grilling time: *13 to 19 minutes*

Yield: *4 servings*

¼ cup fresh lemon juice	2 tablespoons olive oil
1½ teaspoons herbes de provence	1 tablespoon orange blossom honey or other mild honey
1 teaspoon crushed dried untreated lavender	
1 teaspoon salt	4 large boneless, skinless chicken breast halves (1¾ to 2 pounds)

1 In a measuring cup, combine the lemon juice, *herbes de provence,* lavender, salt, olive oil, and honey.

2 Rinse the chicken under cold running water and pat dry with paper towels. With a knife, on a cutting board, cut off and discard any visible fat and gristle from the chicken. Place the chicken in a resealable plastic bag or a shallow, nonreactive baking dish. Pour the lemon lavender marinade over the chicken. Seal the bag or cover the dish and refrigerate for 1 hour.

3 Heat an indoor electric grill, grill pan, or cooktop insert over medium heat for 5 minutes. Drain the chicken and pat dry. If using a grill pan, open grill, or cooktop insert, grill the chicken 12 to 14 minutes or until done, turning several times. (To create decorative crossed grill marks, grill the chicken 4 minutes or until brown grill marks appear on the bottom and then rotate the chicken a quarter turn to the first grill marks, grilling another 2 minutes. Turn the chicken over and repeat.) If using a contact grill, grill the chicken covered for 4 minutes. Lift the cover and turn the chicken over and rotate a quarter turn to create crossed grill marks; then cover and grill 4 minutes longer or until done.

4 Make a small incision in the center of the chicken to determine doneness. The chicken is done when the meat is white and moist with no sign of pink. If the chicken is browning too much, reduce the heat if possible or cover the chicken with a sheet of foil to finish cooking. Transfer the chicken to a serving plate.

Go-With: *Try this dish with Cauliflower Parmesan or Sesame Squash Medley (see Chapter 11).*

Nutrition at a glance (per serving): *calories 233; calories from fat 57; fat 6 g; saturated fat 2 g; cholesterol 110 mg; sodium 241 mg; carbohydrates 2 g; dietary fiber 0 g; protein 40 g*

Chicken with Tomatillo Avocado Salsa

Tomatillos (shown in Figure 9-1) look like small green tomatoes with a papery outer husk, or wrapper. Tangy in taste, they must be cooked and are usually made into tasty salsas. Originally, this recipe was created using Mexican-grown Hass avocados imported during the winter, when California varieties are not available. This avocado variety, which possesses a buttery texture and delicious flavor, is preferred in the sauce with grilled chicken.

Tools: *Grill, saucepan*

Preparation time: *35 minutes*

Grilling time: *20 to 25 minutes*

Yield: *4 servings*

1 pound tomatillos (8 to 10)	*⅛ teaspoon ground black pepper (or to taste)*
1 medium onion, quartered	*¼ cup sour cream*
2 jalapeño peppers, halved lengthwise and seeded	*2 tablespoons water*
½ cup chicken broth	*4 medium boneless, skinless chicken breast halves (about 1½ pounds)*
2 tablespoons olive oil	*1 small, ripe Hass avocado (about 5 ounces)*
½ teaspoon salt (or to taste)	*4 red radishes, trimmed and coarsely chopped*

1 To prepare the tomatillos, remove their papery skins and rinse the tomatillos in water. Pat dry with paper towels. Cut each tomatillo in half. Spray the grill grid with nonstick cooking spray or brush with oil to prevent food from sticking. Heat an indoor electric grill, grill pan, or cooktop insert over medium heat for 5 minutes. Grill the tomatillos, onion, and jalapeños until soft, about 8 to 10 minutes in a grill pan, on an open grill, or on a cooktop insert, or 6 minutes in a contact grill, turning occasionally. As each vegetable softens, remove it to a large cutting board. The tomatillos will soften first in about 5 minutes, then the jalapeños, and lastly the onion. When all the vegetables are tender, coarsely chop the tomatillos and onion and finely chop the jalapeño.

2 In a saucepan, combine the chopped vegetables, the chicken broth, 1 tablespoon of the oil, ½ teaspoon salt (or to taste) and ⅛ teaspoon pepper (or to taste); set salsa aside. In a cup, combine the sour cream and water until smooth. (Put the sour cream mixture into a small squirt bottle, if desired.)

3 Rinse the chicken under cold running water and pat dry with paper towels. With a knife, on a cutting board, cut off and discard any visible fat and gristle from the chicken. In a bowl, coat the chicken breasts with the remaining 1 tablespoon of oil. Sprinkle with salt and pepper.

4 Heat your indoor electric grill, grill pan, or cooktop insert again over medium heat for 5 minutes. If using a grill pan, open grill, or cooktop insert, grill the chicken 10 to 12 minutes or until done, turning several times. (To create decorative crossed grill marks, grill the chicken 3 minutes or until brown grill marks appear on the bottom. Then rotate the chicken a quarter turn to the first grill marks, grilling another 2 minutes. Turn the chicken over and repeat.) If using a contact grill, grill the chicken covered for 4 minutes. Lift the cover and turn the chicken over and rotate a quarter turn to create crossed grill marks; then cover and grill 3 minutes longer or until done.

5 Make a small incision in the center of chicken to determine doneness. The chicken is done when the meat is white and moist with no sign of pink. If the chicken is browning too much, reduce the heat if possible or cover the chicken with a sheet of foil to finish cooking.

6 Transfer the grilled chicken to a cutting board; let stand for a few minutes. Meanwhile, heat the tomatillo salsa until warm. Cut each breast across into ½-inch thick slices. On each of four dinner plates, fan the chicken breast slices in the center. Spoon the tomatillo salsa around chicken and scatter the diced avocado and chopped radishes over the salsa. Drizzle with the sour cream mixture and serve.

Nutrition at a glance (per serving): calories 397; calories from fat 196; fat 22 g; saturated fat 5 g; cholesterol 101 mg; sodium 364 mg; carbohydrates 14 g; dietary fiber 6 g; protein 38 g

Figure 9-1:
To pick the best tomatillos, peel back the husk and select the ones that are golden green rather than dark green, which is an indication of ripeness.

tomatillo

Chicken Tenders Pasta

Every chicken breast has a long slender muscle on the underside called a *tender* or more accurately, the *tenderloin* or *filet*. Packages of these can be purchased in the poultry section of most large supermarkets. If you can't find them, substitute boneless, skinless chicken breasts cut lengthwise into 1-inch-wide strips for this pasta dish.

Tools: *Grill, large pot, large saucepan*

Preparation time: *30 minutes*

Marinating time: *15 minutes*

Grilling time: *9 to 10 minutes*

Yield: *6 servings*

Poultry Dust (see Chapter 4)

1½ pounds chicken tenders (tenderloin)

3 tablespoons olive oil

3 carrots, peeled and chopped

1 medium onion, chopped

½ cup dry red or white wine

26-ounce jar or can tomato-based spaghetti sauce with basil or mushrooms

1 pound thin spaghetti

1 Prepare Poultry Dust. Rinse the chicken tenders and pat dry on paper towels. Place the chicken in a shallow baking dish; toss with 1 tablespoon of the oil and arrange in a single layer in the dish. Sprinkle with 1 teaspoon of the Poultry Dust, turn the tenders over and sprinkle with 1 more teaspoon Poultry Dust. Cover and refrigerate 15 minutes.

2 In a large pot over high heat, bring about 5 quarts of lightly salted water to a boil.

3 Meanwhile, heat the remaining 2 tablespoons oil in a large saucepan over medium heat. Add the carrots and onion; cook 5 to 8 minutes or until the vegetables are softened, stirring occasionally. Add the wine and heat to boiling. Reduce the heat to low and stir in the spaghetti sauce. Simmer, partially covered, for about 5 minutes. While the sauce simmers, add the spaghetti to the boiling water and cook about 8 minutes, or just until al dente.

4 Spray the grill grid with nonstick cooking spray or brush with oil to prevent food from sticking. Heat an indoor electric grill, grill pan, or cooktop insert over medium-high heat for 5 minutes. Place the chicken in a grill pan, on an open grill, or on a cooktop insert and cook 5 minutes, turning once. If using a contact grill, grill 3 minutes, turn and grill 1 minute longer.

5 Drain the spaghetti and return to the pot. Add half of the sauce and toss well. Transfer the spaghetti to a serving dish. Top with grilled tenders and serve with the remaining sauce.

Go-With: *Serve garlic bread and a mixed green salad with this pasta dish.*

Nutrition at a glance (per serving): *calories 546; calories from fat 98; fat 11 g; saturated fat 2 g; cholesterol 63 mg; sodium 407 mg; carbohydrates 74 g; dietary fiber 6 g; protein 35 g*

Tandoori Chicken

The yogurt marinade in this chicken dish imparts a tasty flavor; however, it does leave a residue on the grill. If your grill has a nonstick coating, clean-up will be a breeze.

Tools: *Grill, food processor or blender, resealable plastic bag or nonreactive dish*

Preparation time: *20 minutes*

Marinating time: *30 minutes*

Grilling time: *13 to 15 minutes*

Yield: *4 servings*

½ small onion, coarsely chopped

8-ounce container plain, low-fat yogurt

1 tablespoon paprika

1 tablespoon grated peeled fresh gingerroot

1 teaspoon salt

1 teaspoon ground coriander or ½ teaspoon ground cumin

8 boneless, skinless chicken thighs (1¾ to 2 pounds)

Lime wedges

1 In a food processor or electric blender, process the onion until finely chopped. Add the yogurt, paprika, ginger, salt, and coriander; process the marinade until smooth.

2 Rinse the chicken and pat dry with paper towels. With a knife, on a cutting board, cut off and discard any visible fat and gristle from the chicken. Place the chicken in a resealable plastic bag or a shallow nonreactive baking dish. Pour the yogurt marinade over the chicken. Seal the bag or cover the dish and refrigerate for 30 minutes.

3 Remove the chicken from the marinade, shaking off most of the excess; discard the marinade. Let the chicken drain on paper towels while the grill heats.

4 Spray the grill grid with nonstick cooking spray or brush with oil to prevent food from sticking. Heat an indoor electric grill, grill pan, or cooktop insert over medium heat for 5 minutes.

5 If using a grill pan, open grill, or cooktop insert, grill the chicken 8 to 10 minutes, turning several times. Make a small incision in the center of the chicken to determine doneness. If using a contact grill, grill the chicken covered 5 minutes. Lift the cover and turn the chicken over, rotating a quarter turn to create crossed grill marks. Then cover and grill 3 minutes longer or until done.

6 Make a small incision in the center of chicken to determine doneness. The chicken is done when the meat is white and moist with no sign of pink. If chicken is browning too much, reduce heat if possible or cover chicken with a sheet of foil to finish cooking.

7 Transfer the chicken to a serving plate; garnish with lime wedges if desired. If using a covered grill, pour any juices in the drip pan over the chicken before serving.

Nutrition at a glance (per serving): calories 327; calories from fat 150; fat 17 g; saturated fat 5 g; cholesterol 144 mg; sodium 143 mg; carbohydrates 2 g; dietary fiber 0 g; protein 40 g

Yakitori

This classic Japanese dish features skewers of succulent chicken morsels with onions and pea pods. Chicken thighs are most commonly used but breast meat may be substituted. Due to the removal of the thigh bone, the thickness of some of the meat may be uneven. Therefore, if meat is thin, cut it into about a 1¼- by 2-inch rectangle and, when skewering, fold in half to make the chunk thicker.

Tools: *Grill, shallow dish, medium saucepan, colander, bowl*

Preparation time: *55 minutes*

Grilling time: *13 to 16 minutes*

Yield: *4 servings*

1 large onion	½ cup naturally brewed soy sauce
12 large snow pea pods	½ cup chicken broth
Salt and ground black pepper to taste	⅓ cup mirin (sweet cooking rice wine)
2 tablespoons vegetable oil	¼ cup sugar
8 boneless, skinless chicken thighs (1¾ to 2 pounds)	

1 In a shallow dish, soak eight 9-inch bamboo skewers in cold water for at least 30 minutes. Meanwhile, peel and cut the onion in half lengthwise. Place the cut halves down on a cutting board and cut the halves lengthwise and crosswise to form quarters. Rinse the pea pods and snap off the stem tip; pull off the string to discard it. Cut each pea pod crosswise in half.

2 In a medium saucepan, heat 1 inch of water to boiling over high heat. Add the onion quarters and cook for 2 minutes. Add the pea pods and remove from the heat. Drain the vegetables in a colander and run cold water over them to stop the cooking. (The onion will fall apart into thin layers.) Return the vegetables to the saucepan, sprinkle with salt and pepper to taste. Toss with 1 tablespoon oil and set aside.

3 Rinse the chicken and pat dry with paper towels. With a knife, on a cutting board, cut off and discard any visible fat and gristle. Cut the chicken into 1¼-inch chunks. In a bowl, toss the chicken with the remaining 1 tablespoon of oil and season with salt and pepper.

4 Drain the bamboo skewers and pat them dry. On each skewer, thread a chunk of chicken, a few onion layers, and a pea-pod half. Repeat two more times, ending with a chicken chunk.

5 Spray the grill grid with nonstick cooking spray or brush with oil to prevent food from sticking. Heat an indoor electric grill, grill pan, or cooktop insert over medium heat for 5 minutes. While the grill heats, in a small saucepan, heat the soy sauce, broth, mirin, and sugar to boiling. Remove from the heat and keep warm.

6 Grill the chicken skewers in a grill pan, on an open grill, or on a cooktop insert 9 minutes, turning the skewers over every 3 minutes. Brush the skewers with soy mixture on all sides and grill a few minutes longer or until the chunks are lightly charred and done. Make a small incision in the center of a chicken chunk to determine doneness. For a contact grill, grill the skewers 5 minutes, turn them and brush with soy mixture, then grill 1 or 2 minutes longer. Serve the skewers with the remaining soy mixture.

Vary It! *If mirin is not available, you can use sake, but add 1 tablespoon more sugar.*

Nutrition at a glance (per serving): *calories 467; calories from fat 214; fat 24 g; saturated fat 5 g; cholesterol 144 mg; sodium 2244 mg; carbohydrates 16 g; dietary fiber 1 g; protein 44 g*

Talking Turkey

Turkey isn't just for Thanksgiving! In this section, you can find two savory recipes: one for ground turkey grilled into turkey "steaks" and the other for turkey breasts paired with smooth brandy and oranges.

In addition to the following recipes, check out the Basil Wrap recipe, which calls for turkey cutlets, in Chapter 12.

Salisbury-Style Turkey Steaks with Mushroom Sauce

This poultry version of a hamburger steak is served with a mushroom sauce.

Tools: *Grill, large bowl*

Preparation time: *25 minutes*

Grilling time: *12 to 15 minutes*

Yield: *4 servings*

1 large egg	*¼ teaspoon ground black pepper*
¼ cup dried bread crumbs	*1 teaspoon Worcestershire sauce*
1 tablespoon chopped fresh or 1 teaspoon dried sage leaves	*1½ pounds ground turkey*
1 teaspoon salt	*¼ cup finely chopped scallions or onion*
	Mushroom Sauce (see the following recipe)

1 In a large bowl, with a fork, beat the egg with the bread crumbs, sage, salt, pepper, and Worcestershire sauce until well mixed. Crumble the ground turkey over the egg mixture and sprinkle with the scallions or onion. Lightly toss to mix the crumbs and scallions into the turkey. Divide into four mounds and shape each into four oval patties about ¾-inch thick.

2 Spray the grill grid with nonstick cooking spray or brush with oil to prevent food from sticking. Heat an indoor electric grill, grill pan, or cooktop insert over medium heat for 5 minutes. Grill the turkey steaks in a grill pan, on an open grill, or on a cooktop insert for 8 minutes, turning once or until no longer pink in the center. (To create decorative grill marks, grill the turkey steaks 2 minutes or until brown grill marks appear on the bottom; then rotate a quarter turn to the first grill marks, grilling another 2 minutes. Turn the steaks over and repeat.) If using a contact grill, grill the turkey covered for 4 minutes. Lift the cover and turn the turkey over and rotate a quarter turn to create crossed grill marks; then cover and grill 3 minutes longer or until done.

3 Make a small incision in the center of each steak to determine doneness, or use an instant-read thermometer inserted into the side of the steak. The steak is done when the temperature reaches 160° or when the center is no longer pink.

4 Transfer the steaks to a serving platter and keep them warm. Prepare the Mushroom Sauce and serve.

Nutrition at a glance (per serving): calories 239; calories from fat 110; fat 12 g; saturated fat 3 g; cholesterol 154 mg; sodium 790 mg; carbohydrates 6 g; dietary fiber 0 g; protein 25 g

Mushroom Sauce

Tools: *Saucepan*

Preparation time: *12 minutes*

Yield: *4 servings*

2 tablespoons butter	*13¾-ounce can chicken broth*
½ pound small button or white mushrooms, sliced	*Salt and ground black pepper to taste*
3 tablespoons flour	

In a large saucepan, heat the butter over high heat. Add the mushrooms and cook until tender, about 7 minutes. Continue to cook until most of the mushrooms' juices evaporate. Reduce the heat to medium. Stir the flour into the mushrooms until well mixed. Gradually stir in the chicken broth and cook the sauce until it bubbles and thickens. Season to taste with salt and pepper. Spoon the mushrooms from the sauce over the Salisbury-Style Steaks and pour the rest of the sauce into a small bowl or pitcher to pass.

Go-With: *Mashed potatoes and a tomato salad will complement this dish.*

Nutrition at a glance (per serving): calories 103; calories from fat 69; fat 8 g; saturated fat 4 g; cholesterol 18 mg; sodium 561 mg; carbohydrates 7 g; dietary fiber 1 g; protein 3 g

Brandied Turkey and Oranges

Turkey breasts may be cut into ¼- to ½-inch thick slices and marketed as cutlets, slices, or chops. A contact grill will steam rather than grill such thin slices of turkey, and an open grill or cooktop insert won't hold the brandy. Therefore, only a grill pan is recommended to prepare this recipe.

Tools: *Grill pan*

Preparation time: *15 minutes*

Grilling time: *14 to 15 minutes*

Yield: *4 servings*

2 medium navel or valencia oranges

½ cup chicken broth

1 tablespoon all-purpose flour

1 tablespoon sugar

4 large boneless skinless turkey breast slices or cutlets (about 1¼ pounds)

1 tablespoon olive oil

Salt and ground black pepper to taste

¼ cup brandy

1 On a cutting board, cut one of the oranges lengthwise in half. Place the cut sides down on the board and cut four ¼-inch thick slices from the middle of each half. Set the slices aside. Squeeze the end pieces of the orange to extract its juice in a large measuring cup. Cut the other orange in half crosswise and squeeze the juice into the same cup. Add the chicken broth, flour, and sugar; whisk until smooth. Set the sauce aside.

2 Rinse the turkey under cold running water and pat dry with paper towels. On a plate, coat the turkey with oil. Season with salt and pepper.

3 Spray the grill grid with nonstick cooking spray or brush with oil to prevent food from sticking. Heat a grill pan over medium-high heat for 5 minutes. Grill the orange slices until brown marks appear on the bottom, about 2½ minutes. Turn the slices and grill the other side until grill marks appear. Transfer the slices to a serving platter.

4 Grill the turkey until brown marks appear on the bottom, about 2 minutes. Rotate the turkey a quarter turn to the first grill marks, grilling until crossed marks appear. Turn the turkey over and repeat to grill the other side. Transfer the turkey to a serving platter with oranges. Remove the grill pan from heat. To the grill pan, add the brandy carefully. It will bubble vigorously. Then stir in the broth mixture and bring to boiling over medium heat. Boil and stir the sauce 1 minute and season with salt to taste. Pour the brandy orange sauce over the turkey and serve.

Nutrition at a glance (per serving): calories 256; calories from fat 44; fat 5 g; saturated fat 1 g; cholesterol 103 mg; sodium 335 mg; carbohydrates 13 g; dietary fiber 2 g; protein 38 g

Staying Ahead of the Game with Game Birds

Game birds have a unique taste that you can't get from other types of poultry and are lower in calories and fat than their cousins, chicken and turkey. Because game birds are now raised on farms, you don't have to be a hunter to get your hands on them. One of the two game birds featured in this section, Rock Cornish game hen, isn't a wild bird: It has been breed for years in captivity. Quail, the other game bird that's called for in this section, is a tiny bird that grills up tender and full of flavor. Check the frozen food section of your grocery store or the online suppliers listed at the beginning of this chapter for supplies of both birds.

In addition to Rock Cornish game hens and quail, experiment with other types of game birds, like the ones shown in Figure 9-2. Pheasant, partridge, poussin (poo-SAHN), and grouse, although difficult to find, are all a delicacy if they should fall into your lap (not literally, of course — if that happened, they'd just be a frantic mess of feathers and squawking). Full-flavored and tender when cooked slowly over medium heat, they all benefit from splitting in half and light marinating.

Figure 9-2:
They've got
game.

Honey-Thyme Cornish Game Hens

Splitting the hens in half makes them easier to grill. Nutritionists consider half a tiny game hen as a serving, but you'll likely be hungry unless you eat a whole hen. No matter how much you eat, your grill's surface cooking area determines how many hens can be grilled. While the hens are grilling, prepare the side dishes such as rice and a vegetable or salad.

Tools: *Grill, metal grater*

Preparation time: *15 minutes*

Grilling time: *20 to 40 minutes*

Yield: *4 servings*

1 large lemon	*¼ teaspoon ground black pepper*
2 tablespoons vegetable oil	*2 tablespoons honey*
1 tablespoon fresh thyme leaves	*2 Rock Cornish Game hens*
1 teaspoon salt	*(1¼ to 1½ pounds each)*

1 Using a metal grater, remove the zest from the lemon into a bowl. Add 1 tablespoon of the oil, the thyme, salt, and pepper. Cut the lemon in half and squeeze to extract the juice into a cup; stir in the honey.

2 Remove the neck and giblets from the cavity and trim the excess fat from the game hens. Rinse the game hens, neck, and giblets under cold running water and pat dry with paper towels. Using poultry shears or a knife, on a cutting board, cut the hens in half lengthwise (see Figure 9-3). Remove the back bone; wrap and freeze the back bone with the neck and giblets for soup stock. Fold the wing tips under the top of the shoulders. Rub the lemon zest seasoning paste under the skin of the hens on the breast and, if possible, the thigh. Rub the outside skin of the hens with the remaining 1 tablespoon of oil.

3 Heat an indoor electric grill, grill pan, or cooktop insert over medium heat for 5 minutes. Place the hens, skin sides down, in a grill pan, on an open grill, or on a cooktop insert. Cover with foil and grill the hens 15 minutes. Turn the hens over, cover with foil, and grill 10 minutes longer. Uncover the grill and turn the hens, skin sides down. Grill until the skin crisps up and an instant-read thermometer registers 180° or the juices in the thighs run clear when pierced with a fork. If using a contact grill, grill the hens 10 minutes; turn and rotate the hens a quarter turn to achieve crossed grill marks, and grill 5 minutes longer or until done.

4 Transfer the hens to a serving platter or individual serving plates. Drizzle each hen with some lemon honey and serve.

Nutrition at a glance (per serving): calories 563; calories from fat 355; fat 39 g; saturated fat 10 g; cholesterol 234 mg; sodium 698 mg; carbohydrates 10 g; dietary fiber 0 g; protein 40 g

Quail with Polenta and Peas

Quail may be farm-raised or exist as a wild game bird; the tiny birds grill quickly. It is served here Italian-style with polenta, a Parmesan-flavored cornmeal mush, which complements its delicate flavor.

Tools: *Grill, large resealable plastic bag or large nonreactive baking dish, saucepans*

Preparation time: *45 minutes*

Marinating time: *1 hour*

Grilling time: *13 to 15 minutes*

Yield: *4 servings*

Bird Bath (see Chapter 4)	*1 cup frozen green peas*
8 ready-to-cook quail (about 2 pounds)	*2 tablespoons water*
2 cups milk	*1 tablespoon butter*
1 cup yellow cornmeal	*⅓ cup grated Parmesan cheese*
2 cups chicken broth	*Salt and ground black pepper to taste*

1 Prepare the Bird Bath. Rinse all the quail under cold running water and pat dry with paper towels. With poultry shears or a knife, on a cutting board, cut the quail in half lengthwise along the backbone; open the quail and press the breastbone to flatten. Cut off the neck and the wings at the second joint and discard or freeze for soup stock. Place the quail in a large resealable plastic bag or large nonreactive baking dish. Add the Bird Bath to the bag or dish. Seal the bag or cover the dish and refrigerate for 1 hour.

2 While the quail marinates, prepare the polenta. In a large measuring cup or bowl, combine the milk and cornmeal. In a medium, nonstick saucepan, heat the chicken broth to boiling over high heat. Whisk in the cornmeal mixture. Reduce the heat to low, partially cover and cook, stirring occasionally, until thick, about 15 minutes. Meanwhile, in small saucepan, heat the peas, water, and butter until the peas are tender. Add the cheese to the cornmeal mixture and mix until well combined. Remove the polenta and peas from the heat and keep warm.

3 Drain the quail and discard the marinade. Pat dry with paper towels. Spray the grill grid with nonstick cooking spray or brush with oil to prevent food from sticking. Heat an indoor electric grill, grill pan, or cooktop insert over medium heat for 5 minutes. Place the quail, skin sides down, in a grill pan, on an open grill, or on a cooktop insert. Cook until grill marks appear, about 5 minutes. Turn the quail over, cover with a sheet of foil, and grill 5 minutes longer or until an instant-read thermometer registers 180° or the juices in the thighs run clear when pierced with a fork. If using a contact grill, grill the hens 3 minutes; turn and rotate the hens 45 degrees to achieve crossed grill marks, and grill 5 minutes longer or until done.

4 To serve, spoon a mound of polenta on each dinner plate. Make an indentation in the center and spoon on one fourth of the peas. Top with the grilled quail and serve.

Nutrition at a glance (per serving): calories 655; calories from fat 312; fat 35 g; saturated fat 12 g; cholesterol 154 mg; sodium 1125 mg; carbohydrates 40 g; dietary fiber 5 g; protein 44 g

How to Split a Rock Cornish Game Hen

Figure 9-3:
Splitting up isn't hard to do.

① Place the bird breast side up. Cut along the breast bone from cavity to neck end. Gently pry open.

② Turn the hen over and cut along one side of the backbone, cutting the hen in half.

③ Cut along the other side of the backbone to remove and discard.

discard

Getting Your Ducks in a Row

Duck is a delicacy, but one that you can find in some supermarkets and butcher shops. (See the beginning of this chapter for online suppliers.) Because of its rather high cost and equally high fat content, think of duck as a rare treat, but one that is succulent and worth the cost and calories every now and then.

Asian Greens and Duck

In fancy restaurants today, boneless duck breasts are as popular — and cooked just as rare — as steaks. If overcooked, like steaks, the duck breasts become tough and dry; they are best served pink. This recipe teams bok choy with duck and a soy glaze.

Tools: *Grill, large bowl*

Preparation time: *30 minutes*

Grilling time: *18 to 32 minutes*

Yield: *4 servings*

Orange Soy Glaze (see Chapter 5)

4 heads baby bok choy (12 ounces) or Shanghai pak choi (1 pound)

2 large (¾ pound each) or 4 small boneless duck breasts with skin

1 tablespoon dark (toasted) sesame oil

Salt and ground black pepper to taste

1 Prepare Orange Soy Glaze but keep it warm. Cut each head of the bok choy in half lengthwise. Rinse the bok choy in a large bowl or salad spinner filled with cold water to dislodge any sand or grit. (You may need to run water between the leaves and run your fingers over the inside bottom of the stems to get all the dirt out.) Drain the bowl of water, leaving some water on the leaves of the greens.

2 Rinse the duck breasts under cold running water and pat dry with paper towels. On a plate, season the duck on all sides with salt and pepper. With the tip of a paring knife, score the skin so that fat will drain off during grilling.

3 Heat an indoor electric grill, grill pan, or cooktop insert over medium heat for 5 minutes. Place the bok choy across or perpendicular to the grill's ridges. If using a grill pan, add ⅓ cup water and cover the pan with a sheet of foil. Grill for 5 minutes or until lightly browned on the bottom and tender when pierced with the thin blade of a sharp knife. Turn the greens over and grill uncovered until all the water evaporates and the greens brown on the bottom, about 10 minutes longer. If using an open grill or a cooktop insert, cook greens in a large, covered skillet with the ⅓ cup water. If using a contact grill, grill for 8 minutes, turning the boy choy over once. Transfer the bok choy to a serving dish; drizzle with sesame oil and season with salt and pepper; cover and keep warm.

4 If using large duck breasts, grill them skin sides down for 5 to 6 minutes; turn the duck, cover with foil, and grill 7 to 10 minutes longer or until medium. If using small breasts, grill for 3 to 4 minutes, turn, cover, and grill 5 to 6 minutes longer. Make a small incision in the center of the duck breast to determine doneness. The duck is done when the meat is moist and pale pink, about 160° on an instant-read thermometer. Brush with Orange Soy Glaze and grill 1 minute longer. Transfer to a carving board and let rest a few minutes. Discard fat. Cut the duck breast across into thin slices and arrange on four serving plates. Serve with bok choy and additional soy glaze.

__Note:__ Large duck breasts are individually packaged and sold in meat markets and come from the ducks that have been fattened for foie gras. For the small breasts, you may have to purchase 2 whole ducks and remove the breasts. Freeze the leg-thighs for another recipe.

__Nutrition at a glance (per serving):__ calories 317; calories from fat 157; fat 17 g; saturated fat 4 g; cholesterol 174 mg; sodium 446 mg; carbohydrates 6 g; dietary fiber 1 g; protein 33 g

If you're concerned about calories, you can discard the skin before slicing.

About bok choy

Bok choy, a loose-leaf variety Chinese cabbage, is the best known and most popular of the Asian greens. It is distinguished by its smooth white stalks and dark-green leaves. Shanghai pak choi is similar to bok choy except the stalks are pale green and the baby heads are a bit larger. Although sold primarily in Asian markets or large produce markets with Asian produce sections, you can easily grow bok choy in your home garden.

Chapter 10

Plenty of Fish in the Sea

In This Chapter

▶ Handling seafood safely

▶ Grilling finfish to perfection

▶ Selecting and grilling shrimp and scallops with ease

Seafood grills quickly and tastes succulent. Not a seafood fan? Try some of the recipes in this chapter before you give up for good. Many people cook seafood far too long, resulting in dry, tough meals that taste less than pleasing. Well-cooked fish, on the other hand, has just turned opaque and flakes with a fork. The result is a buttery, rich, delicious flavor.

Seafood is also incredibly healthy. Low in calories and fat (including saturated fat), most seafood contains omega-3 fatty acids, which protects your heart. Three-ounce servings range from under 100 calories for cod and orange roughy to just 150 calories for scallops and salmon. Table 10-1 shows the nutritional labeling information provided by the U.S. Food and Drug Administration (FDA). Most seafood is also high in protein; a 3-ounce serving provides nearly a third of the recommended daily allowance of protein.

Table 10-1	Grilled Seafood Nutrition Chart		
Variety of Seafood	*Calories*	*Total Fat*	*Saturated Fat*
Catfish (3 ounces)	120	5	1
Cod (3 ounces)	90	1	0
Halibut (3 ounces)	120	2	0
Orange roughy (3 ounces)	70	1	0
Salmon (3 ounces)	150	7	0

(continued)

Table 10-1 *(continued)*

Variety of Seafood	Calories	Total Fat	Saturated Fat
Scallop (14 small or 6 large)	150	1	0
Shrimp (3 ounces)	110	2	0
Trout (3 ounces)	130	4	1
Tuna (3 ounces)	120	1	0
Whitefish (3 ounces)	140	6	1

Although many types of seafood are expensive, most grocery stores have weekly sales on at least one variety. If you find a type you like, stock up during sales.

Buying, Storing, and Handling Seafood Safely

Buying, storing, and handling seafood is no trickier than handling pork, beef, or chicken. However, because seafood can contain surface bacteria (that's destroyed by grilling), you want to take precautions when buying, storing, and handling seafood.

When buying and storing seafood, take the following precautions:

✔ **Don't buy seafood that isn't refrigerated or on ice.**

✔ **Buy seafood only from sources you're sure of.** A "great bargain" from a roadside stand doesn't count!

✔ **Avoid buying frozen seafood if the package is damaged in any way.** Also stay away from frozen seafood that shows evidence of frost or ice crystals, which could indicate that the food has thawed, gathered up a bunch of bacteria, and been refrozen. Don't buy frozen seafood if you can't see the food itself inside the packaging.

✔ **Make seafood the last item on your shopping list and grocery shopping the last on your list of errands so that it doesn't spend time at room temperature.** If the seafood is frozen, ask the representative at your fish counter to wrap the package in freezer wrap.

✔ **Place fresh seafood in the meat keeper or at the back of the lowest shelf in your refrigerator, allowing air to circulate around the package.** Wrap frozen seafood in a resealable freezer bag and place immediately into the freezer when you arrive home.

✔ **Thaw frozen seafood in the refrigerator (which usually takes one day or, at least, overnight) or in the microwave.** Avoid thawing seafood on the counter at room temperature. Cook defrosted seafood immediately.

✔ **Use seafood within two days of purchase.**

✔ **Refrigerate seafood while you marinate it.** Discard used marinade and thoroughly wash the dish in which you marinated. (For more tips on marinating, check out Chapter 4.)

Keep the following tips in mind when handling seafood as you prepare to grill it:

✔ Wash your hands with hot, soapy water before and after touching raw seafood.

✔ Before grilling, rinse seafood under running water.

✔ In hot soapy water, wash any knives, cutting boards, and sponges that have come in contact with raw seafood.

✔ If you're using tongs or spatula to turn raw seafood, be sure to wash the tool with hot soapy water before using the same tool to remove cooked food from the grill. Consider using two tongs: one to handle raw foods and the other to handle cooked foods. Wash the raw-food tongs with soapy water after you're finished grilling.

✔ Separate raw and grilled seafood, making sure the juices from the raw seafood don't contaminate the grilled foods.

Preheating times vary among indoor grill manufacturers. Five minutes should be enough to adequately preheat your grill, but check the use and care book that came with your grill — your particular grill may take a bit longer to heat up.

Finfish without Fanfare

Grilling lends itself especially well to meaty fish; that is, any fish that has the word _steak_ associated with it, such as tuna, swordfish, salmon, and halibut. Grilling also works well for thick fillets. Whole fish, discussed in Chapter 14, is another grilled delicacy.

Selecting fillets and steaks

For indoor grilling, choose from three types of finfish cuts, shown in Figure 10-1:

✔ **Whole, thick fillets:** Choose the meatiest fillets you can find. Thin, wimpy fillets won't withstand the heat of your grill, but thicker fillets are a perfect partner for an indoor grill.

✔ **Smaller, round steaks:** These are generally from ¾ to 1 inch thick, have a round shape, and cook well on indoor grills.

✔ **Thicker, larger steaks:** Coming from larger fish, thick steaks can run from 1 inch to 1½ inches in thickness and may weigh a half pound each. Thick steaks are a hearty treat when cooked on your indoor grill.

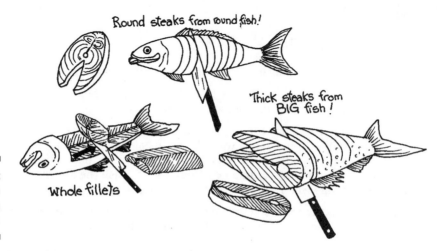

Figure 10-1:
These fish have seen better days.

Grilling up finfish

Timing is everything when grilling finfish, so watch the clock carefully when preparing the recipes in this section. Also, marinating finfish before grilling keeps your catch moist. To keep finfish from sticking to the grill grid, spray your grid or oil it with a brush before placing any food on it.

As a general rule, grill finfish for 10 to 13 minutes per inch of thickness. (Consider keeping a plastic ruler in your kitchen to measure the thickness of steaks and fillets.) Because indoor grills, grill pans, and stovetop inserts can vary so widely in their cooking temperatures, however, use this number only as a guide, adjusting the cooking time by testing for doneness.

You can test whether finfish is done in two ways, both illustrated in Figure 10-2:

- **The nudge of the fork:** Insert the tines of a fork into a fillet and gently twist the fork. If the fish flakes at the surface, your meal is ready!

- **The non-clinging knife:** Place the tip of a knife next to the bone of a steak or into a fillet. If the knife clings to the bone, you've got a few minutes of grilling left.

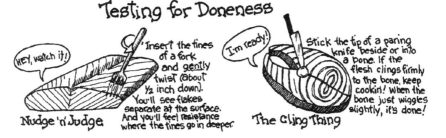

Figure 10-2:
What's done
is done.

Buying seafood online

Buying seafood online sounds a little nutty, doesn't it? Wouldn't the food arrive, days after your order, soggy and smelly? You'd think. But by combining overnight delivery and high-tech packaging, seafood delivered to your door may be even fresher than what you can get at your local supermarket.

The per-pound price of online seafood isn't bad, either. Shipping costs, however, can be prohibitive. Be sure to check shipping rates before ordering.

- **Captain Marden's Seafoods:** Salmon, swordfish, shrimp, scallops shipped fresh from Massachusetts. www.captainmardens.com

- **Charleston Seafood:** More than 30 varieties of fish, plus shrimp delivered fresh from Charleston, South Carolina. www.charlestonseafood.com

- **City Fish:** Scallops, salmon, halibut, and a wide array of other fresh fish fillets. Specializing in local fare from the famous Pike Place Market in Seattle, Washington. www.cityfish.com

- **Freshfish4U.com:** Specializing in freshwater fish from the Great Lakes, including whitefish, perch, walleye, and lake trout. www.freshfish4u.com

- **Lake Superior Fish Company:** Lake trout and whitefish from the waters off Isle Royale National Park in Lake Superior. They also sell wild freshwater trout, whitefish, herring, and walleye from the Great Lakes and Canada. www.lakesuperiorfish.com

For a listing of other seafood sources, check out new.seafood.com/retail/buydirect.html.

For some varieties of finfish, you can also check the color to determine whether it's done. To be safe, however, use an internal thermometer to check whether your seafood is done. The FDA suggests cooking to an internal temperature of 145°. Except for tuna, grilled fish should never appear to be raw.

Keep in mind that the overall weight of your finfish is insignificant when calculating cooking times. The only measure that matters is the thickness of the fillets or steaks.

In addition to the following recipes, check out the Grilled Fish Tacos recipe in Chapter 12.

Zesty Salmon Fillets

In the Pacific Northwest, where five species of wild salmon swim the waters, the supplies are dwindling. If you are fortunate to acquire a wild King (Chinook), Sockeye (red), or Coho (silver) salmon when they are in season (from late spring through fall), try it with this simple recipe. If not, the red-fleshed Atlantic species is farm-raised in many parts of the world and is readily available.

This recipe calls for a sugar- and salt-cured salmon that's typically Scandinavian, but in place of the more-traditional dill, grated citrus peel adds a zesty tropical note.

Tools: *Grill, nonreactive baking dish, large saucepan, peeler*

Preparation time: *30 minutes*

Marinating time: *30 minutes to 4 hours*

Grilling time: *15 to 18 minutes*

Yield: *4 servings*

2 tablespoons sugar	½ pound medium carrots, peeled
1 tablespoon coarse or kosher salt	½ pound sugar snap or snow pea pods
1 tablespoon finely grated lemon or lime peel	1 tablespoon olive oil or butter
¼ teaspoon ground black pepper	Salt and ground black pepper to taste
4 center-cut pieces red salmon fillet with skin, cut about 1¼ inches thick (7 to 8 ounces each)	

1 In a cup, combine the sugar, salt, grated lemon or lime peel, and pepper. Rinse the salmon under cold running water and pat dry with paper towels. Place the salmon, skin side down, in a shallow nonreactive baking dish in a single layer. Rub the sugar mixture on the top and sides of the salmon; cover the dish and marinate in the refrigerator for 30 minutes or up to 4 hours.

2 While the salmon marinates, prepare the vegetables. Cut each carrot in half crosswise. Cut the carrot halves lengthwise into ¼-inch thick sticks. Rinse the pea pods and snap off the stem tip; pull off the string to discard it.

3 In a large saucepan, heat 1 inch of water to boiling over high heat. Add the carrots and cook just until barely tender, about 3 minutes. Add the pea pods and remove the saucepan from the heat. Drain the vegetables and return them to the pan. Add the oil or butter and season with salt and pepper.

4 Spray the grill grid with nonstick cooking spray or brush with oil to prevent food from sticking. Heat an indoor electric grill, grill pan, or cooktop insert over medium heat for 5 minutes. (If your grill has an open grid, use a skillet to sauté the vegetables or they'll fall through.) Add the vegetables and grill 3 to 5 minutes, stirring occasionally, until lightly browned. Transfer the vegetables to a serving platter; cover and keep warm.

5 Drain the salmon and pat dry with paper towels. In a grill pan, on an open grill, or on a cooktop insert, grill the salmon skin side up for a total of 10 minutes, turning once. (If your salmon is thinner, grill 6 to 8 minutes.) If using a contact grill, grill the salmon 7 to 8 minutes, turning once and rotating the salmon a quarter turn. To check for doneness, make a small incision in the center of the fillet with the tip of a thin-bladed knife. The flesh should be pale pink throughout when done. Arrange the salmon over the vegetables and serve.

Go-With: *This dish is excellent with boiled, small, red potato halves.*

Nutrition at a glance (per serving): *calories 383; calories from fat 111; fat 12 g; saturated fat 2 g; cholesterol 133 mg; sodium 561 mg; carbohydrates 12 g; dietary fiber 3 g; protein 53 g*

Mustard-Dill Salmon Steaks

Salmon's attractive color and moist texture make it a popular fish to grill. High in good-for-you omega-3 fatty acids, salmon needs little if any additional fat when cooking. Because salmon steaks are an even thickness all around, they are easy to cook. Mustard and dill are a wonderful tasty topping for this fish.

Tools: *Grill, baking dish, bowl*

Preparation time: *15 minutes*

Marinating time: *15 minutes*

Grilling time: *13 to 15 minutes*

Yield: *4 servings*

4 red salmon steaks, cut about 1 inch thick (about 8 ounces each)

2 tablespoons fresh lemon or lime juice

2 tablespoons spicy brown mustard

2 tablespoons water

2 tablespoons chopped fresh dill

1 tablespoon brown sugar

1 tablespoon vegetable oil

1 Rinse the salmon steaks under cold running water; pat dry with paper towels. Place the steaks in a shallow, nonreactive baking dish in a single layer. Drizzle lemon juice over the steaks in the dish, turning to coat well. Cover and refrigerate for about 15 minutes, turning once.

2 Prepare the mustard dill topping: In a cup or small bowl, combine the mustard, water, dill, and brown sugar until well mixed.

3 Heat an indoor electric grill, grill pan, or cooktop insert over medium heat for 5 minutes. Pat the salmon dry with paper towels. Return the salmon to the dish and drizzle the oil over the salmon and rub the oil on all the sides. Grill the salmon in a grill pan, on an open grill, or on a cooktop insert for about 10 minutes, turning once with a wide spatula. If using a contact grill, grill for 5 minutes; lift the cover, and rotate the salmon a quarter turn; cover and grill 3 minutes longer.

4 To check for doneness, make a small incision in the center of the steak with the tip of a thin-bladed knife. The flesh should be an opaque, pale pink when done. Spoon some of the mustard dill sauce over each steak and serve.

Go-With: *Serve with Zebra Potatoes or Corn Stuffed Tomatoes (see Chapter 11) and a green vegetable, such as steamed green beans or broccoli.*

Nutrition at a glance (per serving): *calories 298; calories from fat 101; fat 11 g; saturated fat 2 g; cholesterol 111 mg; sodium 242 mg; carbohydrates 4 g; dietary fiber 0 g; protein 43 g*

Gingered Halibut with Lime Barbecue Sauce

Halibut is a large flatfish found swimming deep along the bottom of the northern Atlantic and Pacific oceans. Its lean, firm, white flesh is usually marketed as steaks or fillets. When buying halibut, we prefer the solid tail steaks identified by the flesh all around the backbone. Often the steaks are then cut crosswise through the bone.

Tools: *Grill, metal grater, small saucepan (or microwave-safe bowl)*

Preparation time: *15 minutes*

Grilling time: *13 to 15 minutes*

Yield: *4 servings*

2-inch piece fresh ginger, peeled	1 tablespoon olive oil
1 large or 2 small limes	1 teaspoon coarse or kosher salt
¾ cup bottled or homemade barbecue sauce (see Chapter 5)	4 halibut steaks, cut 1 inch thick (7 to 8 ounces each)

1 Using a metal grater, finely grate the ginger onto a large plate, nonreactive baking dish, or cutting board; move the ginger to one side of the plate. Grate the zest or peel of the lime(s)to the other side of the plate. Cut the lime(s) in half and squeeze the juice into a small saucepan or microwave-safe bowl (see Figure 10-3); add the barbecue sauce and stir in half of the ginger. Heat the barbecue sauce just until warm; set aside.

2 On the plate, combine the remaining ginger, lime zest, oil, and salt. Rinse the halibut under cold running water and pat dry with paper towels. On the plate, rub the ginger-lime mixture on both sides of the halibut; set aside while the grill heats.

3 Spray the grill grid with nonstick cooking spray or brush with oil to prevent food from sticking. Heat an indoor electric grill, grill pan, or cooktop insert over medium heat for 5 minutes. Grill the halibut steaks in a grill pan, on an open grill, or on a cooktop insert for 10 minutes, turning once with a wide spatula. If using a contact grill, grill the halibut 4 minutes or until grill marks appear on top of the steak, lift the cover, and rotate the halibut a quarter turn, grilling 4 minutes longer or until done. To test for doneness, make a small incision in the center of the steak with the tip of a thin-bladed knife. The flesh should be opaque, not translucent, when done.

4 Transfer the halibut to serving plates; serve with warm barbecue lime sauce.

Go-With: *A simple baked potato and coleslaw completes this meal.*

Nutrition at a glance (per serving): *calories 263; calories from fat 70; fat 8 g; saturated fat 1 g; cholesterol 62 mg; sodium 769 mg; carbohydrates 7 g; dietary fiber 1 g; protein 42 g*

How to Juice a Lime

Cut a lime in half, across the middle.

Hold a half in one hand at an angle. Use a fork to apply pressure and squeeze out the juice!

Figure 10-3: Pressuring your lime.

Grilled Chive Catfish

Too often, catfish is breaded and deep fried — and is thus laden with calories. A garlicky flavored oil tinted green by herbs serves as a sauce for this grilled farm-raised fish.

Tools: *Grill, small saucepan, paring knife, slotted spoon, mixing bowl, food processor, nonreactive bowl or dish*

Preparation time: *15 minutes*

Grilling time: *12 to 15 minutes*

Yield: *4 servings*

1 small ripe red tomato	2 cloves garlic, peeled
¼ cup thinly sliced fresh chives or scallions	1 teaspoon coarse or kosher salt
2 tablespoons flat-leaf parsley	2 tablespoons fresh lemon juice
¼ cup extra virgin olive oil	4 small catfish fillets (8 ounces each)

1 In a small saucepan, heat 2 inches of water to boiling over high heat. With a paring knife, cut out the stem of the tomato and cut a shallow "X" through the bottom skin. Drop the tomato into boiling water for about 10 seconds and remove with a slotted spoon; rinse under cold water. Starting at the "X," peel off the skin and cut the tomato in half across the middle. Squeeze to remove the seeds and discard. Cut the tomato pulp into ¼-inch dice and set aside in a bowl.

2 In a food processor, combine the chives, parsley, oil, garlic, and salt. Process until the herbs are finely chopped, stopping the motor once to scrape down the side of the container and to force the ingredients down to the bottom. Add the lemon juice and blend a few seconds more.

3 Rinse the catfish under cold running water and pat dry with paper towels. Place the catfish in a nonreactive bowl or dish, and toss with 2 tablespoons of the flavored oil. Set aside while the grill heats.

4 Spray the grill grid with nonstick cooking spray or brush with oil to prevent food from sticking. Heat an indoor electric grill, grill pan, or cooktop insert over medium-high heat for 5 minutes. Fold each fillet crosswise in half. Grill the catfish 8 to 10 minutes in a grill pan, on an open grill, or on a cooktop insert (or 5 to 7 minutes in a contact grill), turning the fish once. The fish is done when it's firm and opaque in the center and flakes easily with a fork.

5 Transfer the catfish to individual serving plates; spoon the remaining flavored oil around the fish and scatter diced tomato over the oil. Serve immediately.

Nutrition at a glance (per serving): *calories 378; calories from fat 266; fat 30 g; saturated fat 5 g; cholesterol 89 mg; sodium 354 mg; carbohydrates 3 g; dietary fiber 0 g; protein 31 g*

Tuna Teriyaki

A sweet syrupy soy is brushed onto the grilled fish just to coat and glaze it (the translation of *teriyaki* is "glaze grilling"). Because of the sugar content, do not brush the sauce on the fish until it is mostly done, and be sure to use a natural (not chemically made) soy sauce.

Tools: *Grill, small saucepan*

Preparation time: *30 minutes*

Marinating time: *15 minutes*

Grilling time: *12 to 15 minutes*

Yield: *4 servings*

⅔ cup naturally brewed soy sauce

⅓ cup sake or dry sherry

¼ cup sugar

4 fresh albacore tuna steaks, cut about
¾ inch thick (7 to 8 ounces each)

3 tablespoons rice vinegar

8 small scallions, roots trimmed off

2 tablespoons vegetable oil

Salt and ground black pepper to taste

1 Prepare the Teriyaki Sauce: In a small saucepan, combine the soy, sake, and sugar; boil until reduced by a third of its volume — 10 to 15 minutes. Watch carefully toward the end of the cooking time, because the sauce may boil over. Cool the Teriyaki Sauce to room temperature (about 15 minutes).

2 While the sauce cools, rinse the tuna under cold running water and pat dry with paper towels. Place the tuna on a plate or nonreactive dish and sprinkle with vinegar. Cover and refrigerate the tuna for 15 minutes to marinate. While the tuna marinates, trim off enough green tops from the scallions so that each scallion is 6 inches long. On a plate, rub 1 tablespoon oil into the scallions.

3 Pat the tuna dry with paper towels. Drizzle the tuna with the remaining 1 tablespoon oil and rub into all sides then season lightly with salt and pepper.

4 Spray the grill grid with nonstick cooking spray or brush with oil to prevent food from sticking. Heat an indoor electric grill, grill pan, or cooktop insert over medium heat for 5 minutes. Grill the scallions in a grill pan, on an open grill, or on a cooktop insert until lightly browned on all sides, about 3 to 5 minutes. Transfer the scallions to a serving plate; cover and keep warm.

5 Grill the tuna in a grill pan or on an open grill until brown grill marks appear on the bottom, 3 to 4 minutes. Turn the tuna over and cook the second side until the fish is just barely opaque inside, 2 to 3 minutes longer. Brush with some Teriyaki Sauce and turn the tuna over again, rotating a quarter turn and brushing with more sauce. If using a contact grill, grill the tuna 3 minutes; lift the cover and brush with Teriyaki Sauce; turn the tuna over and brush with more sauce. Cover and grill tuna 3 minutes longer. Grill just until tuna is medium or has an opaque center, about 1 minute longer.

6 Serve the tuna and scallions. If desired, whip up another batch of Teriyaki Sauce and serve on top.

Nutrition at a glance (per serving): calories 347; calories from fat 78; fat 9 g; saturated fat 1 g; cholesterol 86 mg; sodium 2683 mg; carbohydrates 13 g; dietary fiber 0 g; protein 50 g

Cod Provencal with Basil Oil

Boneless and skinless cod (the small variety is called *scrod* and is a more delicately textured fish) is a delight to grill and goes well with a wide range of sauces. This delicate, white-fleshed fish may fall apart during grilling if the fillet is too thin. Thick fillets are preferable; cooking times will vary with the thickness of the fish. In this recipe, grilled cod is served over a mound of tomato-flecked white beans drizzled with a flavorful oil.

Tools: *Grill, small saucepan, electric blender or food processor, small mixing bowl, nonreactive bowl or dish*

Preparation time: *22 minutes*

Grilling time: *12 to 15 minutes*

Yield: *4 servings*

1 cup fresh basil	1 cup canned diced tomatoes, undrained
½ cup plus 2 tablespoons olive oil	1 teaspoon herbes de provence or dried thyme
1 small onion, sliced	
2 cloves garlic, chopped	Salt and ground white pepper to taste
15½-ounce can cannellini or other white beans, drained and rinsed	1 pound cod or scrod fillets, cut into 4 serving-size portions

1 In a small saucepan, heat 1 inch water to boiling over high heat. Add the basil leaves and blanch for 20 seconds. Drain the wilted basil and rinse with cold water to stop its cooking. Squeeze the leaves until dry and place in an electric blender or food processor. Add ½ cup oil and blend on medium speed until the basil leaves are no longer visible and the oil is tinted green, about 4 or 5 minutes. Pour the basil oil into a small bowl and set aside.

2 In the same small saucepan, heat 1 tablespoon oil over medium heat. Add the onion and cook until soft, about 3 minutes. Add the garlic, beans, tomatoes, and *herbes de provence.* Simmer the beans over low heat for 5 minutes to blend the flavors.

3 While the beans simmer, rinse the cod under cold running water and pat dry with paper towels. Place the cod in a nonreactive bowl or dish, and toss with the remaining 1 tablespoon of olive oil. Set aside while the grill heats.

4 Spray the grill grid with nonstick cooking spray or brush with oil to prevent food from sticking. Heat an indoor electric grill, grill pan, or cooktop insert over medium-high heat for 5 minutes. Grill the cod 8 to 10 minutes in a grill pan, on an open grill, or on a cooktop insert for 5 to 7 minutes in a contact grill, turning the fish once. Fish is done when it is firm and opaque in the center and flakes easily.

5 To serve, spoon a mound of beans in the center of individual serving plates; top the beans with cod and drizzle with 1 or 2 tablespoons of basil oil.

Go-With: *Serve with crusty French bread and a crisp green salad.*

Nutrition at a glance (per serving): calories 431; calories from fat 311; fat 35 g; saturated fat 5 g; cholesterol 30 mg; sodium 356 mg; carbohydrates 15 g; dietary fiber 5 g; protein 16 g

Don't Skimp on Shrimp

Shrimp, served as an appetizer or main course, is a hit with almost everyone, even people who don't normally like seafood. Pair shrimp with sauces, as we've done in this chapter, and you'll convert the stingiest seafood eater into a fan.

Shrimp is low in fat and calories — an entire *pound* of shrimp contains less than 600 calories and just over 5 grams of fat.

Shopping for shrimp

When shopping for shrimp, keep these tips in mind:

✓ **When buying frozen shrimp, look for a label that says it's *IQF —
individually quick frozen*.** This labeling means that the shrimp was frozen immediately after it was caught. Be sure the shrimp isn't clumped together, which could indicate that the shrimp defrosted and refroze during its journey. If you can't see the shrimp inside because of the packaging, don't buy it.

✓ **For fresh shrimp, look for firm, unmushy shrimp without any black spots or yellowing.** If you get a chance to take a whiff of the shrimp, do so: Raw shrimp shouldn't smell fishy; it should smell salty (like the ocean).

Although shrimp is sold by the pound, it's available in various sizes based on the number of shrimp or *count* per pound, as follows:

✓ **Jumbo or extra large shrimp:** 20 or fewer shrimp per pound

✓ **Large shrimp:** 21 to 30 per pound

✓ **Medium shrimp:** 31 to 40 per pound

✓ **Small shrimp:** over 40 shrimp per pound

Although these guidelines hold true for most supermarkets, you may find more or fewer shrimp per pound than what we've listed, so be sure to look for the sign at the fish counter telling you what the approximate count is. In the recipes in this chapter, we've called for specific sizes; however, you can use a different size in the recipe by adjusting the grilling time (larger shrimp need a bit more time to cook).

For appetizers (discussed in detail in Chapter 13), allow five medium or three large shrimp for a serving. Generally, 1 pound of unshelled, raw shrimp yields about 8 ounces of cooked, shelled shrimp.

Grilling perfect shrimp

Shrimp is a breeze to cook on your indoor grill, taking just 2 to 3 minutes of grilling time. Shrimp is done when they are pink and opaque. Don't overcook, however: They'll become dry and rubbery.

In addition to the following recipes, try the Firecracker Shrimp Salad with Blue Cheese Dressing recipe in Chapter 12 or the Grilled Shrimp Cocktail recipe in Chapter 13.

Margarita Marinated Shrimp

Elements of the classic drink are incorporated in this Southwestern inspired dish. Served with a creamy chile tartar sauce, this shrimp dish can be a main dish or an appetizer. *Note:* To further reduce calories and fat, use nonfat mayo instead of low-fat.

Tools: *Grill, large mixing bowl, food processor, small serving bowl*

Preparation time: *30 minutes*

Marinating time: *15 minutes*

Grilling time: *12 to 15 minutes*

Yield: *4 main-dish or 8 appetizer servings*

1½ pounds extra-large or jumbo shrimp (allow 5 or 6 shrimp per main-dish serving or 3 per appetizer), shelled and deveined

3 tablespoons tequila

3 tablespoons fresh lime juice

½ cup reduced-fat mayonnaise

½ cup chunky bottled tomato salsa

2 tablespoons olive or vegetable oil

2 tablespoons fresh orange juice

1 tablespoon chopped cilantro or parsley leaves

1 teaspoon coarse or kosher salt

1 In a large bowl, rinse the shrimp in cold water, draining and changing the water several times. Pat the shrimp dry with paper towels. In a bowl, combine the shrimp with the tequila and lime juice. Cover the bowl and refrigerate the shrimp for 15 minutes to marinate.

2 While the shrimp marinates, prepare a chile tartar sauce: In a food processor, process the mayonnaise and salsa until the sauce is smooth. Pour into a small serving bowl.

3 Spray the grill grid with nonstick cooking spray or brush with oil to prevent food from sticking. Heat an indoor electric grill, grill pan, or cooktop insert over medium-high heat for 5 minutes. Drain the shrimp and pat dry. In a bowl, toss the shrimp with oil. Grill the shrimp in a single layer in a grill pan, on an open grill, or on a cooktop insert until they turn pink, about 3 minutes, turning once. If using a contact grill, grill the shrimp 2 minutes or until the shrimp are pink and opaque. Don't overcook, or they will become dry and rubbery.

4 Transfer the shrimp to a serving dish; drizzle with the orange juice and sprinkle with cilantro and salt. Serve the grilled shrimp with the sauce.

Nutrition at a glance (per serving): *calories 282; calories from fat 161; fat 18 g; saturated fat 3 g; cholesterol 212 mg; sodium 983 mg; carbohydrates 6 g; dietary fiber 1 g; protein 23 g*

TIP

Deveining shrimp

Before grilling shrimp, you'll probably have to shell and *devein* it (that is, remove the shell of the shrimp and the vein that runs the length of the shrimp's back). As the following figure demonstrates, to shell and devein shrimp, first purchase an inexpensive tool called a *deveiner*. For each piece of shrimp, insert the deveiner along the shrimp's backside (away from the legs) and push it toward the tail. The tool removes the shell and the vein in one motion. Run cold water over the now-naked shrimp to remove all traces of the shell and vein.

Of course, you can also purchase shelled and deveined shrimp, but it tends to cost more and isn't always available.

Cleaning and Deveining Shrimp

1. Insert deveiner

2. Push toward the tail vein The tool removes the vein and shell in one motion

3. Clean under cold water

Sweet-and-Sour Grilled Shrimp

Shrimp is one of America's favorite shellfish and with a sweet-and-sour pineapple sauce added, this is bound to be one of your favorite grilled dishes.

Tools: *Grill, large mixing bowl, small saucepan*

Preparation time: *20 minutes*

Marinating time: *15 minutes*

Grilling time: *13 to 17 minutes*

Yield: *4 servings*

1 pound or about 24 large shrimp, shelled

3 tablespoons rice vinegar or cider vinegar

1 teaspoon paprika

Salt

8-ounce can pineapple chunks in juice

1 tablespoon cornstarch

2 tablespoons brown sugar or to taste

1 small onion, halved and then each half quartered

1 green bell pepper, seeded and cut into 1-inch pieces

2 tablespoons vegetable oil

1 In a large bowl, rinse the shrimp in cold water, draining and changing the water several times. Pat the shrimp dry with paper towels. To butterfly the shrimp, with a knife, cut each shrimp lengthwise from top to bottom down the center of the back, without cutting all the way through, and devein the shrimp (see the "Deveining shrimp" sidebar). In a bowl, combine the shrimp, 1 tablespoon of the vinegar, the paprika, and ½ teaspoon salt. Cover the bowl and refrigerate the shrimp for 15 minutes to marinate.

2 While the shrimp marinates, drain the juice from the pineapple into a measuring cup and add enough water to measure ⅔ cup. Set the pineapple aside. In a small saucepan, combine the pineapple juice with the cornstarch, sugar, and the remaining 2 tablespoons vinegar, stirring to dissolve the cornstarch. Bring the sauce to a boil over medium heat, stirring constantly. Add the drained pineapple and season with salt; add more sugar if it's too tart for your taste. Set the sauce aside and keep it warm.

3 Heat an indoor electric grill, grill pan, or cooktop insert over medium heat for 5 minutes. In a bowl, toss the onion and bell pepper with the oil. Grill the vegetables until tender-crisp and lightly charred in spots, 6 to 8 minutes. (If your grill has an open grid, use a skillet to sauté the vegetables or they'll fall through.) Transfer the vegetables from the grill to a bowl.

4 Drain the shrimp and pat dry. Grill the shrimp, opened flat, in a single layer in a grill pan, on an open grill, or on a cooktop insert until they turn pink, about 2 minutes, turning once. If using a contact grill, grill the shrimp 1 to 2 minutes or until the shrimp are pink and opaque. Don't overcook, or they will become dry and rubbery. Transfer the shrimp to the bowl with the vegetables.

5 Pour the pineapple sauce over the shrimp and vegetables; toss until well mixed, and serve.

Nutrition at a glance (per serving): calories 207; calories from fat 69; fat 8 g; saturated fat 1 g; cholesterol 135 mg; sodium 199 mg; carbohydrates 19 g; dietary fiber 1 g; protein 15 g

Successful Scallops

Scallops range from large, meaty sea scallops, which are rich and firm, to bite-sized bay scallops. In this section, we focus on sea scallops, which tend to grill better than their smaller cousins.

Choosing scallops

Bay scallops, the tiny, bite-sized variety, delight your tastebuds in stir-fries and sauces. For grilling, however, they're not especially practical. Instead, choose sea scallops, which can range from 1 to 2 inches in diameter. Sea scallops generally cost more per pound than bay, but they're a treat for special occasions. Look for shiny, opaque, or creamy white scallops at your local fish counter. Ask the person behind the counter to remove the muscle on the side of the scallop (it looks like a tab sticking out) for you. It'll save you a bit of time, but you can do it yourself if you need to.

Grilling succulent scallops

When ready to eat, grilled scallops are firm and turn a milky white color. They cook quickly, in just 3 to 5 minutes, so watch them closely. Overcooked scallops taste rubbery.

Saffron Sea Scallops

These moist and succulent scallops, bathed in delicious saffron butter topped with red onion slivers and plated with a vegetable sauce, make a spectacular meal. Because very high heat is needed to quickly sear the scallops to a golden brown crispness, this recipe is best cooked in a stovetop grill pan instead of on an indoor electric grill.

Saffron is the world's most expensive spice, but you only need a little to add wonderful pungent flavor and burnished orange color to your food. Crumble it before using it to release flavor in the oils.

Tools: *Grill, medium mixing bowl, saucepan*

Preparation time: *40 minutes*

Grilling time: *10 minutes*

Yield: *4 servings*

Veggie Coulis (see Chapter 5)	*2 tablespoons butter*
1½ pounds large sea scallops (16 to 20)	*2 tablespoons fresh lemon juice*
1 tablespoon olive oil	*⅛ teaspoon saffron threads, crumbled*
Salt and ground black pepper to taste	*Chervil or parsley sprigs*
1 small red onion	

1 Prepare carrot or pea version of Veggie Coulis and keep warm.

2 Rinse the scallops under cold water and pat them dry with paper towels. On the side of each scallop, remove and discard its tough white muscle. The edible part of the scallop is the adductor muscle that opens and closes the shell; it can vary in size so, if necessary for even grilling, cut the scallop across into about ¾- to 1-inch thickness. In a bowl, toss the scallops with oil, salt, and pepper.

3 On a cutting board, cut the onion lengthwise in half, and then cut it into thin wedges. In a saucepan, melt the butter over medium heat. Add the onion wedges and cook until just tender, about 3 minutes. Use a slotted spoon to transfer the onion to a bowl, leaving the butter in the pan. Add the lemon juice and saffron to the butter; heat just until the butter turns a golden hue from the saffron. Set the lemony saffron butter aside.

4 Spray the grill grid with nonstick cooking spray or brush with oil to prevent the food from sticking. Heat a grill pan over high heat for 5 minutes. Place the scallops in a single layer on the grill. Grill for 2 minutes; using tongs, turn and grill the other side until crisp and golden brown, 2 to 3 minutes longer. Reduce the heat to medium and grill the scallops until they spring back when pressed lightly and appear opaque in the center and golden brown on the outer cut surfaces. Don't overcook or they will be tough and chewy. Transfer the scallops and onion wedges to individual serving plates. Top scallops with lemony saffron butter.

5 Spoon or squirt the Veggie Coulis on the plate around the scallops; garnish with herb sprigs and serve.

__Nutrition at a glance (per serving):__ calories 318; calories from fat 181; fat 20 g; saturated fat 8 g; cholesterol 60 mg; sodium 932 mg; carbohydrates 18 g; dietary fiber 4 g; protein 17 g

Chapter 11

Vegging Out

- -

In This Chapter

▶ Finding out which vegetables grill well

▶ Grilling up succulent veggies with a variety of recipes

- -

The U.S. Department of Agriculture (USDA) recommends eating three to five half-cup servings of vegetables every day (see Figure 11-1), because they're loaded with vitamins, minerals, and fiber (see the "Choosing Vegetables That Are Great for the Grill — and for You!" section for details). But finding inviting ways to cook veggies can be a challenge. Your indoor grill, however, is an ideal partner for a host of veggies, whether you're a diehard vegetarian or just trying to increase your intake of healthy vegetables. Grilled vegetables are tender, juicy, and loaded with natural flavor, and the recipes in this chapter pair veggies with spices, herbs, and other flavorings that make them even more savory.

Chapter 12 gives you recipes for salads that include grilled foods. Chapter 15 shares recipes for grilled fruits.

Balsamic vinegar

Balsamic vinegar is made from white Trebbiano grape juice from Modena, Italy. Aged in wooden barrels for ten years or longer, this intense, tangy, sweet brown vinegar is great in marinades and salad dressing. A clear balsamic vinegar is also available.

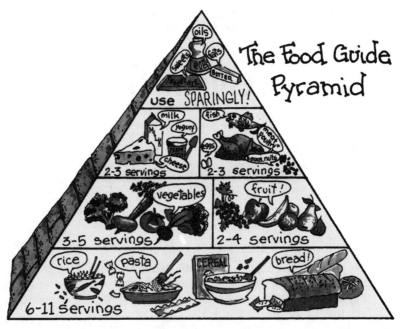

Figure 11-1: The USDA Food Guide Pyramid recommends eating more vegetables than any other food besides grains.

Choosing Vegetables That Are Great for the Grill — and for You!

You can find success on the grill with a variety of vegetables, many of which are shown in Figure 11-2. In addition to tasting delicious when grilled, vegetables are just about the healthiest thing you can eat! The *Journal of the National Cancer Institute*, for example, recently reported that in a study of over 45,000 men, those who consumed broccoli or cabbage once a week showed a lower risk of bladder cancer — protection that lasted ten years! — than men who ate those vegetables less than once a week. Similarly, many other vegetables, including tomatoes and carrots, have been shown to cut cancer risk and/or improve the immune system:

- ✔ **Asparagus:** Rich in beta-carotene, the B-vitamins, vitamin C, and potassium. Helps prevent cancer and heart disease. Check out the Grilled Asparagus Gremolata recipe in this chapter.

- ✔ **Broccoli:** Full of beta-carotene, vitamin C, folic acid, calcium, magnesium, and iron. Protects against diseases of the digestive tract.

- ✔ **Carrots:** A source of beta-carotene and fiber. Good for the skin, immune system, vision, heart, and digestive tract.

- **Cauliflower:** Full of niacin (a B-vitamin), folic acid, vitamin C, and potassium. Enhances the immune system and protects against cancer. See the Cauliflower Parmesan recipe in this chapter for a cheesy, mouth-watering version of cauliflower.

- **Corn:** Filled with beta-carotene, the B vitamins, magnesium, potassium, zinc, protein, and fiber. Can protect against osteoporosis. Flip to the Corn Stuffed Tomatoes recipe for a delicious way to add corn to your diet.

- **Eggplant:** Although not a significant source of vitamins or minerals, cooked eggplant contains just 43 calories per half pound. Turn to the Eggplant Antipasto recipe in this chapter and the Meditortilla Wrap recipe in Chapter 12 for eggplant grilling tips.

- **Mushrooms:** Low in calories and a good source of riboflavin and niacin. Try the Grilled Marinated Mushrooms recipe in this chapter.

- **Potatoes:** Source of potassium, fiber, and iron. May lower blood cholesterol. Try the whimsical Zebra Potatoes recipe in this chapter.

- **Summer squash:** A source of beta-carotene, potassium, magnesium, folic acid, calcium, iron, and fiber. May improve the health of your heart. See the Sesame Squash Medley recipe in this chapter, the Meditortilla Wrap recipe in Chapter 12, and the Herbed Garlic Bread Tomato Salad recipe in Chapter 12 for ideas on how to use summer squash on the grill.

- **Sweet peppers:** Rich in beta-carotene, niacin (a B vitamin), vitamin C, and vitamin E. Boosts the immune system and vision. Get the lowdown on cooking peppers in the Grilled Sweet Peppers recipe in this chapter and the Meditortilla Wrap recipe in Chapter 12.

- **Sweet potatoes:** High in beta-carotene and vitamin C.

- **Tomatoes:** A source of beta-carotene, vitamin C, potassium, and fiber. Lowers blood pressure and protects the colon. Try the Corn Stuffed Tomatoes recipe in this chapter.

For more information on the healthful properties of vegetables, check out *Healing Foods For Dummies* by registered dietitian Molly Siple (published by Hungry Minds, Inc.).

Most vegetables don't require peeling, so before grilling, rinse vegetables with water to remove dirt. Potatoes and carrots may need scrubbing with a vegetable brush. To remove surface bacteria, wax, and residue from pesticides, wash veggies with a vegetable wash or nontoxic soap. To further reduce your exposure to pesticide residues, consider buying organic produce, which is available at health-food stores, cooperatives, and, increasingly, at mainstream grocery stores. Do rinse organic vegetables with running water, however, to remove dirt.

Never, never wash produce with antibacterial soap, which contains harmful residues that may not rinse away.

Figure 11-2:
Five a day
on your
indoor grill.

Grilling Veggies in No Time Flat

Grilling time for vegetables is quick — usually around 15 minutes — so you need to keep a close eye on veggies on the grill to keep them from burning. Before heating the grill, brush the grid with oil or spray with a nonstick cooking spray. This will keep small pieces of vegetables from charring, which doesn't taste good. You can pierce cooked vegetables easily with a fork.

For vegetables that aren't included in the recipes in this chapter, cut the veggies into large chunks and marinate in a simple mixture (see Chapter 4) for 15 minutes to an hour. If you don't have time to make a marinade and wait for your vegetables to soak in it, brush veggies with a bottle marinade or salad dressing as they grill. Watch the vegetables closely and check often for doneness.

Preheating times vary among indoor grill manufacturers. Five minutes should be enough to adequately preheat your grill, but check the use and care book that came with your grill — your particular grill may take a bit longer to heat up.

Cauliflower Parmesan

This is a lower-calorie version of cauliflower with cheese sauce, a popular classic dish. Broth is used in place of milk, and Parmesan cheese is used in place of cheddar or Swiss. This dish is a wonderful accompaniment to poultry, fish, or pork.

Tools: *Grill, medium saucepan, bowl, slotted spoon*

Preparation time: *20 minutes*

Grilling time: *10 to 12 minutes*

Yield: *4 servings*

14½-ounce can store-bought or 1⅔ cups homemade chicken broth

1 pound cauliflower (about ½ head)

1 tablespoon olive oil

1 tablespoon butter, softened

1 tablespoon all-purpose flour

2 tablespoons snipped or sliced fresh chives or finely chopped small scallions

2 tablespoons grated Parmesan cheese

1 In a medium saucepan, heat the broth to boiling over high heat. Meanwhile, trim all the leaves and the center thick core off the head of cauliflower. Rinse and drain the cauliflower. Separate the cauliflower into florets, and cut the florets through the stem as much as possible into ½-inch thick slices. (The flatter the cut surfaces, the easier the florets will be to grill.)

2 Add cauliflower slices to the boiling broth. Cover and return the broth to boiling. Cook the cauliflower 3 minutes or just until tender but still firm. Do not overcook or the florets will fall apart.

3 With a slotted spoon, remove the cooked cauliflower to a serving dish or bowl. Drizzle oil over the cauliflower and toss until well coated. Reserve cooking broth in a bowl or cup.

4 Heat an indoor electric grill, grill pan, or cooktop insert over medium-high heat for 5 minutes. Place the cauliflower, cut sides down, in a grill pan, on an open grill, or on a cooktop insert. Cook until the bottom is flecked with brown, about 5 minutes. Using tongs, turn the slices over. Grill 2 to 3 minutes longer. If using a contact grill, grill the cauliflower 5 minutes. Return the cauliflower to the serving dish or bowl and keep warm.

5 In saucepan, melt the butter over medium heat. Add the flour and whisk; stir in the broth. Heat to boiling, whisking constantly, until the sauce bubbles and thickens slightly. Pour the sauce over the grilled cauliflower and sprinkle with chives and cheese.

Vary It! *Substitute broccoli and Brussels sprouts, both relatives of cauliflower.*

Nutrition at a glance (per serving): *calories 120; calories from fat 85; fat 10 g; saturated fat 3 g; cholesterol 12 mg; sodium 510 mg; carbohydrates 6 g; dietary fiber 3 g; protein 4 g*

Grilled Asparagus Gremolata

Gremolata is an Italian parsley, garlic, and lemon zest seasoning often used on stews and soups. Here it flavors simple, grilled asparagus. In a pound of asparagus, you may get about 19 spears, which makes about 4 servings. However, because asparagus is so good for you, this recipe calls for a bit more.

Tools: *Grill, small saucepan or microwave-safe bowl, peeler, large saucepan*

Preparation time: *15 minutes*

Grilling time: *10 to 13 minutes*

Yield: *4 servings*

1 tablespoon butter	½ teaspoon salt
1 clove garlic, finely chopped	1½ pounds fresh asparagus (½-inch diameter)
¼ cup finely chopped flat-leaf parsley	1 tablespoon olive oil
1 teaspoon finely grated lemon peel	

1 In a small saucepan over low heat, melt the butter and add the garlic. Cook the garlic a few seconds and remove from the heat. Stir in the parsley, lemon peel, and salt; set the gremolada aside.

2 Holding each asparagus spear with one hand at the base (bottom) of the stalk and the other hand about 2 inches up from the base, bend the spear. It should break at the point where the tender stalk starts to toughen. Snap off the woody bottom end of all the spears and discard. With a peeler, peel the skin off the lower half of each spear. Rinse the asparagus spears and pat dry.

3 If you are using a grill pan, an open grill, or a cooktop insert, blanch the asparagus first. The blanched asparagus grills in less time, thus they retain their bright green color. In a large saucepan, bring 1 inch of water to boiling over high heat. Add asparagus and cook (or blanch) for 1 minute. Drain and rinse the asparagus spears with cold water. Pat dry with paper towels. (If you're using a contact grill, you don't need to blanch the asparagus, because the contact grill actually steams while it grills the spears.) On a plate, drizzle oil over the blanched or raw spears and rub to coat them evenly.

4 Heat an indoor electric grill, grill pan, or cooktop insert over medium-high heat for 5 minutes. Place the asparagus across (or perpendicular) to the grill's ridges. Grill 5 to 6 minutes or until lightly browned on all sides and tender when pierced with the thin blade of a sharp knife, turning once or twice. If you're using a contact grill, grill for 8 minutes, turning the spears over once.

5 Transfer the spears to a serving dish. Top with gremolada. Toss before serving to distribute the seasoning.

Vary It! *You can grill asparagus in a grill pan, on an open grill, or on a cooktop insert without blanching them first. They'll take at least 10 minutes to grill and the spears will be yellowish green rather than bright green when tender.*

Nutrition at a glance (per serving): *calories 78; calories from fat 59; fat 7 g; saturated fat 2 g; cholesterol 8 mg; sodium 303 mg; carbohydrates 4 g; dietary fiber 2 g; protein 2 g*

Grilled Sweet Peppers

Peppers abound in a variety of colors — red, orange, purple, white, yellow, and green. They are tasty when grilled for appetizers, sandwiches, and salads.

Tools: *Grill*

Preparation time: *10 minutes*

Grilling time: *12 to 15 minutes*

Yield: *4 servings*

2 large sweet bell peppers   *Salt and ground black pepper to taste*

½ recipe Backbone of Rubs (see Chapter 4)

1 Rinse and dry the peppers. Cut them lengthwise in half and remove the seeds and stem ends. Cut the pepper halves lengthwise into strips about ¾ inch wide. In a bowl, toss the pepper strips with Backbone of Rubs.

2 Heat an indoor electric grill, grill pan, or cooktop insert over medium-high heat for 5 minutes. Grill the peppers in a grill pan, on an open grill, or on a cooktop insert 5 to 6 minutes or until lightly browned, stirring occasionally. If using a contact grill, grill the peppers 3 to 4 minutes or until tender. They will not brown very much. Season grilled peppers with salt and pepper and serve.

Vary It! *Cut the peppers into ½-inch-thick rings instead of strips. Grill and use them to top pizzas or cut the peppers into 1-inch-wide strips and, after grilling, wrap a strip around a small fresh ball of mozzarella cheese, and secure with a toothpick to serve as part of an antipasto plate or appetizer. Grilled peppers can also be pureed in a food processor, turning them into a sauce to drizzle over chicken or lamb.*

Nutrition at a glance (per serving): *calories 104; calories from fat 83; fat 9 g; saturated fat 1 g; cholesterol 0 mg; sodium 293 mg; carbohydrates 6 g; dietary fiber 2 g; protein 1 g*

Eggplant Antipasto

When eggplant is fried in a skillet, it tends to absorb oil like a sponge, and exudes that flavor when the flesh is cooked. By grilling the eggplant, the veggies consume less oil — so you do, too. Salting the eggplant before cooking helps to draw out the moisture and also to remove any bitterness if the eggplant is mature. Use this recipe as a part of an antipasto platter with the addition of other grilled vegetables such as mushrooms, peppers, and zucchini.

Tools: *Grill, baking sheet, small saucepan*

Preparation time: *15 minutes*

Standing time: *30 minutes*

Grilling time: *15 to 21 minutes*

Yield: *4 servings*

1 medium eggplant (about 1¼ pounds), top cap and stem trimmed off	*2 cloves garlic, finely chopped*
Salt	*1 tablespoon chopped fresh basil, oregano, or rosemary*
⅓ cup olive oil	*1 tablespoon balsamic vinegar*

1 Cut eggplant crosswise into ½-inch thick slices. Place the slices in a single layer on a cookie sheet or baking sheet lined with paper towels. Sprinkle both sides of the eggplant slices lightly with the salt. Let the slices stand for 30 minutes.

2 While the slices are standing, in a small saucepan, heat the oil and add the garlic. Remove from the heat and set aside.

3 Heat an indoor electric grill, grill pan, or cooktop insert over medium heat for 5 minutes. Rinse the eggplant under cold running water. Pat the eggplant dry with paper towels. Brush both sides of the eggplant with garlic oil. In a grill pan, on an open grill, or on a cooktop insert, grill the eggplant in a single layer until grill marks appear on the bottom, about 5 minutes. Rotate the slices a quarter turn and grill 3 minutes longer. Turn the slices and grill the other side 3 minutes longer or until they are tender. If using a contact grill, grill the slices 5 minutes. Uncover and turn slices over; then rotate slices a quarter turn. Grill 5 minutes longer or until tender. As each slice becomes tender and lightly browned, transfer it to a serving plate.

4 To the oil remaining in the saucepan, add basil and vinegar. (A couple of spoonfuls should be left. If you have used up most of the oil, add 2 more tablespoons olive oil.) Stir well and drizzle the mixture over the grilled eggplant slices on the plate. Serve warm or at room temperature.

Vary It! *Small baby eggplants as well as Asian eggplants may be used for this recipe. Instead of cutting them crosswise, cut them lengthwise into ⅓-inch-thick slices. Because they're young and tender, they don't need to be salted.*

Nutrition at a glance (per serving): calories 200; calories from fat 163; fat 18 g; saturated fat 3 g; cholesterol 0 mg; sodium 151 mg; carbohydrates 10 g; dietary fiber 3 g; protein 1 g

Grilled Marinated Mushrooms

This recipe uses the common cultivated mushroom. If you like, mix them with any of the cultivated exotic varieties such as Cremini, Shiitake, or Oyster mushrooms.

Tools: *Grill, large mixing bowl*

Preparation time: *15 minutes*

Marinating time: *1 hour*

Grilling time: *13 to 20 minutes*

Yield: *4 servings*

1 pound large white or button mushrooms (about 2 inches in diameter)	*½ teaspoon salt*
	¼ teaspoon dry mustard
¼ cup extra virgin olive oil	*⅛ teaspoon crushed red pepper flakes*
1 tablespoon fresh lemon juice or balsamic vinegar	*1 tablespoon chopped fresh oregano, basil, or parsley*

1 To clean the mushrooms, rinse them under cold running water or place them in a colander and run water over them. (Just don't soak them in water — they will absorb the water like a sponge.) Pat the mushrooms dry with paper towels. On a cutting board, cut the stems flush with the caps. (You can freeze the leftover stems for soup stock.)

2 In a large bowl, whisk together the oil, lemon juice, salt, mustard, and pepper flakes. Add the mushrooms and toss until well mixed. Cover and refrigerate at least 1 hour but no longer than 8 hours.

3 Heat an indoor electric grill, grill pan, or cooktop insert over medium-high heat for 5 minutes. Grill the mushrooms 10 to 12 minutes in a grill pan, on an open grill, or on a cooktop insert, turning occasionally, until tender. If using a contact grill, grill 4 minutes, turn and rotate mushrooms, and grill 3 to 4 minutes longer or until tender. Transfer the mushrooms to a serving dish; sprinkle with chopped oregano and serve.

Nutrition at a glance (per serving): calories 149; calories from fat 122; fat 14 g; saturated fat 2 g; cholesterol 0 mg; sodium 291 mg; carbohydrates 4 g; dietary fiber 1 g; protein 4 g

Zebra Potatoes

The black grill lines embedded in the white potato slices resemble zebra's stripes. Enjoy these potatoes with steaks, burgers, chicken, or pork.

Tools: *Grill, medium saucepan, baking dish*

Preparation time: *15 minutes*

Grilling time: *15 to 17 minutes*

Yield: *4 servings*

1½ pounds baking potatoes (about 3 potatoes)   *Salt to taste*

2 tablespoons vegetable oil

1 Peel and rinse the potatoes. Pat dry with paper towels. On a cutting board, slice the potatoes crosswise into ½-inch-thick slices. Place the slices in a medium saucepan with enough lightly salted water to cover. Cover the pan and bring to a boil. Boil for 5 minutes or until nearly tender when pierced with the blade of a thin, sharp knife; drain thoroughly. Place the potatoes in a large shallow baking dish. Set aside to cool slightly while the grill heats.

2 Spray the grill grid with nonstick cooking spray or brush with oil to prevent food from sticking. Heat an indoor electric grill, grill pan, or cooktop insert over medium heat for 5 minutes. Drizzle the potatoes with oil and sprinkle with salt. Rub the oil into the potatoes to coat the slices on all sides.

3 Grill the potatoes in a single layer in grill pan, on an open grill, or on a cooktop insert until dark grill marks appear on the bottom, about 6 minutes. Turn the potatoes over and continue to grill until the slices are fork-tender, about 6 minutes longer. If using a contact grill, grill the potatoes 10 minutes turning the slices over once and rotating them a quarter turn.

Vary It! *In place of the oil, marinate the potatoes in Backbone of Rubs (see Chapter 4). Try this recipe with sweet potatoes or a waxy potato variety instead of baking potatoes. If you can find them, yellow-fleshed potatoes, such as Yukon Gold, make wonderful grilled potatoes.*

Nutrition at a glance (per serving): *calories 176; calories from fat 62; fat 7 g; saturated fat 1 g; cholesterol 0 mg; sodium 152 mg; carbohydrates 27 g; dietary fiber 2 g; protein 2 g*

Sesame Squash Medley

This vegetable dish has Asian seasonings that will complement pork or poultry dishes. If serving with rice, be sure to cook the rice before you begin preparing this recipe.

Tools: *Grill, large mixing bowl*

Preparation time: *15 minutes*

Grilling time: *14 to 17 minutes*

Yield: *4 servings*

2 small zucchini (about 6 inches long)	½ teaspoon salt
2 yellow summer squash (about 6 inches long)	1 tablespoon naturally brewed soy sauce
1 tablespoon dark (toasted) sesame oil	1 tablespoon toasted sesame seeds
1 teaspoon finely grated fresh ginger or ½ teaspoon ground ginger	

1 Rinse zucchini and yellow squash under cold running water; pat dry with paper towels. On a cutting board, trim and discard the stem ends and cut the squash diagonally into ½-inch-thick slices. In a large bowl, toss the squash slices with sesame oil, ginger, and salt until well mixed.

2 Heat an indoor electric grill, grill pan, or cooktop insert over medium-high heat for 5 minutes. Grill the squash in a single layer in a grill pan, on an open grill, or on a cooktop insert 9 to 12 minutes, turning and rotating slices every 3 minutes to get crossed grill marks. If using a contact grill, grill 9 to 10 minutes, turning and rotating slices every 3 minutes.

3 Transfer the slices to a bowl as they become tender; when all slices are done, toss them with soy sauce and sesame seeds.

Vary It! *You can use patty pan and round zucchini — two summer squash varieties with a different shape — in this dish. Both varieties are easy to grow in the garden and add visual interest to summer meals.*

Nutrition at a glance (per serving): *calories 74; calories from fat 42; fat 5 g; saturated fat 1 g; cholesterol 0 mg; sodium 526 mg; carbohydrates 7 g; dietary fiber 3 g; protein 3 g*

Corn Stuffed Tomatoes

Although this may seem like a very seasonal dish, fresh plum or Roma tomatoes and corn are readily available year-round in many markets. Of course, garden fresh produce is ideal, but purchased produce will do as long as it's ripe. The fresh corn is parched or dry-cooked on an open grill. A contact grill isn't recommended for this recipe, because the corn and tomatoes steam rather than brown.

Tools: *Grill, large mixing bowl*

Preparation time: *25 minutes*

Grilling time: *12 to 17 minutes*

Yield: *4 servings*

4 large ripe plum or Roma tomatoes (about 1 pound)

2 small ears fresh corn, husked and kernels cut off

1 tablespoon butter, softened

1 tablespoon chopped fresh or ½ teaspoon dried oregano

½ teaspoon salt

Ground red pepper (cayenne) to taste

1 Rinse the tomatoes under cold running water and pat dry with paper towels. Cut the tomatoes lengthwise in half.

2 Spray the grill grid with nonstick cooking spray or brush with oil to prevent food from sticking. Heat an open grill, grill pan, or cooktop insert over medium heat for 5 minutes. (If your grill has an open grid, use a skillet to parch the corn.) Add the corn kernels and grill until browned in spots, about 4 to 5 minutes, stirring occasionally. Transfer the corn to a bowl. Stir in the butter, oregano, and pepper to taste; cover and keep the corn warm.

3 Grill the tomato halves, cut sides down, until grill marks appear on the bottom, about 1 minute. Turn and grill the other side 1 to 2 minutes longer. Transfer the tomatoes to a cutting board and with a spoon, scoop out the center and set the tomato shells aside. Coarsely chop the center of the tomatoes. Stir the chopped tomatoes into the corn. If desired, remove the skin from each tomato half.

4 Arrange the tomato shells on a serving plate. Spoon the corn, mounding the mixture, into the tomato shells and serve. Some corn filling may fall on the plate around the tomatoes — that's perfectly okay.

Vary It! *Plum tomatoes are best for this recipe because they have fewer seeds and juice than a regular round tomato and more flesh that won't disintegrate under heat. In a pinch, you can use regular tomatoes, but be careful not to grill them very long.*

Nutrition at a glance (per serving): *calories 82; calories from fat 33; fat 4 g; saturated fat 2 g; cholesterol 8 mg; sodium 307 mg; carbohydrates 12 g; dietary fiber 2 g; protein 2 g*

Chapter 12

Great Wraps and Salads

*W*raps (sandwiches that use a flatbread to wrap the ingredients) and salads may seem out of place in a book on indoor grilling, but all the recipes in this chapter call for grilled ingredients — ranging from grilled cod to grilled zucchini — that are wrapped in flatbread or enveloped in lettuce and other vegetables. The vegetables in wraps and salads are a great source of vitamins, minerals, and fiber (see Chapter 11 for the lowdown on the healthy contribution of veggies) and, when served with soup, make complete meals in little time.

Preheating times vary among indoor grill manufacturers. Five minutes should be enough to adequately preheat your grill, but check the use and care book that came with your grill — your particular grill may take a bit longer to heat up.

Wrapping Up Grilled Meals

Wraps are the quintessential lunchbox or picnic food, and you can leave your knife and fork at home! These handheld, all-rolled-into-one meals take on an endless variety, as indicated by the recipes in this chapter and by the varieties that follow:

> ✔ To make a Greek wrap, use very thinly sliced grilled leg of lamb with a lemony sauce, feta cheese, and fresh mint all in a grilled pita bread.

> ✔ For a boxed lunch to carry to a concert in the park, try a grilled tuna Nicoise. *Nicoise* refers to foods cooked in the style of Nice, France, and may include garlic, tomatoes, green beans, and Nicoise olives. Salad

Nicoise is usually made with potatoes, olives, green beans, and a vinaigrette dressing.

✔ For an Italian flare, grill portobello mushrooms, and then slice and layer with grilled Italian sausages.

See Chapter 7 for a Skirt Steak Fajitas recipe.

Basil Wrap

A spread of basil and mayo envelops this grilled turkey sandwich. Crunchy French fried onion is the secret ingredient that provides bits of "bones" in this tasty roll.

Tools: *Grill, food processor, meat mallet*

Preparation time: *15 minutes*

Grilling time: *9 to 13 minutes*

Yield: *4 sandwiches*

⅔ cup reduced-fat or fat-free mayonnaise

½ cup lightly packed fresh basil leaves

4 boneless skinless turkey breast slices or cutlets (about 1 pound)

Salt and ground black pepper to taste

1 tablespoon vegetable oil

4 handkerchief flatbreads or 10-inch wrappers or fajita tortillas

2 small ripe tomatoes, sliced

2 cups mixed baby salad greens or mesclun

½ to ⅔ cup canned French fried onions

1 In a food processor, process the mayonnaise and basil until the basil is finely chopped and the mayonnaise is tinted a pale green color. Set the basil mayonnaise aside.

2 Between sheets of plastic wrap or waxed paper, using a meat mallet or rolling pin, pound each turkey cutlet to a uniform thickness of ¼ inch or less to ensure even cooking and easy rolling in the sandwich. Remove turkey from the plastic and sprinkle top with salt and pepper. Drizzle some oil over each cutlet and rub to coat both sides.

3 Spray the grill grid with nonstick cooking spray or brush with oil to prevent food from sticking. Heat an indoor electric grill, grill pan, or cooktop insert over medium-high heat for 5 minutes. If the bread wrappers are too stiff to roll, heat each a few seconds on the hot grill, one at a time, until soft and pliable; set the wrapper aside on a pizza pan or large tray for rolling.

4 Grill cutlets in a grill pan, on an open grill, or on a cooktop insert, two at a time, for 1 to 1½ minutes per side or until lightly browned and creamy white. Transfer the cutlets to a plate as they are done. If you're using a contact grill, grill the cutlets for 2 minutes.

5 To assemble each sandwich, spread one fourth of the basil mayonnaise in the center of the bread wrapper. Place a turkey cutlet in the center of the basil mayo, then top with one quarter of the tomato slices, ½ cup salad greens, and 2 or 3 tablespoons of fried onions. To wrap, bring up one side of the flatbread to cover the filling, and then fold in the rest of the wrap to make a tight package. Season as desired.

Vary It! *For an Asian Sandwich, pound and grill the chicken breast halves instead of the turkey. Spread the bread with a hoisin barbecue sauce (see Asian Butterflied Pork Loin) and top with grilled chicken then shredded napa cabbage, cilantro, and crisp noodles.*

Nutrition at a glance (per serving): *calories 592; calories from fat 238; fat 26 g; saturated fat 5 g; cholesterol 95 mg; sodium 934 mg; carbohydrates 49 g; dietary fiber 4 g; protein 37 g*

Grilled Fish Tacos

In Mexico, tacos from street vendors abound much like the hot dog stands in some American cities. This snack food consists of soft fresh corn tortillas wrapped around a filling of your choice. When tacos crossed the borders of the southwest, they became a crisp fried stuffed tortilla. The fish taco emerged 30 or 40 years ago in Baja, California, as a lightly battered and fried chunk of fish served in a fresh corn tortilla with shredded cabbage. Rubio's, a chain of taco outlets in San Diego, is credited with spreading the fish taco to the world. If you want to eat healthy and return to the original taco, try this grilled version.

Tools: *Grill, mixing bowl, plate*

Preparation time: *20 minutes*

Grilling time: *12 to 15 minutes*

Yield: *12 servings*

½ cup low-fat mayonnaise

2 tablespoons nonfat milk

1 tablespoon cider vinegar

1 teaspoon sugar

16-ounce package coleslaw mix (shredded green cabbage and carrots)

Salt and ground black pepper to taste

1 pound boneless, skinless ¾-inch-thick fish fillets such as cod or halibut, cut into 4 pieces

1 tablespoon vegetable oil

½ teaspoon ground cumin

½ teaspoon salt

¼ teaspoon garlic powder

12 corn tortillas

Bottled chunky tomato salsa

1 Prepare the slaw: In a large bowl, combine the mayonnaise, milk, vinegar, and sugar. Add the coleslaw mix and toss to coat with the mayonnaise mixture. Season with salt and pepper to taste. Cover and refrigerate the slaw until you're ready to serve.

2 Rinse the fish under cold running water and pat dry with paper towels. On a plate, rub the oil on both sides of the fish and sprinkle with cumin, salt, and garlic; set aside while the grill heats and the tortillas are warmed.

3 Spray the grill grid with nonstick cooking spray or brush with oil to prevent food from sticking. Heat an indoor electric grill, grill pan, or cooktop insert over medium heat for 5 minutes. Grill the tortillas, about two at a time, until hot. Each will take only a few seconds, turning them over a couple of times to heat evenly; as they are warmed, stack them on a sheet of aluminum foil and wrap to keep them warm.

4 Grill the fish in a grill pan, on an open grill, or on a cooktop insert for 7 to 8 minutes, turning once with a wide spatula. To test for doneness, make a small incision in the center of the fish with the tip of a thin-bladed knife. The flesh should be opaque, not translucent, when done. Place the fish on a plate and cut each into three pieces. (At this point, check the fish to remove any small bones.) If using a contact grill, grill the fish 3 minutes or until grill marks appear on the top. Lift the cover, rotate the fish a quarter turn, and grill 3 minutes longer or until done.

5 To assemble each taco, on each tortilla, place a chunk of fish, a spoonful of slaw, and a spoonful of salsa. Fold the tortilla in half and serve.

Nutrition at a glance (per serving): *calories 124; calories from fat 25; fat 3 g; saturated fat 0.2 g; cholesterol 10 mg; sodium 371 mg; carbohydrates 19 g; dietary fiber 3 g; protein 7 g*

Meditortilla Wrap

Although this Mediterranean-inspired sandwich contains no meat, it is hearty and colorful with delicious grilled vegetables and a hummus (chick pea) spread. Consider making this recipe for a buffet luncheon. The sandwiches are cut diagonally in half and placed cut sides up on a serving platter for presentation.

Tools: *Grill, mixing bowl, plate, salad spinner*

Preparation time: *35 minutes*

Grilling time: *25 to 30 minutes*

Yield: *6 sandwiches*

Backbone of Rubs (see Chapter 4)	*Salt and ground black pepper to taste*
1 small eggplant (about 1 pound), top cap and stem trimmed off	*6 flour tortillas (8 inches in diameter)*
2 small zucchini, about 6 inches long	*¾ cup store-bought hummus*
1 large red bell pepper	*½ pound mozzarella cheese, cut into ½ inch-thick sticks*
1 bunch fresh arugula	

1 Prepare Backbone of Rubs to coat the vegetables. Rinse the vegetables under cold running water and pat dry with paper towels. Remove the tough stems from the arugula and discard. Rinse the arugula leaves, spin dry, and refrigerate until you're ready to use them.

2 Cut the eggplant lengthwise in half. Lay the eggplant halves, cut sides down, on a cutting board and, with a very sharp knife, cut off a ⅛-inch-thick slice lengthwise. Repeat on the opposite side. Discard these slices, because they are mostly peel. Cut the remaining eggplant into ⅓-inch lengthwise slices. Slice the zucchini lengthwise into ¼-inch-thick slices. Trim, seed, and cut the bell pepper lengthwise into ½-inch-wide strips. Place the slices on a large baking sheet and brush the cut sides of the eggplant and zucchini with the Backbone of Rubs. Toss the bell pepper with the remaining Backbone of Rubs.

3 Heat an indoor electric grill, grill pan, or cooktop insert over medium heat for 5 minutes. Grill the eggplant in a single layer in a grill pan, on an open grill, or on a cooktop insert until grill marks appear on the bottom, about 5 minutes. Rotate the slices a quarter turn and grill 3 minutes longer. Turn the slices and grill the other side until they are tender. Transfer the slices as each is tender and lightly browned to a large tray or plate. If using a contact grill, grill the eggplant slices 4 minutes. Uncover and turn the slices over; then rotate the slices a quarter turn. Grill 3 minutes longer or until tender.

4 Grill the zucchini in a single layer in a grill pan, on an open grill, or on a cooktop insert, turning occasionally, until tender, about 10 minutes in the grill pan or 7 to 9 minutes on contact grill. Grill the peppers in a grill pan, on an open grill, or on a cooktop insert 5 to 6 minutes or until lightly browned, stirring occasionally. If using a contact grill, grill the peppers 3 to 4 minutes or until tender. They will not brown very much. Season grilled vegetables with salt and pepper to taste.

5 If the wraps are too stiff to fold, heat them one at a time in a large skillet until soft and pliable. To assemble each sandwich, spread about 2 tablespoons hummus in a thin layer in the center of the lower third of a wrap. Top with one sixth of the grilled vegetables, arugula, and cheese. The filling should be layered compactly so that it is about 5 inches long and about 2½ inches wide. Bring the bottom third of the wrap over the filling, bring each side of the wrap over, and then roll up tightly to enclose the filling (see Figure 12-1).

6 With a serrated or sharp knife and using a sawing motion, cut each sandwich crosswise in half on a slight angle. Place the halves on a plate with the cut sides facing up.

Note: *If you can't purchase hummus, make your own! In a food processor, whirl a 16-ounce can of drained chickpeas, 1 clove of garlic, ¼ cup sesame seeds, the juice of 1 lemon, and ½ cup water until smooth. Season with salt and pepper to taste.*

Nutrition at a glance (per serving): *calories 450; calories from fat 240; fat 27 g; saturated fat 7 g; cholesterol 30 mg; sodium 805 mg; carbohydrates 40 g; dietary fiber 5 g; protein 16 g*

WRAPPING AND ROLLING A TORTILLA

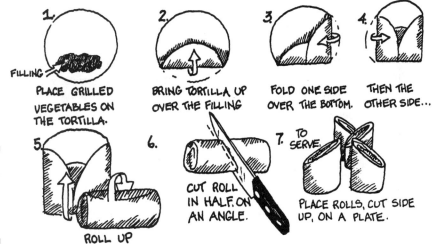

1. PLACE GRILLED VEGETABLES ON THE TORTILLA.

FILLING

2. BRING TORTILLA UP OVER THE FILLING

3. FOLD ONE SIDE OVER THE BOTTOM.

4. THEN THE OTHER SIDE...

5.

6. CUT ROLL IN HALF ON AN ANGLE.

ROLL UP

7. TO SERVE. PLACE ROLLS, CUT SIDE UP, ON A PLATE.

Figure 12-1: Wrappin' and rollin' with a tortilla.

Lettuce Talk about Salads

Salads are healthy, but did you know they can be hearty, too? The three salads in this section are meals unto themselves: a delightful mix of fiery shrimp, celery, tomatoes, and lettuce topped with an out-of-this-world blue cheese dressing; a twist on the traditional Caesar salad that uses tender, grilled, boneless chicken breasts; and an Italian salad that pairs vegetables, basil, and crusty bread.

To remove dirt from lettuce and other vegetable, rinse under running water. To remove pesticide residues and surface bacteria, however, wash in a vegetable wash or nontoxic dish soap (never, however, with an antibacterial soap, which can leave toxic residues of its own behind). Rinse in fast-running water until all traces of soap or vegetable wash are gone. Consider purchasing organic lettuce and other vegetables; you will still need to rinse these, however, because *organic* and *dirt-free* or *bacteria-free* are not synonymous!

Firecracker Shrimp Salad with Blue Cheese Dressing

Spicy hot shrimp — similar in taste to Buffalo wings — top this main-dish salad.

Tools: *Grill, mixing bowl*

Preparation time: *20 minutes*

Marinating time: *15 minutes*

Grilling time: *12 to 15 minutes*

Yield: *4 servings*

1 pound large shrimp (about 24), shelled and deveined

1 tablespoon butter, melted and cooled

1 tablespoon vegetable oil

1 or 2 teaspoons bottled hot pepper sauce

½ teaspoon salt

Blue Cheese Dressing (see the following recipe)

2 stalks celery

2 medium ripe tomatoes (use red, yellow, or favorite tomato variety)

8 cups torn leaf lettuce (use a mixture of red or green leaves)

1 pound gourmet or high quality potato salad

1 In a large bowl, rinse the shrimp in cold water, draining and changing the water several times. Pat the shrimp dry with paper towels. In a bowl, combine the shrimp with butter, oil, hot pepper sauce (1 teaspoon for mildly hot and 2 teaspoons for very hot), and the salt. Cover the bowl and refrigerate the shrimp for 15 minutes to marinate.

2 While the shrimp marinates, prepare the Blue Cheese Dressing.

3 Prepare the ingredients for the salad: Rinse and dry the celery, tomatoes, and lettuce. Cut the celery into 2-inch long by ¼-inch thick sticks. Core the tomatoes and cut the tomatoes into wedges.

4 Heat an indoor electric grill, grill pan, or cooktop insert over medium-high heat for 5 minutes. Grill the shrimp in a grill pan, on an open grill, or on a cooktop insert in a single layer until they turn pink, about 1½ to 2 minutes, turning once. If using a contact grill, grill the shrimp 1 to 1½ minutes or until the shrimp are pink and opaque. Do not overcook, or they will become dry and rubbery.

5 To assemble the salad, on four serving plates, put a bed of the torn lettuce, dividing evenly. Place a mound of shrimp in the center and surround with celery sticks, tomatoes, and potato salad. Pass the Blue Cheese Dressing.

Go-With: *Serve with crisp bread sticks or toasted flatbread such as foccacia.*

Nutrition at a glance (per serving, without condiments): *calories 322; calories from fat 151; fat 17 g; saturated fat 4 g; cholesterol 220 mg; sodium 1135 mg; carbohydrates 20 g; dietary fiber 5 g; protein 20 g*

Blue Cheese Dressing

Tools: *Mixing bowl, whisk*

Preparation time: *5 minutes*

Yield: *1½ cups (24 tablespoons)*

½ cup reduced-fat mayonnaise	*1 tablespoon cider or white wine vinegar*
½ cup nonfat sour cream	*½ cup crumbled blue cheese*
2 to 3 tablespoons milk	*Salt and ground black pepper to taste*

In a mixing bowl, stir the mayonnaise and sour cream until smooth. Stir in the milk and vinegar, adding more of the milk if the dressing seems a little thick. Fold in the cheese and season with salt and pepper to taste. Pour into a small serving bowl.

Nutrition at a glance (per tablespoon): *calories 32.3; calories from fat 23.3; fat 2.6 g; saturated fat 0.9 g; cholesterol 4.4 mg; sodium 107.9 mg; carbohydrates 1.3 g; dietary fiber 0 g; protein 0.9 g*

To further reduce the calories and fat in this recipe, substitute fat-free mayo for reduced-fat.

Grilled Chicken Caesar Salad

This popular variation of the classic Caesar salad is enjoyed by everyone. Without the raw egg that's often used in the classic, the dressing isn't as rich or creamy as the real thing, but it's much better for you.

Tools: *Grill, mixing bowl*

Preparation time: *25 minutes*

Marinating time: *1 hour*

Grilling time: *12 to 15 minutes*

Yield: *4 servings*

⅔ cup olive oil

⅓ cup fresh lemon juice

2 teaspoons Dijon-style mustard

1 teaspoon Worcestershire sauce

2 cloves garlic, finely chopped

6 oil-packed flat anchovies, drained and finely chopped

4 small boneless skinless chicken breast halves (about 1¼ pounds)

Salt and ground black pepper to taste

1 small head romaine lettuce or 2 or 3 hearts of romaine, rinsed and dried

½ cup grated Parmesan cheese

1 cup garlic croutons

1 In a large measuring cup, whisk together the oil, lemon juice, mustard, Worcestershire, garlic, and anchovies. Set the dressing aside.

2 Rinse the chicken under cold running water and pat dry with paper towels. With a knife, on a cutting board, cut off and discard any visible fat and gristle. Place the chicken in a resealable plastic bag or a shallow, nonreactive baking dish. Pour ¼ cup dressing over the chicken. Seal the bag or cover the dish and refrigerate for 1 hour.

3 Heat an indoor electric grill, grill pan, or cooktop insert over medium heat for 5 minutes. Drain the chicken, discarding the marinade. If using a grill pan, open grill, or cooktop insert, grill the chicken 8 to 10 minutes or until done, turning several times. (To create decorative crossed grill marks, grill the chicken 3 minutes or until brown grill marks appear on the bottom; then rotate the chicken a quarter turn to the first grill marks and then grill another 1 minute. Turn the chicken over and repeat.) Cut the chicken to determine doneness. The chicken is done when the meat is white and moist with no sign of pink when the thickest part of the chicken is cut. If the chicken is browning too much, reduce the heat if possible or cover the chicken with a sheet of foil to finish cooking. If using a contact grill, grill the chicken covered for 4 minutes. Lift the cover and turn the chicken over and rotate a quarter turn to create crossed grill marks; then cover and grill 2 minutes longer or until done.

4 Transfer the grilled chicken to a cutting board, season with salt and pepper and let stand a few minutes. Meanwhile, tear the romaine into small pieces. Cut each breast across into ½-inch thick slices. On each of four serving plates, place a mound of romaine and sprinkle with half of the cheese and the croutons. Arrange chicken breast slices in the center. Whisk the remaining dressing until well mixed and spoon over the salad. Sprinkle with the remaining cheese before serving.

Vary It! *If you don't like anchovies, substitute 1 tablespoon of chopped sun-dried tomatoes packed in oil. If desired, top the salad with 1 small red onion, cut into thin rounds.*

Nutrition at a glance (per serving): *calories 709; calories from fat 452; fat 50 g; saturated fat 8 g; cholesterol 93 mg; sodium 1033 mg; carbohydrates 22 g; dietary fiber 2 g; protein 42 g*

Herbed Garlic Bread Tomato Salad

At the end of the gardening season, this Italian salad incorporates the abundance of fresh ripe tomatoes and vegetables. This is a vegetarian luncheon salad but at times we vary it by adding shaved fresh Parmesan cheese, cubes of mozzarella cheese, or even pepperoni slices.

Tools: *Grill, mixing bowl, saucepan, whisk*

Preparation time: *30 minutes*

Grilling time: *17 to 20 minutes*

Yield: *4 servings*

¼ cup olive oil

2 cloves garlic, minced

2 tablespoons finely chopped fresh oregano

½ teaspoon coarse or kosher salt

½ loaf crusty Italian bread, halved horizontally (about an 8-inch piece)

2 zucchini or yellow summer squash, sliced

⅓ cup extra virgin olive oil

2 tablespoons red wine vinegar

2 cups cubed fresh tomatoes (consider using a mixture of tomato varieties — red, orange, white, green, and striped)

Salt and ground black pepper to taste

1 cup grape tomatoes, halved

1 cup lightly packed small fresh basil leaves (if the leaves are large, tear into bite-size pieces)

½ cup Kalamata or other brine-cured black olives, pitted and halved

1 Heat an indoor electric grill, grill pan, or cooktop insert over medium heat for 5 minutes. In a small saucepan, heat the oil until hot. Remove from the heat and add garlic. Let stand a few minutes to flavor the oil. Stir in the oregano and salt.

2 Brush the cut surfaces of the bread with herbed garlic oil. Grill the bread, cut sides down, until golden brown, about 5 minutes in a grill pan, on an open grill, or on a cooktop insert or 2½ minutes in a contact grill. Turn the bread over and grill the other side until crispy, about 2 minutes longer. Transfer the bread to a cutting board. Cut the bread into 1 inch chunks.

3 In a mixing bowl, toss the zucchini with the remaining herbed garlic oil. Grill 7 to 8 minutes until tender, turning once. Return the grilled zucchini to the bowl.

4 In a small bowl, whisk the extra virgin oil and vinegar until blended. Whisk in the cubed tomatoes and salt and pepper to taste. In a salad bowl, toss the tomato dressing with bread cubes. Let stand 5 minutes or until the bread absorbs all the dressing.

5 Just before serving, top the bread cubes with grilled zucchini, grape tomatoes, basil, and olives; toss and serve.

Go-With: *A summer fruit tart topped with frozen yogurt or berries is a wonderful dessert to go with this main-dish salad.*

Nutrition at a glance (per serving): *calories 483; calories from fat 330; fat 37 g; saturated fat 5 g; cholesterol 0 mg; sodium 757 mg; carbohydrates 35 g; dietary fiber 4 g; protein 7 g*

Part IV
Dressing Up for Dinner

The 5th Wave   By Rich Tennant

"I'm pretty sure it's grilled game. That would explain the meat tasting like a Monopoly game board."

In this part . . .

This part helps you make a party or meal that your guests will remember. We've included chapters on creating grilled appetizers, grilling unique dishes like venison and whole trout, and using grilled fruits and cakes to create distinctive, delicious desserts.

Chapter 13

Warming Up the Crowd with Appetizers

In This Chapter

▶ Using your indoor grill to create delicious appetizers

▶ Making a range of recipes from veggie treats to chicken wings

▶ Understanding how many appetizers are enough

Appetizers are small tidbits of food that are served before the main meal (when guests are getting to know each other) or throughout a party that doesn't include a meal. In the case of bread-based appetizers, consider serving them as a part of the meal itself.

The quality of your appetizers can be the difference between a delightful formal dinner or party and a dud. By using your indoor grill to create delicious bites of food, you'll make the meal or party inviting and memorable.

Although traditional appetizers are always a hit, consider including lower-calorie and lower-fat options for your guests. Guests will appreciate your keeping their health in mind.

This chapter gives you a wealth of options: traditional appetizers such as chicken wings and kielbasa, lower-fat varieties such as shrimp cocktail and salmon, and vegetarian (but sometimes higher-fat) options like bruschetta and stuffed mushrooms. This chapter also lets you know how many appetizers you'll need for your crowd.

Knowing How Much Is Enough

If your appetizers will simply whet your guests' appetite before dinner, don't serve too many appetizers or they won't be hungry for dinner. Provide enough for each guest to eat one or two servings. For a party, during which guests will nosh and nibble for several hours, provide about five servings per person.

You can estimate appetizer servings (and the impact on your budget) as follows:

- ✓ **Meat, poultry, and finfish:** A serving includes three tidbits of meat, poultry, or finfish. Each servings calculates to about ⅛ pound for boneless and ¼ pound for bone-in. Depending on the types and cuts you choose, appetizers made with these ingredients can range from inexpensive to a budget-stretching delicacy.

- ✓ **Shrimp and scallops:** A serving is about three pieces of shrimp or scallops. These can be expensive, so provide a small sampling of shrimp and/or scallops with a larger offering of less expensive appetizers.

- ✓ **Bread:** One serving is equal to half of a tortilla (cut into quarters) or one slice of bread (cut into halves). If you're serving bread as part of the main meal (as the recipes in this chapter assume you will), double this amount. Bread-based appetizers tend to be extremely inexpensive.

- ✓ **Cheese:** A serving is about 1 ounce of cheese. Because a pound of cheese weighs 16 ounces, you can get 16 servings from 1 pound. Depending on the variety you choose, cheese can be moderately priced or inexpensive.

- ✓ **Veggies:** For one serving, provide about three large pieces of vegetables, such as three large strips of pepper, three half carrots (equal to six or eight peeled baby carrots), or three tomato quarters. Keep in mind that although veggies are healthy and delicious, they aren't nearly as filling as other appetizers and can be expensive when not in season.

Stretch your food budget by providing nongrilled appetizers, too. Include baby peeled carrots, sliced celery, cherry tomatoes, pickles and olives (buy on sale to save on these rather pricey appetizers), crackers, cheese spreads, and salad spreads made from chicken, ham, and tuna.

Creating Traditional Appetizers on Your Indoor Grill

In this section, you'll find old favorites — chicken wings, kielbasa, and shrimp cocktail — along with a delicious recipe for healthy and tasty salmon. Be sure to check the chapters in Part III for additional recipes for which you can adapt the serving sizes and use them as appetizers.

Preheating times vary among indoor grill manufacturers. Five minutes should be enough to adequately preheat your grill, but check the use and care book that came with your grill — your particular grill may take a bit longer to heat up.

Grilled Chicken Wings

Grilled chicken wings are a hit with any crowd. You can make the dry rub and barbecue sauce ahead of time so that you can quickly prepare these finger-licking morsels when you need them.

Preparation time: *15 minutes*

Grilling time: *15 to 30 minutes*

Yield: *6 appetizer servings (18 pieces)*

1½ pounds (about 9) small chicken wings

2 teaspoons Poultry Dust (see Chapter 4)

¼ cup Basic Barbecue Sauce (see Chapter 5)

1 Rinse the chicken wings under cold running water; drain and pat dry with paper towels. Cut the tips off the chicken wings and freeze for soup stock. Cut each remaining wing between the joints to separate them.

2 On a large plate, sprinkle the wings with Poultry Dust until evenly distributed on all sides.

3 Spray the grill grid with nonstick cooking spray or brush with oil to prevent food from sticking. Heat an indoor electric grill, grill pan, or cooktop insert over medium heat for 5 minutes. Grill the wings in a grill pan, on an open grill, or on a cooktop insert in a single layer for 20 minutes, turning several times. If using a contact grill, grill for 10 minutes, turning once.

4 Brush the wings on the top sides with barbecue sauce; turn the wings and brush the remaining side with sauce. Grill the wings 1 minute; turn the wings, brush them again, and grill another minute or until the wings are fork tender.

Vary It! Brush wings with the Hoisin Barbecue Sauce from Asian Butterflied Pork Loin (see Chapter 8).

Nutrition at a glance (per serving): calories 147; calories from fat 80; fat 9 g; saturated fat 2 g; cholesterol 37 mg; sodium 344 mg; carbohydrates 5 g; dietary fiber 0 g; protein 12 g

Grilled Shrimp Cocktail

The classic shrimp cocktail begins by cooking shrimp in a court bouillon or seasoned stock. For this new grilled classic, that solution is turned into a brine to marinate the shrimp prior to grilling. Unlike traditional shrimp cocktail, this shellfish is skewered and grilled, giving them a subtle smokiness. (See Chapter 10 for additional seafood recipes.)

Note that you're better off using a grill pan, open indoor grill, or cooktop insert for this recipe: Your contact grill may not get hot enough to cook the shrimp correctly.

Tools: *Grill, small saucepan, mixing bowl*

Preparation time: *25 minutes*

Marinating time: *4 hours*

Grilling time: *10 to 15 minutes*

Yield: *8 appetizer servings (at least 24 shrimp)*

1 cup water	1 tablespoon lemon juice
2 bay leaves	2 teaspoons coarse or kosher salt
2 slices onion	1 pound large (21 to 30 count) shrimp
8 peppercorns	½ cup or more bottled seafood cocktail sauce

1 In a small saucepan, bring ⅓ cup water, the bay leaves, onion slices, and peppercorns to boiling over medium heat. Simmer the mixture for 1 minute and remove from the heat. Pour into a bowl and add the remaining ⅔ cup water, the lemon juice, and the salt. Stir well to dissolve the salt. Refrigerate the brine while you prepare the shrimp.

2 Shell and devein the shrimp (see Chapter 10 for more on deveining). Rinse the shrimp in a bowl of water and drain. Add the shrimp to the cooled brine; cover and refrigerate 4 hours to marinate. About 30 minutes before you're planning to grill, soak enough 6-inch bamboo skewers to match the number of shrimp that you have brined. After brining, drain the shrimp and rinse under cold water. Drain the shrimp and pat dry with paper towels. To thread a shrimp, insert the skewer (parallel) through the shrimp from the cut head end to the tail. (This will straighten the shrimp so you'll have a shrimp on a stick!) Be sure the point of the skewer doesn't go beyond the tail end.

3 Spray the grill grid with nonstick cooking spray or brush with oil to prevent food from sticking. Heat an indoor electric grill, grill pan, or cooktop insert over medium-high heat for 10 minutes to get it really hot. Grill the shrimp in a grill pan, on an open grill, or on a cooktop insert in a single layer (in two batches) 1½ to 2 minutes, turning once, until they turn pink and opaque. Do not overcook, or they will become dry and rubbery.

4 Transfer the shrimp to a serving plate with a bowl of seafood sauce.

Vary It! If you can't find ready-made cocktail sauce, mix ½ cup tomato-based chili sauce or ketchup with 1 tablespoon prepared horseradish, 1 tablespoon lemon juice, 1 teaspoon Worcestershire sauce, and a few dashes Tabasco or hot pepper sauce.

Nutrition at a glance (per serving): calories 49; calories from fat 5; fat 0.5 g; saturated fat 0.1 g; cholesterol 67 mg; sodium 286 mg; carbohydrates 3 g; dietary fiber 0 g; protein 7.5 g

Glazed and Grilled Kielbasa

Smoked sausages make a popular, easy-to-prepare appetizer because most sausages on the market are fully cooked products. The turkey version is the least caloric and is preferred here, but any of the other smoked sausages can be grilled. See Chapter 6 for more sausage recipes.

Tools: *Grill, small mixing bowl, whisk, microwave-safe bowl or small saucepan*

Preparation time: *10 minutes*

Grilling time: *7 to 8 minutes*

Yield: *8 appetizer servings (about 26 pieces)*

Mustard Dipping Sauce	1 pound turkey kielbasa
¼ cup spicy brown or Dijon-style mustard	¼ cup apple jelly
¼ cup orange juice	1 tablespoon balsamic or red wine vinegar
1 tablespoon sugar	

1 Prepare Mustard Dipping Sauce: In a small mixing bowl, whisk together the mustard, orange juice, and sugar until smooth. Pour into a small serving bowl.

2 Heat an indoor electric grill, grill pan, or cooktop insert over medium heat for 5 minutes. While the pan heats, cut the kielbasa into ¾-inch-thick slices. Using a microwave-safe bowl in the microwave or a small saucepan over low heat, heat the apple jelly and vinegar to boiling. Set the glaze aside.

3 Grill the kielbasa in a grill pan, on an open grill, or on a cooktop insert, cut sides down, until grill marks appear on the bottom, 3 to 4 minutes. Turn each piece over and grill 1 to 2 minutes longer or until heated through. Brush each piece on all sides with some glaze. Transfer the kielbasa to a serving plate with the Mustard Dipping Sauce and a tiny cup filled with round wooden toothpicks or cocktail picks.

4 If using a contact grill, grill the sausages 2 minutes. Brush with glaze. Transfer the grilled sausages to a serving plate. Serve with toothpicks to dip into Mustard Dipping Sauce.

Go-With: *Sliced pumpernickel bread or small rolls work well with this appetizer.*

Nutrition at a glance (per serving): calories 129; calories from fat 45; fat 5 g; saturated fat 2 g; cholesterol 37 mg; sodium 604 mg; carbohydrates 11 g; dietary fiber 0 g; protein 9 g

Rosemary Skewered Salmon

For this recipe, having a rosemary shrub nearby is helpful. Because this herb grows like a weed at Lucy's family's Arizona home, she often make skewers from the woody branches to spear seafood, chicken, lamb, and even chunks of bread that she toasts on the grill. For this appetizer, use rosemary for skewers if you have some; otherwise, use cocktail picks instead.

Tools: *Grill, nonreactive bowl*

Preparation time: *15 minutes*

Marinating time: *1 hour*

Grilling time: *10 to 15 minutes*

Yield: *8 appetizer servings (about 24 pieces)*

1 pound center-cut red salmon fillet, cut 1 inch thick

⅓ cup orange juice

1 tablespoon finely chopped fresh rosemary

1 tablespoon lemon juice

½ teaspoon salt

¼ teaspoon Tabasco

About 24 3-inch sprigs fresh rosemary

Lemon wedges

1 Rinse the salmon under cold running water and pat dry with paper towels. Pull or trim the skin off the fillet and discard. Cut the salmon into 1-inch chunks. Place the salmon in a small nonreactive bowl. Add the orange juice, rosemary, lemon juice, salt, and Tabasco to the salmon. Toss gently with a spoon to mix the ingredients. Cover the bowl and refrigerate the salmon for 1 hour to marinate.

2 While the salmon marinates, prepare the rosemary skewers. Rinse the rosemary in cold water; drain and, if possible, use a salad spinner to spin dry. Remove the leaves from the lower half of each sprig, leaving a tuft of leaves on top.

3 Spray the grill grid with nonstick cooking spray or brush with oil to prevent food from sticking. Heat an indoor electric grill, grill pan, or cooktop insert over medium-high heat for 5 minutes. Drain the salmon, discarding the marinade, and place the salmon on a tray lined with paper towels.

4 Grill the salmon in a grill pan, on an open grill, or on a cooktop insert for a total of 6 to 7 minutes, turning each chunk to brown on all sides. If using a contact grill, grill salmon for 2½ minutes. The flesh should be pale pink throughout when done. Arrange the salmon on a platter. Insert a rosemary skewer into each chunk. Garnish the platter with lemon wedges and serve.

Vary It! *Each salmon chunk may be served on a cucumber slice without the rosemary skewer.*

Nutrition at a glance (per serving): *calories 63; calories from fat 17; fat 2 g; saturated fat 0 g; cholesterol 28 mg; sodium 72 mg; carbohydrates 0 g; dietary fiber 0 g; protein 11 g*

Grilling Vegetarian Appetizers

This section shares a variety of vegetarian snacks from bready varieties like quesadillas and bruschetta to cheesy mixtures that incorporate Brie and mozzarella. Your vegetarian friends will appreciate your providing options for them, but you don't have to be vegetarian to enjoy the appetizers in this section! Die-hard meat eaters will relish these tasty treats, as well.

Quesadillas

This traditional southwestern snack food is a Mexican cheese sandwich — a tortilla folded over a filling of chile and cheese. In Mexico, quesadillas are made by folding uncooked corn tortillas over filling and frying them in oil. In the United States, flour tortillas are preferred. By grilling the tortillas, you'll eliminate the oil used in frying. We usually serve this as a prelude to a Tex-Mex meal; for a crowd, double or triple the recipe.

Preparation time: *10 minutes*

Grilling time: *10 to 15 minutes*

Yield: *4 appetizer servings (or 16 pieces)*

Four 8-inch flour tortillas

1⅓ cups shredded mild cheddar or Monterey Jack cheese

⅓ cup bottled chunky tomato salsa

Guacamole (optional)

Sliced cherry tomatoes (optional)

1 Spray the grill grid with nonstick cooking spray or brush with oil to prevent food from sticking. Heat an indoor electric grill, grill pan, or cooktop insert over medium heat for 5 minutes. Heat each tortilla a few seconds on the hot grill, one at a time, until soft and pliable; transfer the tortilla to a pizza pan or large tray for filling.

2 Sprinkle ⅓ cup shredded cheese over half of each tortilla. Drop dabs of 1 rounded tablespoon salsa on the cheese. Fold the tortilla over the filling. Place the folded tortilla on the grill, two at a time, and grill until the cheese begins to melt and the tortilla browns slightly, turning once or twice, about 2 to 3 minutes.

3 Serve the quesadillas whole or place the quesadillas on a cutting board and cut each into four wedges. If desired, top each with a small mound of guacamole and a cherry tomato slice. Serve immediately.

Vary It! *If you can only find the smaller 6-inch tortillas, just make a stack of two tortillas for each quesadilla. You can make a meal of quesadillas by serving two of them per person. Consider adding sliced green onions or fresh cilantro to the filling. You can add dollops of refried beans or cooked beef, pork, or chicken to the cheese filling.*

Go-With: *With a mixed green salad, you'll have a tasty supper or lunch.*

Nutrition at a glance (per serving): *calories 320; calories from fat 143; fat 16 g; saturated fat 9 g; cholesterol 39 mg; sodium 619 mg; carbohydrates 30 g; dietary fiber 2 g; protein 14 g*

Bruschetta

Bruschetta (bru-SKET-ta) are slices of grilled or toasted country bread rubbed with garlic and drizzled with a fruity olive oil. As the original Italian garlic bread, bruschetta is now served as a base for a wide variety of toppings.

Tools: *Grill, medium saucepan, paring knife, large mixing bowl, nonreactive bowl or dish, skillet (if using an open electric grill or cooktop insert)*

Preparation time: *23 minutes*

Grilling time: *15 to 18 minutes*

Yield: *4 appetizer servings (8 slices)*

1 pound (4 large) ripe plum tomatoes	Salt and ground black pepper to taste
1 medium onion	One 6- to 7-inch round loaf sourdough or crusty country bread, sliced ¾ inch thick
2 large cloves garlic	
¼ pound small fresh cremini or baby portobello mushrooms	3 tablespoons thinly sliced fresh or 1 teaspoon dried basil
3 tablespoons olive oil	1 tablespoon balsamic vinegar

1 In a medium saucepan, heat 1½ inches water to boiling over high heat. With a paring knife, cut out the stem of each tomato and cut a shallow "X" through the bottom skin. Drop the tomatoes into boiling water for about 30 seconds; remove with a slotted spoon and rinse under cold water. Starting at the "X," peel off the skin and cut the tomato in half across the middle. Squeeze to remove the seeds and discard. Cut the tomato pulp into ¼-inch dice and set aside in a large mixing bowl.

2 Rinse the onion, garlic, and mushrooms under cold running water and pat dry with paper towels. Cut the onion lengthwise in half and then into slivers of wedges. Cut the garlic crosswise in half. Cut the mushrooms into sixths or quarters. Place the onion slivers and mushrooms in a nonreactive bowl or dish, and toss with 1 tablespoon of the oil and some salt and pepper. Set aside while the grill heats.

3 Spray the grill grid with nonstick cooking spray or brush with oil to prevent food from sticking. Heat an indoor electric grill, grill pan, or cooktop insert over medium heat for 5 minutes. Grill the bread on an open grill, a grill pan, or a cooktop insert 2 to 3 minutes on each side or until grill marks appear. If using a contact grill, grill bread 5 to 6 minutes. Brush the bread on one side with the remaining oil and rub the oiled surface with the cut side of the garlic. Set the bread, garlic-rubbed side up, on a large serving platter. After using the garlic, finely chop them and add to the onions and mushrooms.

4 If using a grill pan or contact grill, grill the onions and mushrooms, covered, for 3 to 5 minutes, stirring occasionally. If using an open electric grill or a cooktop insert, you'll have to use a skillet over medium heat to sauté the mushroom mixture. Toss the mushroom mixture with tomatoes, basil, and vinegar. Spoon the tomato-mushroom mixture onto the grilled bread and serve.

Go-With: *A corn or potato chowder and a marinated green bean salad will make this a fine meal.*

Vary It! *If you use smaller slices of bread, you'll end up making crostini or "little toasts." For crostini, use a 16-inch loaf (about 3 inches wide) of French or Italian bread. Cut bread into ½-inch thick slices.*

Nutrition at a glance (per serving): *calories 271; calories from fat 109; fat 12 g; saturated fat 2 g; cholesterol 0 mg; sodium 464 mg; carbohydrates 36 g; dietary fiber 4 g; protein 7 g*

Brining

This technique of using salty water, called a *brine,* is usually applied to large cuts of meat, such as beef, as a way to preserve it and add flavor and moisture over a period of time. We usually brine pork loin, turkey, and chicken before grilling. They are delicious and moist when done. Brining also infuses flavor into food if the brine contains herbs or spices, citrus peel, or onions. You might call brine a salty marinade!

Be sure to use a nonreactive container made of glass, plastic, stainless steel, or ceramic material — never aluminum. (Salt reacts chemically with aluminum to discolor the food and produces an off flavor. See Chapter 3 for more information.)

As for salt, we prefer to use coarse or kosher salt because it is pure and additive-free. The grains are much larger than regular table salt. You can also use sea salt, which is preferred by chefs (although it is more expensive). Sea salt is made by evaporating seawater; it contains minerals from the sea.

Leaf-Wrapped Grilled Brie

Enveloped in grape leaves rather than rich puff pastry, this already rich, warm appetizer goes well with plain bread or crackers, and firm fruit slices make a refreshing alternative.

Tools: *Grill, large mixing bowl, pizza pan (optional), butcher string*

Preparation time: *15 minutes*

Grilling time: *10 to 15 minutes*

Yield: *15 appetizer servings*

12 large brined grape leaves (about 5 to 6 inches across, if leaves are smaller, you'll need more leaves)	*1 long slender loaf French baguette, thinly sliced, or plain crackers*
5-inch wheel mini or baby Brie (15 ounces)	*2 large red or golden apples, cored and sliced*
Coarsely ground black pepper or chopped fresh parsley or chervil	

1 In a large mixing bowl, rinse the grape leaves in cold water to remove the excess salt from the leaves. Pat the leaves dry with paper towels. With a knife, cut off and discard the tough stem end of each leaf.

2 On a work surface or a pizza pan, overlap 8 leaves to form about a 12-inch circle. Place 2 leaves in the center. Cut the rind off the top of the Brie to expose the cheese. Place the cheese, cut side up, on the center grape leaves and sprinkle the top lightly with pepper or herbs. Cover the top of the cheese with the remaining leaves. Bring the leaves around the cheese up and over the top. Tie securely with butcher string to form a package (see Figure 13-1 for illustrated instructions). (The cheese can be prepared up to this point and refrigerated a day before grilling. However, remove cheese from refrigerator a half hour before grilling.)

3 Heat an indoor electric grill, grill pan, or cooktop insert over medium heat for 5 minutes. Spray the grape leaves on both sides of the cheese package with nonstick cooking spray or brush with oil. Grill the cheese package, top side down, in a grill pan, on an open grill, or on a cooktop insert for 3 to 4 minutes. Turn the cheese over with a wide spatula and grill 4 minutes longer or until the center of the cheese feels soft. When you finish grilling, the top side of the cheese should be upright.

4 Transfer the cheese to a large serving platter. Cut and remove the string. Unroll the leaves around the cheese down and remove the top leaves covering the cheese. Surround the cheese with baguette or fruit slices. Insert several cheese spreaders or butter knives into the cheese. Let your guests serve themselves by spreading the warm cheese onto bread slices, crackers, or apple slices.

Note: *Grape leaves are sold in jars in the ethnic section of your market with Greek foods. If you have fresh grape leaves, boil them in salted water until they're soft and pliable.*

Nutrition at a glance (per serving): *calories 178; calories from fat 86; fat 10 g; saturated fat 5 g; cholesterol 28 mg; sodium 360 mg; carbohydrates 16 g; dietary fiber 2 g; protein 7 g*

GRAPE-LEAF WRAPPING OF BRIE

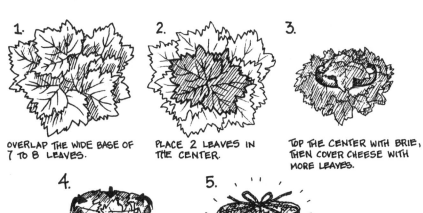

1. OVERLAP THE WIDE BASE OF 7 TO 8 LEAVES.

2. PLACE 2 LEAVES IN THE CENTER.

3. TOP THE CENTER WITH BRIE, THEN COVER CHEESE WITH MORE LEAVES.

4. BRING LEAVES UP OVER CHEESE TO ENCLOSE THE BRIE.

5. TIE BRIE UP WITH A STRING TO LOOK LIKE A PACKAGE !

Figure 13-1:
The grapes (leaves) of wrap.

Veggie-Stuffed Mushrooms

Chopped carrots seasoned with dill fill these bite-size lemony mushroom caps. They're healthy and tasty, too!

Tools: *Grill, metal grater, mixing bowls, small saucepan*

Preparation time: *25 minutes*

Marinating time: *15 minutes*

Grilling time: *13 to 15 minutes*

Yield: *8 appetizer servings (24 pieces)*

1 small lemon

24 1¾- to 2-inch white or button mushrooms

2 tablespoons olive oil

½ teaspoon salt

2 tablespoons butter

2 shallots or 1 scallion, finely chopped

⅓ cup finely chopped fresh carrots

½ cup fresh bread crumbs

1 tablespoon chopped fresh dill or 1 teaspoon dill weed

Salt and ground black pepper to taste

1 With a metal grater, finely grate the peel or zest from the lemon into a medium mixing bowl; set aside. Cut the lemon in half and squeeze its juice into a large bowl, discarding any seeds. Rinse the mushrooms under cold running water; pat dry with paper towels. Remove the mushroom stems from the caps and reserve. Place the caps in the bowl with the lemon juice; add the oil and salt; toss the mushrooms; set aside to marinate for 15 minutes, tossing occasionally.

2 On a cutting board, with a knife, finely chop enough of the mushroom stems to measure about 1 cup, discarding any leftover stems or freezing them for soup stock. In a small saucepan, heat the butter over medium heat. Add the shallots and sauté 1 minute. Add the mushroom stems and carrots and cook, stirring often, until the carrots are tender, about 6 minutes. Transfer the cooked vegetables to the bowl with grated peel; stir in the bread crumbs and the dill. Season with salt and pepper to taste.

3 Heat an indoor electric grill, grill pan, or cooktop insert over medium heat for 5 minutes. Drain the mushrooms, discarding the marinade. Pat the mushrooms dry on paper towels. Grill the mushrooms in a grill pan, on an open grill, or on a cooktop insert for 10 to 13 minutes, turning several times until tender. If using a contact grill, grill mushrooms 7 to 8 minutes, turning and rotating mushrooms one time for even browning. Drain mushroom caps of any juices that accumulate in the cavity. Transfer the mushroom caps, stemmed sides up, to a serving plate. Spoon the filling into the mushrooms caps, dividing evenly (see Figure 13-2). Garnish the plate with sprigs of fresh dill, if desired, and serve.

Nutrition at a glance (per serving): *calories 88; calories from fat 60; fat 7 g; saturated fat 2 g; cholesterol 8 mg; sodium 239 mg; carbohydrates 6 g; dietary fiber 1 g; protein 3 g*

STUFFING MUSHROOMS

Figure 13-2:
Stuffing
mushrooms
is kid stuff.

1.

2. REMOVE STEMS AND GRILL MUSHROOM CAPS.

3. SPOON FILLING INTO MUSHROOM CAPS.

Swiss Chard Bundles

After grilling, these carrot and cheese bundles resemble stuffed grape leaves. If you grow you own chard, you'll have an easier time counting the leaves for this recipe, but the store-bought variety works well, too. If you don't have enough large leaves, piece smaller leaves together.

Tools: *Grill, small mixing bowl, large saucepan*

Preparation time: *40 minutes*

Marinating time: *4 hours or overnight*

Grilling time: *13 to 15 minutes*

Yield: *8 appetizer servings (24 pieces)*

⅓ cup extra virgin olive oil

1 clove garlic, finely chopped

1 tablespoon chopped fresh oregano or basil leaves

½ teaspoon salt

¼ teaspoon crushed red pepper flakes

12 fresh baby (1-inch) mozzarella balls, drained if packed in water (about 4 ounces)

½ of a 1-pound package peeled baby or mini-cut carrots

24 large Swiss chard leaves (about 2 bunches)

1 In a small mixing bowl, whisk together the oil, garlic, oregano, salt, and red pepper. Cut each mozzarella ball into 4 wedges. Place the mozzarella in the flavored oil; cover and refrigerate at least 4 hours or overnight.

2 In a large saucepan, heat 2 inches of water to boiling over high heat. Add 24 carrots and cook until fork-tender, about 10 minutes. While the carrots cook, on a cutting board, with a knife, cut the stems off the Swiss chard; wrap and refrigerate to use in stir-fries or other recipes. Rinse the trimmed leaves and set aside.

3 With a slotted spoon, transfer the cooked carrots to a bowl of cold water to stop their cooking. To the same boiling water, with tongs, dip the chard leaves, one at a time, for 30 seconds to blanch. Place the blanched leaves in a colander to drain them and when they're cool enough to handle, squeeze the leaves to rid them of all moisture. Place the leaves between paper towels to dry. Drain the carrots and pat them dry; cut each carrot lengthwise in half.

4 On a work surface, spread out one leaf, with the cut stem end away from you. About an inch from the rounded end of the leaf, place 2 carrot halves parallel to each other across the stem; top with 2 drained mozzarella quarters in between. (Reserve the mozzarella's oil marinade.) Fold the sides over the filling and roll up the leaf away from you to enclose the filling (see Figure 13-3). Place on a plate. Repeat with the remaining leaves and marinated mozzarella. Brush the Swiss chard bundles on all sides with the reserved marinade, coating well.

5 Heat an indoor electric grill, grill pan, or cooktop insert over medium heat for 5 minutes. Grill the chard bundles in a grill pan, on an open grill, or on a cooktop insert in a
single layer (in two batches) for 4 to 5 minutes, turning once, until the leaves are lightly
browned. If using a contact grill, grill the bundles for 2 to 3 minutes. Transfer the bundles to a serving plate as they are grilled. Arrange the bundles around the edge of the
plate and fill the center with the remaining baby carrots.

*Nutrition at a glance (per serving): calories 159; calories from fat 112; fat 12 g; saturated fat 3 g; cholesterol 11 mg;
sodium 482 mg; carbohydrates 8 g; dietary fiber 3 g; protein 5 g*

MAKING SWISS CHARD BUNDLES

Figure 13-3:
These Swiss
chard
bundles are
anything but
neutral.

1. WITH FILLING AT ONE END OF A BLANCHED CHARD LEAF...

2. BRING LONG SIDES OF LEAF OVER THE FILLING.

3. ROLL UP TO ENCLOSE

ZUCCHINI ROLLUPS

Figure 13-4:
Rockin' and
rollin' with
zucchini.

1. START WITH A GRILLED SLICE OF ZUCCHINI WITH PARMESAN AND HERBS.

2. ROLL UP THE ZUCCHINI

3. SKEWER ROLL WITH A TOOTHPICK.

Zucchini Rolls

When you have an abundance of zucchini or when they're in season and very inexpensive, this is one simple way to use them up. Just be sure to select the smaller squash so that the rolls are bite-size and don't use a contact grill for this recipe, because the thin zucchini slices will steam and soften instead of grilling. You can insert a small strip of prosciutto or a quartered piece of sun-dried tomato in place of the cheese. For serving as a first course in a meal, serve the rolls over a pool of fresh tomato sauce.

Preparation time: *15 minutes*

Grilling time: *21 to 29 minutes*

Yield: *8 appetizer servings (24 to 26 pieces)*

6 medium zucchini (6 to 7 inches long), as straight as possible	*4 tablespoons finely chopped fresh herb (parsley, mint, oregano, or mixture of your choice)*
4 tablespoons grated Parmesan cheese	*Lettuce leaves (optional)*

1 Rinse and dry the zucchini. Trim off the ends. On a cutting board, with a sharp thin-bladed knife, make a paper-thin lengthwise slice to remove the skin of the first slice. Repeat to peel off the skin from the opposite side, then start slicing the zucchini into ¼-inch-thick lengthwise slices. (The straighter the squash, the more easily the zucchini can be sliced.) When your get down to the last two slices, you may have to lay the remaining zucchini down and cut parallel to the cutting board. You should yield at least 4 or 5 slices from each zucchini.

2 Spray the grill grid with nonstick cooking spray or brush with oil to prevent the food from sticking. Heat an indoor electric grill, grill pan, or cooktop insert over medium heat for 5 minutes. Grill the zucchini slices in a grill pan, on an open grill, or on a cook-top insert in a single layer (in two or three batches) for 4 to 5 minutes on each side or until tender and soft. Drain the slices on paper towels.

3 While the slices are warm and pliable, sprinkle each with ½ teaspoon grated cheese and ½ teaspoon chopped herbs. Roll up the zucchini and secure with a round wooden tooth-pick (see Figure 13-4). Arrange the rolls on a plate lined with lettuce leaves, if desired.

Vary It! *If you grow your own squash, use the leaves of a zucchini plant instead of lettuce as a liner for your food. Substitute golden zucchini for some of the green zucchini to add visual interest to your plate.*

Nutrition at a glance (per serving): *calories 36; calories from fat 10; fat 1 g; saturated fat 1 g; cholesterol 3 mg; sodium 64 mg; carbohydrates 5 g; dietary fiber 2 g; protein 3 g*

Chapter 14

Making the Occasion Special

Sometimes, a meal just has to be perfect: You're celebrating, your boss is coming to dinner, or you have a hot date! Regardless of the occasion, preparing foods on your indoor grill is a great idea because the house will smell enticing and cleanup will be easy.

The first step to making an occasion memorable is dressing up your table with a special tablecloth and napkins, the good china and silverware, and wine glasses. Step two is choosing unique foods, so this chapter features recipes for lamb, whole trout, venison, and veal.

See Chapter 18 for ten more ideas for making a memorable meal.

Dressing Up Your Meal

So, you're going to make this a special meal — one that your guest(s) will remember months from now. But how do you get started? Start by setting a gourmet table:

> ✔ **Use an attractive tablecloth or special placemats.** Put away the plastic-coated *101 Dalmations* placemats and, instead, use pretty cloth to set the stage.

> ✔ **At each setting, pull out your best china and set the table using as many plates as possible.** Use your largest plates, called *dinner plates* (if they're very large, they may be called *charger plates*) for the center of the place setting (see Figure 14-1). You may also want to place a *salad plate* (a plate that's slightly smaller than the dinner plate) in the middle of the dinner plate, taking away the salad plate after that course is eaten. Some china sets have a salad *bowl* instead of a plate.

Also set out a *bread plate* (sometimes called a *bread and butter plate*, which may be identical to the salad plate or slightly smaller) for rolls or slices of bread. Put this plate above and to the left of the dinner plate. Keep *dessert plates* (even smaller plates than salad or bread plates, but you can use either salad plates or bread plates if you don't have any that are specifically designed for dessert) in the kitchen until you're ready to serve dessert.

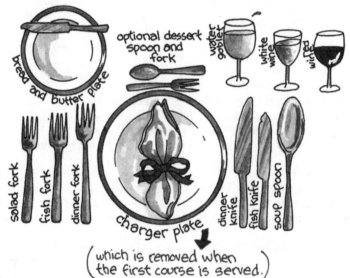

A Place Setting with the Works!

bread and butter plate

optional dessert spoon and fork

water goblet

white wine

red wine

salad fork

fish fork

dinner fork

dinner knife

fish knife

soup spoon

charger plate

(which is removed when the first course is served.)

Figure 14-1:
The whole kit and caboodle.

- ✔ **If you usually use paper towels or paper napkins, get hold of some attractive cloth napkins (preferably ones that coordinate with the tablecloth or placemats), and tie them up with ribbon or a napkin ring.** Place a napkin in the center of each dinner plate (or salad plate).

- ✔ **Set out two wine goblets — a larger one for water, and a smaller one for wine or soda (if you don't consume alcohol) — above and to the right of the dinner plate.** Not sure which wine to use with which meal? Table 14-1, gleaned from the pages of *Wine Buying Companion For Dummies,* 2nd Edition, by Ed McCarthy and Mary Ewing-Mulligan (Hungry Minds, Inc.), can help. (If you've never heard of these wines, don't fret. Take this list along to a wine shop and have the sales clerk help you hunt down one of the selections.)

✓ **Clean up your silverware (sometimes called *flatware*), and set it for your guests.** The dinner fork is the longest; the salad fork is the next smallest. You may also have a fish fork, which goes in between the dinner and salad forks. Place the forks to the left of the dinner plate. To the right of the dinner plate, put a knife and large spoon (called a *soup spoon*). If you have a very small knife in your collection, place it on the butter plate (refer to Figure 14-1). Keep dessert spoons and forks with the dessert plates (in the kitchen) until you serve dessert. If you don't have dessert forks in your collection, use salad forks in their place.

✓ **Along with the dessert plates and silverware, keep cups and saucers in the kitchen for after-dinner beverages such as coffee, tea, or hot chocolate.**

Table 14-1	Wine Selections Recommended by *Wine Buying Companion For Dummies*
Main Grilled Dish	*Wine to Serve*
Burgers	Australian Cabernet, Chilean Cabernet, lighter U.S. Cabernet, U.S. Merlot, lighter Zinfandel, Côtes du Rhône
Chicken	U.S. Chardonnay, white Burgundy, Tuscan Sangiovese, U.S. Pinot Noir
Darker fish	Australian Semillon, U.S. Chardonnay, Viognier, white Burgundy, U.S. Pinot Noir, lighter Zinfandel, Napa Valley brut Champagne
Grilled steak	Australian Cabernet, California Cabernet, South African Cabernet/Merlot blend, Zinfandel, Bordeaux, Chianti Classico, Rioja Reserve
Lamb chops	Chilean Cabernet, red Bordeaux, Chianti Classico, rosé Champagne
Pork chops	Australian Shiraz
Salmon	Napa Valley brut Champagne, red Burgundy, U.S. Pinot Noir
Turkey	Lighter Chianti, U.S. Chardonnay
Vegetables	California Cabernet, California Chardonnay
Venison	Barolo, Chianti Classico Riserva, Lagrein, Minervois, Gigondas, hearty Provence red, California Syrah, U.S. Cabernet

Your special table is set, but you can still add special touches to your meal in the following ways:

- Don't forget to use your best serving bowls and utensils and a basket for rolls or bread. Also put out your best salt and pepper shakers and any sauces, spreads, or garnishes in nice-looking bowls.

- Add an attractive centerpiece (flowers are always appropriate).

- Use candles, making sure that they're short enough or arranged such that all the guests can see each other.

- Turn off or turn down the lights.

- Turn on your favorite music (not too loud!) and set it to play continuously so that you're not jumping up in the middle of the meal to change tapes or CDs.

All that's left is to grill your meal. We suggest making one of the four recipes in this chapter your main dish, adding the following as complements:

- Serve Grilled Shrimp Cocktail, Leaf-Wrapped Grilled Brie, or Veggie-Stuffed Mushrooms (see Chapter 13) as appetizers. Or, if you really like seafood, consider serving Margarita-Marinated Shrimp, Sweet-and-Sour Grilled Shrimp, or Saffron Sea Scallops (see Chapter 10) as appetizers.

- Grill Bruschetta (see Chapter 13) as bread to go along with the meal. If this is too much bread for you, serve it as an appetizer.

- Make smaller versions of Firecracker Shrimp Salad with Blue Cheese Dressing, Grilled Chicken Caesar Salad, or Herbed Garlic Bread Tomato Salad (see Chapter 12) for the salad.

- Prepare Grilled Asparagus Gremolata, Grilled Marinated Mushrooms, Grilled Sweet Peppers, Sesame Squash Medley, or Corn Stuffed Tomatoes (see Chapter 11) as vegetable side dishes. (The Veal Chops on Spinach with Red Potatoes recipe has vegetables as part of the recipe, so you may not need additional veggies.)

- Serve any of the desserts in Chapter 15.

Preheating times vary among indoor grill manufacturers. Five minutes should be enough to adequately preheat your grill, but check the use and care book that came with your grill — your particular grill may take a bit longer to heat up.

Two Shakes of a Lamb's Tail

Lamb is the original grilled food: In the early days of cooking, when our ancestors did it over an open flame, kebabs were always made with lamb pieces. Although today's indoor grills are much more tame than an outdoor barbecue pit, lamb is still a perfect partner for the grill.

You'll find lamb in a variety of cuts (see Figure 14-2). Loin cuts tend to be the most tender, but nearly any cut of lamb will work on the grill. Our recipe calls for boneless leg or shank half.

Buy lamb just before you plan to use it and look for meat that is bright red in color.

Remember to follow the usual precautions when handling raw meat: Wash your hands with hot, soapy water before and after touching raw lamb; in hot soapy water, wash any knives, cutting boards, and sponges that have come in contact with raw lamb; and separate raw and grilled lamb, making sure the juices from the raw lamb don't contaminate grilled foods.

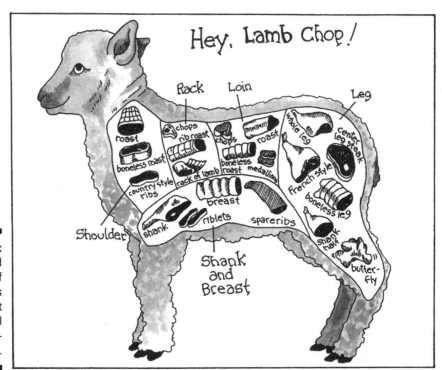

Figure 14-2:
You can find many of these cuts of lamb at your local super-market.

Grilled Lamb with
Vegetable Couscous

This is an ideal springtime dish because fresh lamb is plentiful then. A mint marinade doubles as a sauce for the meat. With grilled asparagus (see Chapter 11) served along-side the instant couscous, you'll have an easy-to-make dinner. Fresh strawberries would be a fitting dessert to conclude this seasonal menu.

Tools: *Grill, mixing bowl, resealable plastic bag or shallow nonreactive baking dish, microwave-safe bowl or pitcher, medium saucepan*

Preparation time: *15 minutes*

Marinating time: *2 hours or overnight*

Grilling time: *13 to 20 minutes*

Yield: *4 servings*

14½-ounce can or 1⅔ cups homemade beef broth	*1¾-pound boneless leg of lamb or 3¼-pound shank half leg of lamb, boned*
½ cup dry red wine	*1 cup water*
1 cup lightly packed fresh mint leaves without stems, finely chopped	*1 small onion, finely diced*
	2 large carrots, peeled and finely diced (about 1 cup)
2 tablespoons brown sugar	
1 teaspoon salt	*1¼ cups instant couscous*
½ teaspoon ground black pepper	*Salt to taste*

1 In a mixing bowl, mix together 1 cup broth with the wine, mint, brown sugar, salt, and pepper. Refrigerate the remaining ⅔ cup broth for the couscous.

2 With a knife, on a cutting board, cut off and discard any visible fat and gristle from the lamb. If any part of the lamb is thicker than 1¼ inches, butterfly or split the muscle in half without cutting all the way through. Place the lamb in a resealable plastic bag or a shallow, nonreactive baking dish. Pour 1 cup of the marinade over the lamb. Seal the bag or cover the dish and refrigerate for at least 2 hours or overnight. Pour the remaining mint marinade to serve as a sauce in a microwave-safe bowl or pitcher; cover and refrig-erate. While the lamb is marinating, you can prepare the vegetables for the couscous.

3 After the lamb has marinated, drain the marinade and discard. Pat the lamb dry on paper towels. Heat an indoor electric grill, grill pan, or cooktop insert over medium heat for 5 minutes. If you're using a grill pan, open grill, or cooktop insert, place the lamb on the grill pan and cover with a sheet of aluminum foil. Grill the lamb for 15 min-utes or until medium to rare, turning several times. Make a small incision in the center of the lamb to determine doneness. The lamb is done when the meat is reddish pink. If the lamb is browning too much, reduce the heat if possible. With an instant-read ther-mometer, the lamb should be 130° for medium-rare in the thickest part; it will be medium in the thin pieces. If using a contact grill, grill the lamb covered for 4 minutes. Lift the cover and turn the lamb over, rotating a quarter turn to create crossed grill marks. Then cover and grill 4 minutes longer or until done to your preference. Pour any juices from the drip pan over the lamb before serving. (If you want, you can use these juices in place of some of the water in the couscous.) Let the lamb stand 10 minutes loosely covered with a sheet of aluminum foil before slicing.

4 While the lamb is standing, prepare the Vegetable Couscous: In a medium covered saucepan, heat the remaining ⅔ cup broth, the water, onion, and carrots to boiling over high heat. Reduce the heat to medium-low and cook until the vegetables are tender, about 5 minutes. Stir in the couscous. Remove from the heat and let stand for 5 minutes. Reheat the remaining mint marinade or sauce until hot. With a fork, fluff the couscous and season with salt to taste. Slice the lamb and serve with couscous. Pass the remaining mint sauce to serve over the lamb.

Vary It! In place of the carrots, if you have leftover cooked vegetables such as peas, cut green beans, or broccoli, toss them into the boiling liquid to reheat before adding the couscous. You can also add a few chopped herbs such as chives, dill, or tarragon to the couscous before serving.

Nutrition at a glance (per serving): calories 485; calories from fat 92; fat 10 g; saturated fat 3 g; cholesterol 98 mg; sodium 1007 mg; carbohydrates 53 g; dietary fiber 5 g; protein 39 g

A Fine Kettle of Whole Fish

Whole fish is a rare treat, so if you don't spend your spare time fishing, make it a point to make friends with some fishermen. Our recipe calls for whole trout, but you can grill any whole fish, including bass, red snapper, and rockfish, the same way. We recommend leaving the head intact, but if it grosses you out, ask the representative at your fish counter to cut it off.

If you can't hook up with any friends who fish, consider ordering whole fish online. Through high-tech packaging and overnight delivery, you can have fresh, whole fish delivered to your door. Because shipping costs can be expensive, however, but sure to find out what costs will be added to your order before purchasing.

For a list of companies that carry seafood, check out `new.seafood.com/retail/buydirect.html`.

Keep the following tips in mind when handling seafood as you prepare to grill it:

- ✔ Wash your hands with hot, soapy water before and after touching raw seafood.

- ✔ Before grilling, rinse seafood under running water.

- ✔ In hot soapy water, wash any knives, cutting boards, and sponges that have come in contact with raw seafood.

- ✔ Separate raw and grilled seafood, making sure the juices from raw seafood don't contaminate grilled foods.

Look for more seafood recipes in Chapter 10.

Grilled Trout Amandine

A delicate, smoky brine enhances fresh trout, whether just caught or bought, for a light meal for two individuals. Double the recipe if you have a larger grill.

Tools: *Grill, resealable plastic bag or shallow nonreactive baking dish, small saucepan*

Preparation time: *10 minutes*

Marinating time: *30 minutes*

Grilling time: *13 to 15 minutes*

Yield: *2 servings*

1 cup water	2 tablespoons butter
1½ tablespoons brown sugar	¼ cup sliced or slivered blanched almonds
1 tablespoon coarse or kosher salt	2 tablespoons finely chopped parsley or chives
1 teaspoon hickory liquid smoke seasoning	
2 rainbow, brook, or brown trout (about 9 to 10 ounces each), gutted with head intact (11- to 12-inch-long fish)	Lemon wedges

1 In a measuring cup, combine the water, brown sugar, salt, and liquid smoke. Set the brine aside.

2 Rinse the trout under cold running water and pat dry with paper towels. With a knife, on a cutting board, make four ¼-inch-deep slashes on each side of the fish, spaced about 1 inch apart (see Figure 14-3). Place the trout in a resealable plastic bag or a shallow, nonreactive baking dish. Pour the brine over the trout. Seal the bag or cover the dish and refrigerate for 30 minutes, turning the fish over once.

3 Spray the grill grid with nonstick cooking spray or brush with oil to prevent food from sticking. Heat an indoor electric grill, grill pan, or cooktop insert over medium heat for

5 minutes. While the pan heats, in a small saucepan, melt the butter and add the almonds and cook over medium-low heat until the almonds are lightly browned, about 3 to 5 minutes. Remove from the heat immediately to prevent the almonds from over-browning. Add the parsley and set aside.

4 Drain the trout, discarding the brine; rinse under cold water and pat the fish dry with paper towels. Grill the trout on an open grill, in a grill pan, or on a cooktop insert for 8 to 10 minutes, turning once or until done. If using a contact grill, grill the trout for 3 minutes; lift the cover, turn, and rotate the trout a quarter turn to create crossed char marks; grill 2 minutes longer or until done. Check through one of the incisions in the center of the fish to determine doneness. When done, the flesh is white and opaque.

5 Transfer the trout to dinner plates. Top each with the almond-butter mixture. Serve with lemon wedges.

Go-With: A green vegetable such as broccoli or green beans, asparagus, or zucchini can be paired nicely with this dish. While the fish is marinating, you can make a wild rice pilaf.

Nutrition at a glance (per serving): calories 297; calories from fat 203; fat 23 g; saturated fat 9 g; cholesterol 83 mg; sodium 218 mg; carbohydrates 4 g; dietary fiber 2 g; protein 20 g

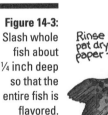
Figure 14-3:
Slash whole fish about ¼ inch deep so that the entire fish is flavored.

The Merchant of Venison

Venison may refer to any wild or farm-raised antlered game animal, such as moose, caribou, antelope, and elk, but it usually refers to the meat of a deer. (The word *venison* comes from the Latin word *venatus,* which means "to hunt.") Many deer are farmed in some areas of the U.S. and New Zealand; farmed venison is more tender and less gamy than its wild counterpart.

You can find farmed venison at the following online stores:

- **Old World Venison Company:** www.upstel.net/~pbingham/venison.html
- **Grandview Farms:** ultimate.org/sites/gvf/price.html
- **Shaffer Farms:** www.igateway.com/clients/shafrfam/
- **Underhill Farms:** www.underhillfarms.com/venison/
- **Highbourne Deer Farms:** www.highbournedeerfarms.com/

Whether you're a hunter, the lucky recipient of venison from a hunting friend, or an online shopper, request choice cuts such as boneless saddle, tenderloin, or rib chops for special occasions.

The saddle contains the two short loins or backstraps lying parallel to each side of the back bone and can be boned (boneless loin or backstrap) and cut crosswise into medallions (restaurants call them *saddle of venison*) or sawed with bone into T-bone steaks and loin chops. The tenderloin is found under the saddle and may be cooked whole or sliced into medallions. A venison steak can also be sliced from the hind legs or haunches.

Grill the lean, tender parts of venison to no more than rare or medium rare so that it doesn't become dry and chewy.

Use caution when handling raw venison. See the "Two Shakes of a Lamb's Tail" section, earlier in this chapter, for a list of precautions.

Venison Steak with Port Wine Cranberry Sauce

This autumnal feast of boneless loin steaks is served accompanied by a cranberry sauce — not the sauce that's served with turkey, but a special one for game made with port wine and currant jelly.

Tools: *Grill, resealable plastic bag or shallow nonreactive baking dish, medium saucepan, bowl*

Preparation time: *20 minutes*

Marinating time: *1 hour or overnight*

Grilling time: *11 to 13 minutes*

Yield: *6 servings*

1 boneless whitetail or red deer loin (backstrap) or ¾ mule deer loin (about 1¾ pounds)

1 cup Meat Soaker (see Chapter 4)

Watercress sprigs (optional)

Port Wine Cranberry Sauce

1½ cups fresh or frozen cranberries

1 tablespoon butter

2 shallots or white part of 2 scallions, chopped

⅓ cup ruby port wine

¼ cup beef broth

½ cup red currant jelly or apple jelly

1 If the venison has been packaged in plastic, rinse the venison under cold running water and pat dry with paper towels. With a knife, on a cutting board, cut off and discard any visible fat and gristle from the venison. Cut the venison loin crosswise into 1½-inch thick slices. Place the slices on the cutting board, cut sides down, and press with the heel of your hand to flatten each to about a 1¼-inch thickness. Place the venison in a resealable plastic bag or a shallow, nonreactive baking dish. Pour the Meat Soaker over the venison. Seal the bag or cover the dish and refrigerate for 1 hour or overnight.

2 Prepare the Port Wine Cranberry Sauce: Rinse and pick over the cranberries. In a medium saucepan, melt the butter over medium heat and add shallots. Sauté the shallots for 1 minute. Stir in the cranberries, port, and broth. Heat the cranberries to boiling, and then add the jelly. Cook over medium-low heat, stirring occasionally, until the cranberries have popped open, about 15 to 20 minutes. Transfer the sauce to a serving bowl and set aside. (You can make the sauce up to a day ahead; just cover and refrigerate it until needed. Reheat before serving.)

3 About 15 minutes before serving time, remove the venison from the marinade and pat dry on paper towels. Spray the grill grid with nonstick cooking spray or brush with oil to prevent food from sticking. Heat an indoor electric grill, grill pan, or cooktop insert over medium-high heat for 5 minutes. If using a grill pan, open grill, or cooktop insert, grill the venison for 8 minutes or until rare to medium-rare, turning several times. (To create decorative crossed grill marks, grill for 3 minutes or until brown grill marks appear on the bottom; then rotate the venison a quarter turn to the first grill marks and grill another 1 minute. Turn the venison over and repeat.) Make a small incision in the center to determine doneness. The venison is done when the meat is reddish pink for medium-rare. If using a contact grill, grill the venison covered for 4 minutes. Lift the cover and turn the venison over, rotating a quarter turn to create crossed grill marks. Then cover and grill 2 minutes longer or until done to your preference. Pour any juices from the drip pan over the venison before serving.

4 To serve, on a large plate with a rim, spoon some of the liquid and a few berries from the Port Wine Cranberry Sauce. Arrange the venison in the sauce. Garnish with watercress. Pass the remaining sauce.

Go-With: Baked sweet potatoes and Cauliflower Parmesan (see Chapter 11).

Vary It! Boneless venison loin or backstrap from New Zealand is available in major meat markets. If you can't find it, use venison rib chops or the tenderloin. You can also grill slices of venison round steak, cut from the hind legs, but this cut won't be as tender as the loin.

Nutrition at a glance (per serving): calories 319; calories from fat 109; fat 12 g; saturated fat 4 g; cholesterol 112 mg; sodium 148 mg; carbohydrates 22 g; dietary fiber 1 g; protein 29 g

The Veal Deal

Veal (meat from young calves) is expensive but worth having for a special meal. Veal is usually more tender and milder in flavor than beef because the muscles have not had the time to mature and toughen. Our recipe calls for veal rib chops, but you can also purchase loin roasts, rib roasts, rump roasts, loin chops, and cutlets. These tender cuts all grill well. Less tender cuts, which are less suitable for the grill, include shanks, shoulder roasts, breasts, riblets, and round steaks. As in the following recipe, veal is enhanced by brief marinating.

Veal is low in calories and fat: A 3-ounce portion has just 166 calories and under 6 grams of fat, less than 2 of which are saturated. Veal is also an excellent source of niacin, vitamins B-12 and B-6, and zinc.

Take care when handling raw veal. See the "Two Shakes of a Lamb's Tail" section, earlier in this chapter, for a list of precautions.

Veal Chops on Spinach with Red Potatoes

Marinated veal chops are served here on a bed of sautéed spinach along with grilled potatoes.

Tools: *Grill, nonreactive baking dish, medium saucepan, salad spinner, resealable plastic bag*

Preparation time: *20 minutes*

Marinating time: *1 hour or up to 6 hours*

Grilling time: *17 to 22 minutes*

Yield: *2 servings*

4 tablespoons vegetable or olive oil

2 tablespoons Worcestershire sauce

1½ teaspoons finely chopped fresh or ½ teaspoon dried rosemary

2 veal rib chops, cut about ¾ inch thick (9 to 10 ounces each)

8 baby red potatoes, about 1¼-inch diameter

4 cups fresh spinach (about 10 ounces)

1 small red onion, sliced

1 teaspoon balsamic or red wine vinegar

Salt and ground black pepper to taste

1 In a nonreactive baking dish, combine 2 tablespoons oil, the Worcestershire, and rosemary. Add the veal to the dish; turn to coat. Cover and refrigerate at least 1 hour or up to 6 hours.

2 While the veal marinates, scrub the potatoes and cut each in half. In a medium saucepan, heat 2 inches of water to boiling. Add the potatoes and cook just until fork tender, about 10 minutes. While the potatoes cook, rinse the spinach and spin dry in a salad spinner. Remove the stems and tear any very large spinach leaves in half. Place the spinach in a plastic bag; seal and refrigerate until ready to sauté. Drain the potatoes; return to the pan and toss with 1 tablespoon oil. Set aside until ready to grill.

3 Drain the veal, discarding the marinade, and pat dry with paper towels. Heat an indoor electric grill, grill pan, or cooktop insert over medium heat for 5 minutes. Place the veal in the center of the grill pan or grill. Place the potatoes, cut sides down, around the veal. Grill the veal and potatoes 12 minutes, turning several times. (To create decorative crossed grill marks, grill the veal 4 minutes or until brown grill marks appear on the bottom, and then rotate the veal a quarter turn to the first grill marks, grilling another 2 minutes. Turn the veal over and repeat, unless you're using a contact grill.) Make a small incision next to the bone of the veal to determine doneness. The veal is done when the meat is pinkish and moist.

4 While the veal is grilling, in a large skillet, heat the remaining 1 tablespoon oil over medium heat and add onion. Sauté the onion until tender, about 5 minutes. Remove the chops from the grill and let them rest on a plate for 5 minutes, loosely covered with a sheet of aluminum foil. Add the spinach to the onion; sauté until wilted, about 2 minutes. Sprinkle with vinegar; season with salt and pepper.

5 Divide the spinach and onion slices between two plates. Top with veal and serve with potatoes.

Nutrition at a glance (per serving): *calories 409; calories from fat 155; fat 17 g; saturated fat 3 g; cholesterol 137 mg; sodium 489 mg; carbohydrates 20 g; dietary fiber 4 g; protein 42 g*

Chapter 15

Getting Your Just Desserts

*B*y grilling fruits and cakes on your indoor grill, you can create the perfect end to a meal. Fast, simple, and (in most cases) light and healthy, the grilled desserts in this chapter yield flavorful treats that even the pickiest eaters will love.

In this chapter, you can find tips for selecting fruits that grill well, using those fruits at the peak of ripeness, and combining grilled fruits with grilled cakes and sumptuous sauces to create delightful desserts.

Selecting Fruits for the Grill

The best fruits to grill are those that are soft yet hearty (some would say "meaty" but that just doesn't sound appetizing!), and are just ripened. Pears, bananas, pineapples, avocados, papayas, mangos, peaches, nectarines, cantaloupe, and apples all fill the bill. Other fruits aren't off limits, however; experiment with grilling whatever fruits you have on hand to see how they turn out. Or use other fruits, especially small berries that may fall through your grill grid, as topping for grilled cakes.

The key to selecting fruit for the grill is to use them at the peak of ripeness. This happens in two ways: For fruit that's doesn't ripen after it's harvested, use care when selecting them at your local market. For fruit that ripens after harvesting, ripen the fruits at home and use them when they're at exactly the right texture, color, and flavor. The two following sections guide you through the ins and outs of both types of fruit.

Selecting ripened fruit at the store

When some fruits, including the following, are harvested before their time, they lack flavor and sweetness. You must use care when selecting these fruits.

- Apples
- Cherries
- Citrus
- Pineapples
- Soft berries
- Strawberries
- Watermelon

For these types of fruits, use the following tips to determine whether they're ripe:

- **Go by color:** Look for colors that are deep and intense. For apples and watermelon, green is an acceptable color; for other fruit in this category, it's not.

- **Go by smell:** Ripe fruit smells full and fruity. Okay, saying that fruit should smell "fruity" seems like a no-brainer, but it's true: Underripe fruit doesn't smell like much.

- **Go by feel:** Except for apples, don't select fruit that's rock-hard. The fruit should give slightly when you squeeze it. Apples, on the other hand, should be firm to the touch.

- **Go by weight:** Choose small, heavy fruits over larger, lighter ones. Ripe fruit feels strangely heavy for its size.

Ripening fruits after purchasing them

Other fruits can be harvested early because they continue to ripen after they've been picked. Fruit that you purchase before it's ripe and allow to ripen at home includes the following:

- Avocados
- Bananas
- Cantaloupe

- Kiwi
- Mangos
- Nectarines
- Papayas
- Peaches
- Pears
- Plums

You can purchase these fruits when they're hard, odorless, and green. They'll gradually ripen to their full color, peak flavor, and succulent juiciness.

To ripen fruit after you've purchased it, place the fruit in a small, brown paper bag, fold down the top, and keep the bag at room temperature for one to three days. The fruit inside will quickly ripen to its full flavor, so check it regularly.

To ripen avocados, bananas, and cantaloupe even more quickly, place an apple inside the paper bag: The ethylene gas that apples give off naturally can encourage ripening in these fruits.

Never, never, never store unripe fruit in the refrigerator: These fruits will either never ripen or will become mealy.

Mastering the Subtleties of Grilling Desserts

With your indoor grill, you can create mouth-watering desserts without a lot of fuss. Using the recipes in this section, you can create a variety of grilled treats: Some are homey favorites, but with a creative twist; others are light options, ideal after a rich meal, that are low in calories and fat.

When grilling fruit, use only a medium heat and watch carefully as it cooks. Grilled fruit can burn quickly!

Preheating times vary among indoor grill manufacturers. Five minutes should be enough to adequately preheat your grill, but check the use and care book that came with your grill — your particular grill may take a bit longer to heat up.

Caramel Pears over Gingered Crumbs

Plentiful during the autumn and into spring when you'll be grilling indoors, pears assume a mellow flavor when grilled. Bosc pears, a brown-skinned variety that holds its shape well, is recommended for this recipe. However, Bartlett pears can also be cooked as long as they're still pale green (not yet completely yellow), a sign that they're firm and not fully ripe.

Tools: *Grill, small saucepan, microwave-safe bowl (optional), melon baller or small spoon, food processor*

Preparation time: *15 minutes*

Grilling time: *10 to 15 minutes*

Yield: *4 servings*

½ cup sugar	*2 large Bosc pears*
1 tablespoon water	*4 squares graham crackers (2 whole rectangles)*
2 tablespoons lemon juice	
2 tablespoons unsalted butter	*½ teaspoon ground ginger*

1 In a heavy small saucepan, heat the sugar with the water over medium heat, stirring with a metal spoon, until the sugar melts and begins to turn a golden caramel, 7 to 10 minutes. Remove the pan from the heat and carefully add the lemon juice down the side of the pan (the caramel will bubble and steam, so be careful). Return the pan to low heat and cook, stirring, until the caramel is syrupy. Set the caramel aside; reheat to warm before serving.

2 In a microwave-safe bowl in a microwave oven or in a small saucepan over low heat, melt the butter and set aside. Heat an indoor electric grill, grill pan, or cooktop insert over medium heat for 5 minutes. While the grill is heating, peel the pears and cut each pour lengthwise in half. With the tip of a small spoon or melon baller, scoop out the cores; remove the stems and blossom ends. Lightly brush the pear halves on all sides with some melted butter.

3 Place the pears, cut sides down, on a grill grid. Cover with a sheet of aluminum foil and grill for 5 minutes. While the pears grill, into a food processor, crumble the crackers and then process until coarse crumbs form; you can use ⅓ cup packaged graham cracker crumbs if you prefer.

4 Add the crumbs and ginger to the bowl of melted butter; toss with a fork until well mixed. Turn the pears over; cover with foil and grill 3 to 4 minutes longer or until the flesh looks opaque and is soft when pierced with a fork through the thickest part. If using a contact grill, grill pears for 8 minutes, turning and rotating them once to create crossed char marks.

5 To serve, spoon the gingered crumbs onto four dessert plates. Top with the grilled pear halves and drizzle with the caramel syrup. Serve warm or at room temperature.

Vary It! *Instead of the caramel, serve the pears with a fruit coulis. This uncooked fruit sauce is easily made by pureeing 1 cup fresh strawberries or mango with sugar to taste. The sauce can be smooth or coarse, but should be just thin enough to pour. (Couler is French for "to run.") If the coulis is too thick, thin with orange juice, orange liqueur, or lime juice. In place of the pears, use any firm cooking apple variety, such as Golden Delicious, Jonagold, Pink Lady, Gravenstein, Pippin, or Winesap.*

Nutrition at a glance (per serving): *calories 242; calories from fat 62; fat 7 g; saturated fat 4 g; cholesterol 16 mg; sodium 44 mg; carbohydrates 47 g; dietary fiber 3 g; protein 1 g*

Banana Brochettes
on Chocolate Sauce

This dessert is a light version of a combination hot fudge sundae and banana split. Although most homemade chocolate sauces call for heavy cream or butter, this simple version uses neither yet tastes rich and yummy. To grill bananas, one of the most popular fruits in the world, choose firm, just-ripe fruit. Overripe ones are too soft to grill. In addition, for this recipe, use the straightest bananas you can find. Use a grill pan, open electric grill, or cooktop insert for this recipe; avoid using a contact grill.

Tools: *Grill, bamboo skewers, small double boiler or heatproof bowl, saucepan, heatproof rubber spatula*

Preparation time: *30 minutes*

Grilling time: *7 to 12 minutes*

Yield: *4 servings*

½ cup semisweet chocolate chips	*4 scoops vanilla ice cream*
¼ cup water	*4 small sprigs fresh mint (optional)*
4 bananas (6 to 7 inches long)	
4 tablespoons chopped unsalted roasted peanuts	

1 Soak eight 6-inch bamboo skewers in water for 30 minutes. (If you can't find short skewers, cut four 12-inch skewers in half.) Place the chocolate and water in a small double boiler or a heatproof bowl, and set the pan or bowl over a saucepan with an inch of boiling water. Heat the chocolate and water, stirring with a heatproof rubber spatula, until melted smooth. Remove from the heat. Set the sauce aside.

2 Spray the grill grid with nonstick cooking spray or brush with oil to prevent food from sticking. Heat an indoor electric grill, grill pan, or cooktop insert over medium heat for 5 minutes. Drain and dry the skewers. Peel one banana and trim off about ¼ inch of the pointed ends. Cut the trimmed banana crosswise into 1-inch-thick slices. (Cut the slices evenly so that they will touch the grill surface evenly.) Place the slices, cut sides up (or down) in two rows. Insert a skewer through each row through the side of each banana slice. You should have half a banana on each skewer. Repeat to skewer the remaining bananas. (*Note:* By threading a row of bananas, the banana's cut surfaces should be at the same level for even grilling.)

3 Place the skewers of bananas on a grill grid. Grill the brochettes 1 minute or until grill marks appear on the bottom; turn the skewers and grill 1 minute longer.

4 For each serving, spoon 2 tablespoons chocolate sauce in a swirl across the center of a dessert plate. Place two skewers with the point of the skewers touching each other at the edge of the plate and the opposite ends about 3 inches apart. Place a scoop of ice cream on the plate in the opening between the skewers. Sprinkle each plate with some peanuts. Garnish with mint, if desired.

Vary It! *If you don't have mint, scatter a few raspberries or strawberries on the plate to add color. You can also replace peanuts with shelled pistachios, almonds, or hazelnuts.*

Nutrition at a glance (per serving): *calories 397; calories from fat 163; fat 18 g; saturated fat 8 g; cholesterol 29 mg; sodium 55 mg; carbohydrates 59 g; dietary fiber 4 g; protein 6 g*

Glazed Pineapple Wedges

Grown in tropical regions of the world, the pineapple is named for its pinecone-like appearance. Pineapples don't ripen after they're harvested, so select a pineapple that has a golden-yellow skin, rather than green, with fresh-looking leaves on top. Choose a small, yet heavy fruit. This recipe combines wedges of fresh pineapple with a delicious orange sauce.

Tools: *Grill, microwave-safe cup or small saucepan*

Preparation time: *10 minutes*

Grilling time: *16 to 25 minutes*

Yield: *8 servings*

1 ripe pineapple (about 3½ pounds)

¼ cup orange marmalade

1 tablespoon orange liqueur (Triple sec or Cointreau) or orange juice

1 tablespoon unsalted butter

1 Trim and cut the pineapple using Figure 15-1 and the following instructions as your guide: On a cutting board, with a sharp knife, cut the top fronds off. Cut a thin slice off the bottom. Stand the pineapple up and cut off the rind to remove the eyes. (In some areas, you may be able to purchase pineapples that are already trimmed and cored. If you buy one this way, skip the preceding and proceed with the rest of this step.) Cut the pineapple lengthwise in half, and then cut each half lengthwise so that you have 4 lengthwise wedges. Cut the core from the wedges and cut each wedge into 8 slices. Place the pieces on a tray lined with paper towels; pat the cut surfaces dry.

2 Heat an indoor electric grill, grill pan, or cooktop insert over medium-high heat for 5 minutes. While the grill is heating, in a microwave-safe cup in a microwave oven or small saucepan over low heat, heat the orange marmalade with the orange liqueur and butter until syrupy in consistency.

3 Place the pineapple, half of them at a time, on the grill grid of an open grill, a grill pan, or a cooktop insert, with one of the flat cut sides down. Cover the pan with a sheet of aluminum foil. Grill the pineapple until grill marks appear on the bottom, about 2½ to 5 minutes. Turn the pineapple to the other flat side and grill 2 to 4 minutes longer. Turn the pineapple so that the cored side is up and grill the rounded, skinned side down for 1 minute. If using a contact grill, place the pineapple on the grill grid with one of the flat cut sides down for about 2 minutes. Transfer the grilled pineapple to a plate with the cored side up and brush each flat side with orange glaze.

Nutrition at a glance (per serving): calories 89; calories from fat 17; fat 2 g; saturated fat 1 g; cholesterol 4 mg; sodium 7 mg; carbohydrates 20 g; dietary fiber 1 g; protein 0 g

Grilled Angel Cake and Blueberry "Cobbler"

The topping for this whimsical cobbler is a tender, grilled cake instead of the buttery biscuit topping that's most often associated with old-fashioned cobblers. And although the classic usually requires several steps in its preparation and about three-quarters of an hour of oven baking, this unusual version is quick and contains little cholesterol and fat.

Tools: *Grill, medium saucepan, serrated knife*

Preparation time: *15 minutes*

Grilling time: *10 to 12 minutes*

Yield: *6 servings*

½ cup sugar

2 tablespoons cornstarch

1 cup bottled unsweetened apple juice

10- or 12-ounce package frozen blueberries

1 tablespoon lemon juice

10½-ounce loaf bakery angel food cake

¼ cup sliced almonds, toasted

1 In a medium saucepan, combine the sugar and cornstarch until mixed. Stir in the apple juice until smooth. Cook the mixture over medium heat, stirring constantly until thickened and bubbly. Reduce the heat to low and stir in the frozen blueberries; heat just until bubbles appear around the side of the saucepan. Stir in the lemon juice. Pour the blueberries into an 8-inch glass cake dish or casserole dish. Cover and keep warm. (Or make this ahead and microwave to reheat just before grilling.)

2 Spray the grill grid with nonstick cooking spray or brush with oil to prevent food from sticking. Heat an indoor electric grill, grill pan, or cooktop insert over medium heat for 5 minutes. While the grill is heating, with a serrated knife and using a sawing motion, cut the cake horizontally in half to split the cake into two layers. Wrap and use one half in another recipe. Cut the remaining cake half into 8 chunks. Grill the cake chunks, turning frequently, until lightly browned on all sides, about 5 to 7 minutes. Using a contact grill may take a minute or two less, but keep rotating the cake chunks to keep them from burning.

3 Just before serving, use your fingers to tear each cake chunk in half so that they're irregular pieces. Dot the top of the blueberries with a layer of grilled cake, pressing the torn sides of the cake down into the blueberries. Sprinkle the "cobbler" with toasted almonds and serve.

Vary It! *Serve with a dollop of nonfat sour cream or vanilla nonfat yogurt.*

Nutrition at a glance (per serving): *calories 214; calories from fat 26; fat 3 g; saturated fat 0 g; cholesterol 0 mg; sodium 188 mg; carbohydrates 46 g; dietary fiber 3 g; protein 3 g*

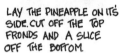

Figure 15-1:
Trimming and cutting a pineapple isn't as difficult as you may think.

TRIM AND CUT PINEAPPLE

1. LAY THE PINEAPPLE ON ITS SIDE. CUT OFF THE TOP FRONDS AND A SLICE OFF THE BOTTOM.

2. WITH THE PINEAPPLE UPRIGHT, CUT OFF THE EYES WITH A KNIFE.

3. CUT IN HALF

4. CUT AGAIN INTO WEDGES OR SLICES.

You can reduce fat even further by removing the almonds from this recipe, but keep in mind that almonds contain "good" fat: According to the Almond Board of California, adding 3 ounces of almonds a day to your healthy diet can lower cholesterol as much as 30 points in 30 days.

Toasted Buttery Pound Cake with Rum Syrup and Grilled Oranges

Rich, buttery pound cake has a wonderful affinity with rum, all enhanced with a cinnamon-spiced syrup dotted with cranberries. Oranges offer a tart contrast to this sweet dessert.

Tools: *Grill, small saucepan*

Preparation time: *15 minutes*

Grilling time: *16 to 17 minutes*

Yield: *8 servings*

½ cup water	Two 3-inch cinnamon sticks
¼ cup light or golden rum	4 medium navel oranges
¼ cup dried cranberries or cherries	10¾-ounce loaf frozen all-butter pound cake, thawed
2 tablespoons sugar	

1 Prepare the Rum Syrup: In a small saucepan, combine the water, rum, dried cranberries, sugar, and cinnamon sticks. Bring to boiling over medium heat. Reduce the heat to low and simmer for 3 minutes. Remove the syrup from the heat and let stand while you prepare the rest of the dessert.

2 On a cutting board, with a sharp knife, trim the tops and bottom off the oranges. Then cut all the peel and white pith from the flesh of the oranges. Cut each orange crosswise into ½-inch-thick slices. Drain the slices on a tray lined with paper towels. Cut the pound cake into 8 slices.

3 Spray the grill grid with nonstick cooking spray or brush with oil to prevent the food from sticking. Heat an open grill, a grill pan, or a cooktop insert over medium heat for 5 minutes. Grill the pound cake slices until grill marks appear on the bottom, about 1 minute. Turn the slices over and grill until marks appear on the other side. Rotate the cake slices a quarter turn and grill until crossed marks appear. Turn the slices over and repeat to create crossed marks on the other side. (It will take a total of about 5 minutes to grill the cake slices.) If using a contact grill, heat for 5 minutes over medium heat and grill the pound cake for 2 minutes, turning and rotating slices one time for crossed char marks. Transfer the cake slices to a round serving plate, arrange them around the edge.

4 Grill the orange slices in a single layer on an open grill, in a grill pan, or on a cooktop insert until grill marks appear on the bottom, about 4 minutes. Turn the slices and grill 2 to 3 minutes longer. If using a contact grill, grill slices 8 to 10 minutes, lifting the cover several times to let the excess moisture escape. Place the grilled oranges in the center of the plate with some over the cake slices. Discard the cinnamon sticks, if desired, and spoon rum syrup with cranberries over the pound cake and orange slices.

Vary It! In place of the cinnamon, make the syrup with star anise or whole cloves.

Nutrition at a glance (per serving): calories 199; calories from fat 59; fat 7 g; saturated fat 4 g; cholesterol 54 mg; sodium 139 mg; carbohydrates 33 g; dietary fiber 2 g; protein 3 g

 Check your grocery store for low-fat or nonfat pound cakes.

Indoor S'mores

By grilling indoors, you can enjoy this popular sweet gooey treat any time of the year. Because you can't roast marshmallows on an indoor electric grill, in a grill pan, or on a cooktop insert, the next best thing is to grill the graham crackers to melt the chocolate. This recipe shows you how.

Tools: *Grill*

Preparation time: *2 minutes*

Grilling time: *8½ to 11 minutes*

Yield: *4 servings*

1 Hershey's milk chocolate candy bar (1.55 ounces)	*8 squares graham cracker (2 whole rectangles)*
4 tablespoons marshmallow cream	

1 Heat an indoor electric grill, grill pan, or cooktop insert over medium heat for 5 minutes. Break the candy bar crosswise into quarters with 3 rectangles in each piece. Top half of the cracker squares with a quarter piece of candy bar placed in the center. Spread marshmallow on the remaining 4 crackers. Place a marshmallow cracker, marshmallow side down, on top of the chocolate cracker. Press together.

2 Grill the crackers with the chocolate side down on the grill grid until chocolate begins to soften, about 3 to 5 minutes; turn and grill the other side 30 seconds to 1 minute longer or until chocolate melts.

Vary It! *For a S'mores Club, spread peanut butter on four cracker squares and put them, buttered side down, on top of the chocolate candy before adding the marshmallow squares.*

Nutrition at a glance (per serving): *calories 177; calories from fat 44; fat 5 g; saturated fat 2 g; cholesterol 2 mg; sodium 100 mg; carbohydrates 32 g; dietary fiber 1 g; protein 2 g*

Part V
The Part of Tens

The 5th Wave　　By Rich Tennant

FOR ADDED REALISM, THE BENSONS USE ANT FARMS FOR CENTERPIECES AT THEIR INDOOR GRILL PICNIC

What is this-some sort of sick joke?

In this part . . .

This part is a quick read — each chapter, made up of ten "bests," takes just a minute to peruse — but covers essentials such as making your grilled meals lean and healthy and your grilled meals as memorable as possible.

Chapter 16

Ten Great Reasons to Grill Indoors

· ·

In This Chapter

▶ Discovering ten benefits of grilling indoors

▶ Finding out why your next meal should be a grilled one!

· ·

*G*rilling indoors is fun, easy, inexpensive, and delicious! This chapter shares ten fantastic reasons to grill indoors.

Grilling Is a Healthy Form of Cooking

Grilling ranks right up there with broiling, boiling, and baking as one of the healthiest ways to cook meat. A 3-ounce grilled chicken breast, for example, weighs in at 120 calories and 2 grams of fat. Take that same chicken breast, roll it in flour, and deep-fry it, and you've increased the calories to 220 with 7 grams of fat!

Grilling cannot, however, make fatty foods healthier for you. If you cook two identical pieces of meat, one on a grill and one in a frying pan (not a deep-fat fryer that uses grease to boil food, but a flat pan on which you cook hamburgers, grilled cheese, and pancakes), the fat content will be identical, in spite of the fact that the former will not be sitting in grease on the grill and the latter *will* be in the frying pan.

To get the most out of the health benefits of grilling, choose lean foods (veggies, seafood, lean meats, skinless poultry), and trim all visible fat from foods. Check out Chapter 18 for ideas on how to keep your meal lean. Reference the chapters in Part III for tips on how to choose lean cuts of a variety of meats, poultry, and seafood.

Grilled Food Tastes Delicious!

Because grilled meats aren't sitting in grease as they cook, you taste the flavor of foods, not the flavor of *grease.* The flavor of vegetables and fruits, too, is enhanced by a few minutes on the grill, as long as you take care not to burn these tender foods. (See Chapters 11 and 15 for tips on grilling vegetables and fruits, respectively.)

Those Char Marks Look Cool

Face it — char marks are hip, which makes grilling hip. Baked and broiled foods have no personality; they're just plain as can be. Perhaps char marks give people a psychological boost, too: In the middle of winter, grilled food makes people think of lazy summer days.

Indoor Grills Are Cheaper than Outdoor Grills

The most expensive indoor grills on the market cost roughly $100. The most expensive gas grills cost more than a brand-new small car. Outdoor grilling experts frequently reference a growing phenomenon, in which people are "taking the kitchen outside" and spending on their outdoor grill areas what they may have spent remodeling their kitchens. But here's the key to indoor grilling: Instead of taking the kitchen outside and spending $10,000, you can bring the outside to the kitchen and spend from $20 to $120.

Of course, some people do both: They grill on their outdoor rigs when the weather cooperates and grill indoors when it doesn't.

You Can Grill Regardless of the Weather

Snow, sleet, rain, or extreme heat don't have to change your decision to grill. Oh sure, you'll get a reputation for being hardy if you don a hat, gloves, boots, and a heavy coat in order to grill your dinner in the middle of the snowstorm, but wouldn't you rather just wear sweats and slippers, stand at your stovetop or countertop, and experience the same great taste?

Grilling indoors lets you grill whenever you want, in any weather, at any time of the day.

You Can Grill Every Day

This is a corollary to the preceding section: If you can grill regardless of the weather, it stands to reason that you can grill every day. Some people think of grilling as a "special" way to cook — once in a while or when company comes — and instead, microwave, bake, and broil the rest of the time. But with a conveniently located indoor grill, grill pan, or cooktop insert, you can literally grill every day. And why not? It's healthy, tasty, and hip!

Indoor Grills Heat Up Faster than Outdoor Grills

The preceding section discusses grilling every day, made possible by indoor grillers' blatant disregard for weather conditions *and* by the fact that indoor grills warm up so quickly. One reason that people save grilling for special times is that no one has time to spend 20 to 30 minutes heating up a charcoal grill (or 10 to 15 minutes heating up a gas grill). Grill pans and most indoor electric grills and cooktop inserts preheat in five to ten minutes, which considerably cuts your time spent preparing a meal.

Be sure to read the instructions that come with your grill or cooktop insert. You may find that your particular model requires more than five minutes to preheat, although most models don't.

Indoor Grills Don't Take Up Much Space

Compared to outdoor models, indoor grills are space savers. Many are smaller than a breadbox (or a bread machine); you can probably store yours on a shelf, in a cupboard, or in a deep drawer. Wherever you keep it, be sure to keep it handy so that you can grill every day.

Indoor grills are growing in size and a few come with their own stands, so you may soon see a time when they don't take up any less space than outdoor grills. In fact, the indoor grill market is expanding to include indoor/outdoor grills in an effort to capture more of the outdoor grilling market, too.

You Can Grill on a Balcony or in an Apartment

Although most condominium associations and apartment managers place restrictions on using outdoor grills anywhere near living areas, the same isn't usually true of indoor grills. Because indoor grills don't cook on open flames (as gas and charcoal grills do), they pose little danger to the community.

This doesn't mean, however, that indoor grills don't have to be watched. Keep a close eye on your indoor grill as you cook, watching for overheating.

Cleanup Is Fast and Easy

Many indoor grills boast nonstick surfaces and dishwasher-safe parts, so cleanup is a cinch. No metal cleaning brushes and scrapers required: All you usually need is a soapy sponge. Cleaning a grill pan is a little trickier, but not by much. See Chapter 3 for the lowdown on cleaning your grill, grill pan, or cooktop insert.

Chapter 17

Ten Ways to Make Grilling Healthy and Safe

· ·

In This Chapter

▶ Maintaining your grill properly

▶ Marinating safely

▶ Handling food correctly

· ·

*I*ndoor grilling is a safe way to cook, but as with all cooking, you need to take certain precautions. This chapter shares 11 tips (we got a bit carried away!) for making your indoor grilling experience safe and healthy.

Chapter 3 gives additional tips for staying safe when grilling. The chapters in Part III also share food-specific safety tips.

Buy Meats, Poultry, and Seafood Last

Make the meat, poultry, and seafood sections of your supermarket the last place you visit before going to the checkout counter. Food can spoil in your cart while you shop for other items on your list.

In hot weather, bring a cooler and some ice packs in your car and place meat, poultry, and seafood into the cooler for the ride home.

Shop Carefully

Check the sell-by dates on all products and look for mushiness, off colors, or strong smells. If you're the least bit in doubt about whether to buy a product, don't. Chances are, the food has begun to spoil and could sicken you and your family if you eat it.

Check out the chapters in Part III for details on what to look for as you shop for specific types of foods.

Thaw Foods in the Refrigerator

Don't thaw meat, poultry, or seafood on the countertop. By planning ahead (moving food for the next day's meal from the freezer to the fridge before you go to bed), you can cook with thoroughly defrosted foods without letting it spoil.

If you get into a time crunch, use your microwave to defrost foods. Many microwaves have an auto-weight defrost feature. Enter the weight of the meat or poultry you're defrosting, and it does the rest, prompting you to turn or flip the food from time to time. Microwaves are powerful, however, so keep a close eye on the food as it defrosts so that the food doesn't actually start to cook.

Marinate Foods in the Refrigerator

Marinating on the countertop is exactly like thawing on the countertop; both can expose you to spoiled food. Instead, marinate all foods in the refrigerator.

Don't Use Metal Pans to Marinate Food

All metal containers (except for stainless steel) react with the marinade and give an awful, metallic flavor to marinated foods. Be sure the bowl is *nonreactive;* that is, not made of a metal such as aluminum. Use glass, ceramic, or plastic containers, which won't react with the acids in the marinades. See Chapter 3 for more tips on marinating.

Throw Away Your Marinade after You Use It

Back when people didn't think so much about bacteria, people used to pour excess marinade over cooked foods to add additional flavor. Don't do this today. Marinades pick up whatever bacteria may be on the foods you're grilling (this bacteria is killed by cooking to the proper temperature — see the following section), so by pouring a marinade over cooked food, you could be pouring bacteria over food just before you eat it. If you must reuse the marinade, heat it to boiling to kill whatever may be in there. A better bet, however, is to whip up a new batch for the pour-over.

Always Grill to the Proper Temperature

To kill bacteria that may linger in uncooked meat, poultry, and seafood, you must grill these foods to a certain temperature. The chapters in Part III, as well as the Cheat Sheet in the front of this book, spell out the proper temperatures for a variety of foods. Use a thermometer (see Chapter 2) to check the temperature as your food grills.

Don't insert the thermometer until the outside of the food is seared, or the thermometer itself could carry bacteria into the interior of the food.

Don't Cross-Contaminate

The bacteria that may be present in, say, your hamburger, can cross-contaminate your tomatoes if you put the raw burger and tomatoes on the same plate or touch the tomatoes after handling the raw meat. Keep cooked and uncooked foods completely separate.

After the burger is cooked, of course, tomatoes are a perfect partner.

Wash Hands, Knives, Cutting Boards, and Sponges with Soapy Water

Because you can cross-contaminate foods in your kitchen, wash everything (hands, knives, cutting boards, countertops, faucet knobs) that may have touched raw meat, poultry, or seafood. We've heard stories recently of families handling raw hamburgers or chicken breast, and then tearing up lettuce for a salad without washing their hands. The result? Entire families are sickened, not by the hamburger or chicken breast, because they were cooked to the proper temperature, but by the lettuce, which harbored bacteria that came from the food before it was cooked.

Also wash your sponge by adding liquid detergent to it and squeezing the sponge until the suds disappear. Run your sponge through the dishwasher every few days and replace it every few weeks.

Position Your Grill away from Cabinets

Although indoor grills don't cook with an open flame, grills can build up quite a bit of heat. Position your indoor grill so that it's away from the upper cabinets in your kitchen. If you're unsure whether your grill is heating the cabinets, touch the bottom of your cabinets as soon as you turn off your grill. If the cabinet is hot to the touch, position your indoor grill elsewhere in the future.

Use Long-Handled Utensils

As the size of *grill grids* (the surface on which you grill foods) increases on indoor grills, so, too, does the risk that you can burn yourself as your arm or face gets too close to the grid. When indoor grill grids were small, grillers could use regular-sized kitchen utensils to work with the food on the grill; a better bet these days is to buy long-handled utensils — spatulas, forks, tongs, mitts, and brushes — that were originally created for outdoor grillers.

Many longer-handled grilling tools tend to be metal, because they're designed for outdoor grills, which don't feature a nonstick coating. Many indoor grills use a nonstick coating on the grill grid, however, and metal tools will eventually scratch the coating. As manufacturers begin to design longer-handled nylon grilling tools, we predict you'll see a large variety of long-handled, nonstick grilling tools in the near future.

Be sure that tools designed for nonstick surfaces are labeled as being "heat resistant," preferably up to about 500 degrees.

Chapter 18

Ten Ways to Stay Lean and Healthy

In This Chapter
▶ Finding ways to make your meals healthier
▶ Reducing fat and calories in grilled foods

*M*any people purchase an indoor grill in the hopes that, by cooking with it, their foods will be healthier. Here's the reality: Grilling is, hands down, one of the healthiest ways to cook, but it can't make unhealthy foods any healthier. For that, you have to make some changes in your diet. This chapter gives you 10, er, 11, ways to make simple changes that add up to a real difference in how you look and feel.

Eat a Variety of Foods

Eating a variety is essential: If, say, you eat hash browns and a sausage sandwich for breakfast; a burger, fries, and a soda for lunch; and a grilled steak with potatoes for dinner, the "grilled" part of "grilled steak" isn't going to make you any healthier. You've eaten only beef, potatoes, bread, and a soda throughout your day, which isn't much of a variety. Instead, you want to eat something like this:

   ✔ **Breakfast:** Fresh fruit, a small bowl of oatmeal, and yogurt

   ✔ **Lunch:** Roast beef sandwich on pumpernickel, baby carrots and red pepper strips, and tomato juice

   ✔ **Dinner:** Grilled salmon with almonds, steamed broccoli, rice dish, and a bowl of ice cream

Although this isn't necessarily a low-fat or low-calorie diet, it is filling and healthy, giving you whole grains, a wide variety of fresh fruits and vegetables, dairy products, healthy nuts, lean meat, and omega-3 fatty acids (see Chapter 10). If, the next day, you add more variety and develop this as a habit, before long, your health will improve dramatically.

An easy way to determine whether you're eating a variety of foods is to look at colors and textures. If everything you eat is tan-colored and fairly mushy, you're mostly eating the same foods. But if you're eating foods that are bright red, orange, off-white, dark brown, pink, and dark green and if the textures range from soft to crunchy with everything in between, chances are, you're eating a healthy diet.

Consider Your Condiments

Condiments, such as sauces, spreads, and toppings, can add fat and calories to your meal. Whenever possible, go condiment-free or choose lower-fat, lower-calorie condiments such as salsa, chutney, mustard, and Tabasco sauce. See Chapter 5 for some light sauce ideas.

To add additional flavoring without adding many calories or much fat, consider marinating your foods before grilling it. Chapter 4 gives you a variety of marinade recipes, many of which are low in fat and calories.

Eat Seafood

Seafood is incredibly healthy. Low in calories and fat (including saturated fat), most seafood also contains omega-3 fatty acids that protect your heart. In fact, omega-3 fatty acids are considered "good fat"; nutritionists recommend eating foods high in omega-3s once or twice per week. A 3-ounce serving of seafood ranges from 70 to 150 calories, with 1 to 7 grams of fat. Most seafood is also extremely high in protein. See Chapter 10 for great grilled seafood recipes.

Go Vegetarian

Although becoming vegetarian is difficult in a fast-food culture, it is an option for improving your health. Most foods that are high in saturated fats come from animals, so by eliminating animal products, you can eliminate many opportunities to consume fat-laden calories. And by combining beans and rice at the same meal, you can still give your body an excellent source of protein.

Many people are going "mostly" vegetarian, meaning that they eat seafood once or twice per week, and occasionally eat lean cuts of poultry and beef, focusing most of their eating on vegetarian fare. This way, they still eat foods that pack plenty of healthy vitamins and minerals while eating more than their share of vegetables, fruits, and whole grains. Chapter 11 gives you a wide variety of grilled vegetable recipes, and Chapter 15 has recipes for grilled fruit.

You can still be unhealthy as a vegetarian. If you consume mostly peanut products, for example, your diet won't have the variety you need in order to be healthy. As a vegetarian, you have to work even harder than consumers of meat, poultry, seafood, and dairy to eat a well-rounded, nutritious, varied diet.

Don't Count Meat Out

Lean beef is a high-quality source of protein, B-vitamins, zinc, and iron, so unless you're a vegetarian, don't count it out. Grilled cuts of lean beef can be good for you! See Chapter 7 for the lowdown on grilled beef.

Look for Cuts of Beef That Have "Loin" or "Round" in the Name

Beef cuts with the words "loin" or "round" in the name are the leanest you can buy. Look specifically for these words when shopping for beef, and make a habit of steering clear of other cuts of beef.

Buy Extra-Lean Ground Beef

You don't have to cut out burgers to consume a healthy diet. Just make each burger a healthier one, and limit your intake to one every week or so. To make a healthy burger, do the following:

- ✔ Buy extra-lean ground beef — it's usually labeled "96 percent fat-free."

  You can also buy ground turkey breast, which is often 98 percent fat-free. It'll make a burger that tastes a bit like turkey, but it'll still be a tasty sandwich. Don't bother with ground turkey that isn't made from turkey breast; it's not very lean.

- ✔ Use a whole-wheat or pumpernickel bun or bagel instead of a standard white-bread bun.

- ✔ Add healthy veggies like tomatoes, pickles, red or green pepper strips, and lettuce. In fact, consider grilling tomatoes and pepper strips before adding them to your burger.

- ✔ Use low-calorie, low-fat condiments, such as salsa, ketchup, and mustard. Avoid higher-fat mayonnaise, cheese, and bacon on your burger.

See Chapter 6 for delicious grilled burger recipes.

Look for Pork Tenderloin

Pork can also be a healthy meat, if you don't consume it often and if you stick to pork tenderloin over other cuts of meat. Pork tenderloin has only 140 calories and 4 grams of fat per 3-ounce serving: That's less than nearly all lean cuts of beef! See Chapter 8 for information on and recipes for grilled pork.

Pork tenderloin can be pricey, but buy it on sale and freeze it for future use.

Trim All Fat from Meat

The old rule was that you left ⅛ inch of fat around cuts of meat to add "flavor." More modern research suggests that leaving any visible fat adds only fat and calories to meat. Before grilling any meat, cut away any fat that you see around the edge of the cut. If you buy pork tenderloin or beef loin and round cuts, you won't see much fat, but cut what you see anyway.

Choose White Meat over Dark

Ground turkey breast (white meat) is much healthier than ground turkey thigh (dark meat). A chicken breast (white meat) has far less fat than a chicken drumstick (dark meat). So here's the rule: No matter what kind of poultry you're selecting, choose white meat over dark. See Chapter 9 for the goods on grilling poultry.

Remove the Skin from Poultry

For a 3-ounce portion of poultry (that's about the size of a deck of cards), skin adds from 40 to 60 calories and adds 5 grams of fat. It's not worth it. Start taking the skin off, and within a month or two, you'll wonder why you were ever interested in such a fat-laden piece of food.

Chapter 19

Ten Ways to Make Your Grilled Meals Memorable

. . . .

In This Chapter

▶ Creating an inviting atmosphere

▶ Planning a memorable meal

▶ Finding other ways to make your dinner special

. . . .

Chapter 14 gives you ideas for making a meal special, both in the setting and in the foods you prepare, and shares four distinctive, delicious recipes for special days. This chapter builds off that idea, giving you ten quick ways to take an everyday meal and make it extraordinary.

Make an All-Grilled Meal

Go hog-wild and make a meal that has char marks on every possible piece of food. Start with grilled appetizers (see Chapter 13), add a salad made with grilled foods (see Chapter 12), serve a grilled main dish (see the chapters in Part III), prepare a grilled vegetable side dish (see Chapter 11), and create a grilled dessert (see Chapter 15)!

Because most indoor grills aren't very expensive, use two or three at a once to make an all-grilled meal in no time.

Create an Indoor Picnic

Because you and your trusty indoor grill have an advantage over outdoor grillers, you can create an indoor picnic, barbecue, or party any time of the year. Invite your friends to a winter solstice barbecue or a Fourth of February picnic. Set out blankets to sit on and serve grilled burgers (see Chapter 5), grilled chicken wings (see Chapter 13), and other sunny favorites.

Vary Your Food Routine

If you find yourself eating the same types of foods day in and day out, use the recipes in Parts III and IV to liven up your routine. If you always make burgers, consider trying grilled shrimp (see Chapters 10 and 13). If you've never eaten grilled lamb, check out the recipe in Chapter 14. Try grilled veggies (Chapter 11) and fruits (Chapter 15), and you'll make your dinner guests (even if that's just your family!) sit up and take notice.

Consider the Presentation

Plan your meal so that each plate displays an array of colors and textures. Instead of serving plain chicken breast (off-white), potatoes with butter (off-white), and corn (light yellow), make Chicken with Tomatillo Avocado Salsa (Chapter 9), Eggplant Antipasto and Corn Stuffed Tomatoes (Chapter 11), and Grilled Angel Cake and Blueberry "Cobbler" (Chapter 15). That's off-white, green, purple, light yellow, red, white, and blue. Such a blaze of color will make any dinner memorable!

Begin with Appetizers

Chapter 13 gives you about a dozen appetizer recipes that you can prepare simply and quickly on your indoor grill. And by leafing through the chapters in Part III and adjusting the servings accordingly, you can use dozens of other recipes in this book to make delicious, appealing appetizers that will brighten any meal.

Dine by Candlelight

Want to stir things up? Light some candles and turn off the lights. Your roommates, friends, spouse, and/or children won't know what happened to their boring old dinner routine. Add a delicious grilled meal, and they won't complain about having a hard time seeing their plates.

Serve a Vintage Wine or Other Delicious Beverages

Serve whatever your guests love, regardless of whether it's an "appropriate" dinner beverage. Kids love Kool-Aid? Go for it! Hot chocolate in the middle of summer? Why not? Lemonade in winter? Sure! Grilled foods go with nearly any kind of beverage.

When you want to break out a tasty wine for the adults at your meal but aren't sure which type to serve, check out *Wine For Dummies,* 2nd Edition, by Ed McCarthy and Mary Ewing-Mulligan (Hungry Minds, Inc.).

Finish with a Scrumptious Dessert

Flip through Chapter 15, and you'll find half a dozen of the most interesting desserts you can imagine — and all made on the grill. From Banana Brochettes on Chocolate Sauce to Indoor S'mores, you'll find something to liven up your meal.

Invite Interesting People to Dinner

This is a bit of a no-brainer: If you invite your neighbor Rhoda to dinner, and she talks about her root canal, you're going to have a less interesting meal than if, say, you invite the Dalai Lama or Oprah to dinner. (No guarantee that they'll come, of course, but the fact that you invited them — and, at best, they politely declined or, at worst, took out a restraining order — could make interesting dinner conversation.)

Invite Kids and Pets to Your Dinner

Kids and pets always make meals lively, which, under the right circumstances, could be translated as "interesting" or "memorable." Kids often spill things, say the darndest things, ask funny questions, and complain about new foods. Pets may beg for food, pull down tablecloths, and occasionally jump up on people's laps. No one can ever claim that wasn't memorable.

Appendix

Resources

• •

*W*e've designed this appendix to give you additional indoor grilling resources. Here, you can find a list of major grill manufacturers (and a couple of retailers), a few Web sites that offer additional grilling information, additional sources of recipes, and a listing of online retail food shops.

We've listed every resource alphabetically within its section so as to avoid favoritism.

Grill Manufacturers

We had originally planned to list all the indoor grills that we could find at the time of this printing and give information on each. What we found, though, is that new grills are introduced just about every month, so the list would be hopelessly out of date within six months of printing this book. Instead, we've listed the major grill manufacturers. (Check out indoor grills offered by All-Clad, Calphalon, KitchenAid, Krups, and Lodge as well.)

- ✔ **Black and Decker:** Black and Decker has marketed their first indoor grill, an open electric model. They've built in some interesting features, such as a Flavor Scenter Well (for marinades, liquid smoke, sauces, or fruit juices) that enhances the aroma of foods and a splatter shield that protects your walls and countertop from grease. Their model features variable temperature control, a nonstick grill grid, and dishwasher-safe parts. Visit them online at www.householdproductsinc.com/cooking.htm, and click on Indoor Grills/Skillets, and then click on Product Information. You can also reach Black and Decker at 800-231-9786.

- ✔ **DeLonghi:** DeLonghi makes a range of incredibly innovative (and good looking!) indoor grills. Their Web site is the best way to view their products, which you can also purchase at department stores and specialty retailers. Visit www.delonghi.com/sitodl98en/index.htm and click on the Contact Grills or Indoor Barbecues tabs for more information.

- **Farberware:** In addition to manufacturing an *electric grill pan* (a round, open indoor grill with a cover) that's worth checking out, Farberware makes what is possibly the most unique indoor electric grill on the market — one with a rotisserie attachment. A *rotisserie* cooks above the grill grid, turning food at a slow, constant speed so that it never burns. It's perfect for grilling roasts, leg of lamb, or any other large pieces of meat. We don't cover rotisserie cooking in this book because most indoor grills can't be used in this way. For tips on using a rotisserie, check out *Grilling For Dummies* by Marie Rama and John Mariani (Hungry Minds, Inc.).

  To view Farberware's grills online, visit `www.farberware.com:80/catalog/The_Salton_Web_Page.htm`. Click on the View Our Products link, and then click on Farberware Electric Healthy Gourmet Grill Pan or Farberware Open Hearth Smokeless Indoor Grill/Rotisserie. Note that, although both of these grills are marketed under the Farberware name, Farberware is part of the same company as Salton-Maxim, the people who make the George Foreman grills.

- **Hamilton Beach:** Go to `www.hamiltonbeach.com`, click on the Hamilton Beach home appliance button, and click on the Indoor Grills link. There, you'll find pictures and information on their wide variety of well-made Health Smart and Meal Maker indoor grills and contact grills, many of which have adjustable temperature controls, nonstick surfaces, and dishwasher-safe parts. You can also call Hamilton Beach at 800-851-8900. *Note:* Hamilton Beach and Proctor-Silex are part of the same company; Proctor-Silex is just beginning to market indoor electric grills, so look for more of these in the future.

- **Le Creuset:** Le Creuset makes fabulous porcelain enamel on cast-iron grill pans. Visit them online at `www.lecreuset.com` or call 877-CREUSET. To see an array of all the great colors in which you can purchase one of their grill pans, log on to `www.greattable.com/productguide_lc2.php?line=1`. Granted, the exterior color of your grill pan isn't that important, but if you can get colors like "flame" or "saffron" into your kitchen, why not?

- **Oster:** Oster manufactures an open electric grill that includes variable temperature control that shows the actual temperature (instead of "low," "medium," and "high"), nonstick surface, and dishwasher-safe parts. The owner's manual also contains several recipes. Visit `www.oster.com/productpantry/ourproducts.asp` and select Indoor Grills in the drop-down menu. You can also call their Customer Service hotline at 800-526-2832.

- **Philips:** The same people who mass-manufactured the world's flat-panel television have also created the Philips Indoor/Outdoor grill, an easy-care, multi-featured open electric grill that features adjustable temperature control, a nonstick grill grid, dishwasher-safe parts, and a special area of the grill that's for keeping foods warm after they're finished cooking. It's worth a look at `philipsonline.com/specs/Specs.cgi?Model=HL4500`.

✔ **Salton (George Foreman grills):** To look at the multitude of George Foreman grills that Salton manufactures, visit `www.salton-maxim.com/salton/default.asp`, click on the George Foreman's Grilling Machine link, and click on the View Our Products link. There, you'll find information on nearly a dozen contact grills and grill pans. In addition, Salton gives information on what we think is the future of indoor grills: the George Foreman Indoor/Outdoor Electric Bar-B-Que Grill, a large, open electric grill, complete with a removable stand, that has a domed lid, which makes the grill cook like an outdoor charcoal grill. You get the ease of indoor grilling with the taste and control of larger, outdoor grills. And because this product is on a stand, you can use it outdoors. Salton plans to market an entire line of indoor/outdoor grills in the future. See Chapter 2 for more information.

✔ **T-Fal:** T-Fal, the original creators of nonstick cookware, feature a variety of indoor grills, including a cool double-decker model that keeps grilled foods warm while you grill more for your meal. Visit them at `www.t-fal.com/products/appliance/barbecue/bbq.html`, and keep in mind that they call their indoor grills "barbecues," so look for this link as you search their site.

✔ **West Bend:** West Bend manufactures a well-priced electric grill (called the Heart Smart electric indoor grill) that has an adjustable temperature control, nonstick grill grid, and dishwasher-safe parts. Look for more information on their Web site at `www.westbend.com`, by clicking on "Specialty Electrics." You can also order replacement products directly from their site.

When shopping for an electric grill, remember to look for an adjustable temperature control, dishwasher-safe parts (especially the drip tray), a large grill grid, and a steam vent (for contact grills). When looking for a grill pan, shop for a heavy-duty one that is either made of cast iron or has a nonstick coating, and be sure to use a mitt or handle glove if the handle doesn't stay cool. Chapter 2 has more information about electric grill and grill pan features.

If you're looking for a cooktop insert (see Chapter 2), check out the Jenn-Air, GE, and Amana Web sites, or visit your local major appliance store for more information.

Grilling Web Sites

Web sites that specialize in indoor grilling are few and far between, so we've created one that we'll keep adding to and improving with time. To stay current, search the Web for "indoor grilling," "grilling," and "grill." Most of what you'll find are product-specific sites that sell everything from bottled marinades to grills, but they may be of help to you. See the following section for sites that specialize in grilling recipes.

✔ **About.com:** About.com features information about nearly everything under the sun, and the information at `bbq.about.com/food/bbq/` is no different. Although this site is geared toward outdoor grilling, you can still glean some useful indoor grilling information from it.

✔ **The Grilling Institute of America:** This site has traditionally provided expert advice at `www.grillinginstitute.com/`. Although their site is temporarily down as of the writing of this book, we've included the site in the hopes that it'll be up and running in the near future.

✔ **The Indoor Grilling Web site:** Admittedly, this is a shameless plug for our Web site at `www.indoorgrilling.com`, but we're not selling anything on it (besides copies of this book), so we feel good about advertising what is, essentially, more information about indoor grilling.

Web Recipe Resources

Although this book contains over 80 delicious recipes, you may decide you need even more — good for you! Check out the following Web sites for even more recipes and be sure to check your local supermarket throughout the year for recipe cards that feature grilled foods:

✔ **All Recipes:** All Recipes at `www.allrecipes.com/directory/1499.asp`, features a wealth of grilling recipes, including several vegetarian ones.

✔ **Better Homes and Gardens:** The Better Homes Kitchen at `www.bhg.com/food/grillguide/grill1.htm` has cooked up some scrumptious grilling recipes.

✔ **Culinary Café:** Visit `www.culinarycafe.com/Barbeque.html` for an extensive buffet of recipes for grilled foods, including ones that are low in fat and calories.

✔ **Epicurious Food:** You can find an array of recipes, including several for marinades at `www.epicurious.com/e_eating/e04_out_grill/out_intro.html`.

✔ **Hamilton Beach:** Hamilton Beach, makers of one of the widest selections of indoor grills, gives a bunch of helpful recipes on their Web site. Go to `www.hamiltonbeach.com`, click on the Hamilton Beach home appliance button, click on the Indoor Grills link, and click on the Recipes tab.

✔ **Laura's Lean:** Laura's Lean beef comes from cattle raised on natural grains and grasses, without the use of growth hormones or antibiotics. But even if you don't use their products, check out their Web site at `www.laurasleanbeef.com` and click on the Reluctant Chef tab. There you'll find plenty of beef recipes that you can cook up on your indoor grill.

✔ **Salton-Maxim:** The makers of the George Foreman grills shares delicious recipes, many designed especially for contact grills, at `www.salton-maxim.com/salton/grill/georgeforeman.asp` (click on Scrumptious Recipes).

✔ **Tabasco:** The Tabasco Sauce Web site at `www.TABASCO.com/html/recipes_sauces_condiments.html`, has delightful recipes for marinades and sauces.

Mail-Order Foods

When you're looking for something unique or just don't want the hassle of trying to find fresh meats in your area, check out the Internet for mail-order foods. Online sellers use high-tech packaging that keeps foods fresh and send packages via overnight delivery. Chances are, your online purchases will be kept more consistently cold than grocery store purchases that sit in your cart and car.

Be sure to check out the shipping costs before you order. Some companies charge an arm and a leg for shipping their products using next-day delivery. Before submitting the order, know what you're going to pay!

Here are some great places to turn if you want (or need) to order your food by mail:

✔ **Captain Marden's Seafoods:** Captain Marden's features salmon, swordfish, shrimp, and scallops shipped fresh from Massachusetts. Visit `www.captainmardens.com`.

✔ **Charleston Seafood:** Charleston Seafood at `www.charlestonseafood.com` features more than 30 varieties of finfish, plus shrimp delivered fresh from Charleston, South Carolina.

✔ **City Fish:** Specializing in local fare from the Pike Place Market in Seattle, Washington, City Fish (`www.cityfish.com`) sells scallops, salmon, halibut, and a wide array of other fresh fish fillets.

✔ **Culver Duck:** Culver Duck in Middlebury, Indiana, sells duck breasts and whole duck. Visit them online at `www.culverduck.com`.

✔ **D'Artagnan:** D'Artagnan, out of Newark, New Jersey, sells fresh duck and quail, as well as a variety of other game birds and other animals. Visit their site at `www.dartagnan.com`.

✔ **Freshfish4U:** Specializing in freshwater fish from the Great Lakes, including whitefish, perch, walleye, and lake trout. Freshfish4U.com is at `www.freshfish4u.com`.

- **Grandview Farms:** Grandview Farms ships fresh venison (from steaks to ground meat) and bison (roasts, steaks, and burgers) from their location in Ontario, Canada. Visit them on the Internet at `ultimate.org/sites/gvf/price.html`.

- **Highbourne Deer Farms:** Highbourne Deer Farms breeds red deer for venison at their Dallastown, Pennsylvania, location. Check out `www.highbournedeerfarms.com` for pricing and shipping information.

- **Lake Superior Fish Company:** Lake Superior Fish Company sells fresh lake trout and whitefish from the waters off Isle Royale National Park in Lake Superior. They also sell wild freshwater trout, whitefish, herring, and walleye from the Great Lakes and Canada. Visit them at `www.lakesuperiorfish.com`.

- **Old World Venison Company:** Old World Venison Company, located in Randall, Minnesota, sells elk and deer products — including steaks, tenderloins, and roasts — online. Visit them at `www.upstel.net/~pbingham/venison.html`.

- **Select Gourmet Foods:** Select Gourmet Foods, Inc., in Kenmore, Washington, sells a variety of game. Visit `selectgourmetfoods.com` for information.

- **Shaffer Farms:** Shaffer Farms, located in Dalmatia, Pennsylvania, sells venison chops, steaks, tenderloin, and sausage at `www.igateway.com/clients/shafrfam`.

- **Underhill Farms:** Underhill Farms offers a wide variety of venison steaks, chops, and sausage at excellent prices. Check out their Web site at `www.underhillfarms.com/venison`.

Index

● *C* ●